PURIFIED BY FIRE

A History of Cremation in America

STEPHEN PROTHERO

University of California Press

Berkeley   Los Angeles   London

University of California Press
Berkeley and Los Angeles, California

University of California Press, Ltd.
London, England

Library of Congress Cataloging-in-Publication Data

Prothero, Stephen R.

   Purified by fire : a history of cremation in America /
Stephen Prothero.
     p .   cm .
   Includes bibliographical references and index.
   ISBN 0-520-20816-1(cloth : alk. paper)
      1. Cremation—United States—History.
   2. Cremation—United States—Public opinion.
   3. Funeral rites and ceremonies—United States—
   History.   4. Public opinion—United States.
   5. United States—Social life and customs.   I . Title.

GT3330 .P76 2001
393'.2—dc21   00-059005

Manufactured in Canada
9   8   7   6   5   4   3   2   1   0

10   9   8   7   6   5   4   3   2   1
The paper used in this publication meets the
minimum requirements of ANSI / NISO Z39
0.48-1992(R 1997) (Permanence of Paper). ∞

To the memory of my grandparents
Mr. and Mrs. Clifford Anderson

Why hide Reason's, or Affection's eyes?
The grave pollutes, the furnace purifies.

THE URN (1895)

Contents

Illustrations

Acknowledgments

THIS BOOK IS DEDICATED TO THE MEMORY of my maternal grandparents, Alphild and Clifford Anderson. They helped put me through college and, by relaying stories about my Swedish and Norwegian ancestors, instilled in me both a curiosity about history and a respect for the dead. Their cremated remains now lie across the street from my boyhood home in Osterville, Massachusetts, in the memorial garden at St. Peter's Episcopal Church.

All books are collaborations. The American Academy of Religion got this project under way with a research assistance grant in 1992. Georgia State University contributed additional financial support. Students in my "Death and Immortality" courses at Georgia State University and Boston University stimulated my thinking, and some, notably Dawn Huff and Clay Shelton, conducted independent research that proved useful to me. I also received help from departmental colleagues, including Timothy Renick in Atlanta and Peter Berger, John Clayton, David Eckel, Paula Fredriksen, Jonathan Klawans, Livia Kohn, and Frank Korom in Boston. Shanny Luft prepared the index.

Portions of this book appeared earlier as chapters in *Lived Religion in America: Toward a History of Practice* (1997), edited by David D. Hall; and *One Nation under God: Religion and American Culture* (1999), edited by Marjorie B. Garber and Rebecca L. Walkowitz. All three editors gave me valuable criticisms. Colleagues in history, religious studies, anthropology, ritual studies, and American studies also offered much-appreciated advice. They include Andrew Bernstein, Carolyn Walker Bynum, David L. Chappell, Richard Wightman Fox, Ron Grimes, David Hackett, William Hutchison, Edward C. Johnson, Gary Laderman, Laurie Maffly-Kipp, Joel Martin, Colleen McDannell, Michael McNally, Robert Orsi, Leigh Schmidt, Richard Seager, Theophilus Smith, and Thomas Tweed. Madeline Duntley read the entire manuscript carefully and critically, and the book is much better for it. My editors at University of California Press, Doug Abrams Arava and Reed Malcolm, ably steered the book to publication and provided encouragement along the way.

Judith Harding guided me expertly through the vast holdings of the National Center for Death Education at Mount Ida College in Newton Centre, Massachusetts, and Lisa Carlson of the Funeral and Memorial Society of America answered a number of questions via e-mail (often within minutes). I also received help from the staffs at the Massachusetts Historical Society; the Washington County Historical Society in Washington, Pennsylvania; the John Crerar Library at the University of Chicago; Boston University's Interlibrary Loan Office; Boston Public Library; and Harvard University's libraries.

When I began this project, I thought people in the funeral industry would be reluctant to speak with me. In almost all cases I was proved wrong. Ron Hast of *Mortuary Management,* Michael Kubasak of Service Corporation International, Howard Raether of the National Funeral Directors Association, and Jack Springer of the Cremation Association of North America all agreed to be interviewed (some of them on multiple occasions), as did dozens of operators and trustees of crematories and cemeteries across the United States. At Mount Auburn Cemetery, Meg Winslow and Janet Heywood were particularly helpful. At Forest Hills Cemetery I received assistance from the whole staff, and archivist Rachel Sideman graciously shared with me her own research on cremation.

Finally, I want to thank my wife, Edye Nesmith, and my children, Molly and Lucy, for supporting me as only they could. Death is a grueling topic. Their collective love of life made this book possible.

Introduction

DEATH IS A SORT OF ALCHEMY. IT changes us in an instant into something completely new. Spirit, soul, and mind flash away, and what was once a living body becomes a new creation. This new thing, the corpse, is most evidently flesh and bones: pound after pound of inert ligaments, veins, arteries, organs, nails, skin, and hair. But it is also a powerful symbol, charged with meanings as many and varied as human cultures and individual personalities. The corpse represents, among other things, a threat to social order, an economic burden to the family, a reminder of our mortality, an offense to sight and smell, an affront to hopes of eternal life, and a reason to believe in the bodily resurrection.

Corpses ask no questions but prompt many. How am I going to get along without her pay check? Why wouldn't he listen when I told him to stop drinking? What's my cut of the inheritance? Is now the time to get right with God? How could God have allowed this to happen? Is there really a heaven? A hell? But after all these questions have been answered or, more likely, as they resound without resolution, the corpse remains a brute fact. In this flesh, these bones, inheres a responsibility. What to do with a dead body?

In every human society the living care for the corpse. This care may include cleaning it, shaving it, dressing it, putting it on display, speaking to it, praying over it, caressing it, lavishing praise on it, offering it food, and otherwise facilitating its entrance into whatever, if anything, lies ahead. When all is said and done, however, a dead body has to be disposed of, banished, so the tasks of the living can proceed. Death rites remind us that corpses are feared as well as feted. Though the dead arrive at funerals as honored guests, at the party's climax they are summarily shown the door. The remnants of father or mother, husband or wife are precious. But as long as they continue to decay they are polluted too, heavy with the dangers of transitional states.

How then to get rid of a corpse and its dangers? Earth burial is one obvious choice. However, a dead body can also be placed in a tomb or a crypt, buried at sea, cremated, launched into outer space, donated to a medical school for dissection, or stored in a freezer to await some future revitalization. It can be mummified or embalmed, cooked by cannibals, boiled by souvenir-seeking admirers intent on dividing the relics, or left out in the open as carrion for birds and beasts. Each of these options admits of assorted variations and combinations, as, for example, when the organs of a British car crash victim are harvested for transplanting before burial, or when a fallen warrior in Venezuela's Yanoama tribe is cremated only to be consumed with food and drink in a communal meal. The possibilities are limited, in fact, only by the boundaries of good taste and ritual propriety. In an utterly secularized (and thus utterly imaginary) society, it might be possible simply to throw a corpse in the trash along with the rest of the refuse. But we don't do that, at least not in the United States.

American Ways of Death

What Americans usually do is bury. To be more specific, they call the funeral director, who arrives promptly and respectfully and in all likelihood at the hospital, where the vast majority of contemporary deaths occur. He (or she—the female ranks are swelling in the dismal trade) bags the body; drives it to the funeral home; cleans it; embalms it; dresses it; does its hair; daubs makeup on its face, neck, and hands; and places it in an appropriate casket. At the visitation that follows, the body (now beautified via embalming) will in all likelihood be displayed in the funeral home's "slumber room." If the casket is open, those who have come to pay their respects may feel obliged to say the deceased appears to be sleeping peacefully. Typically a funeral service follows, at either a religious site or the funeral home. Prayers are spoken, scripture is read, music is sung, and the priest, minister, rabbi, or other officiant delivers a short, uplifting homily.

The body is then transported to the memorial park by hearse, followed by a line of cars whose headlights have been turned on. At the grave site workers will have prepared the soil with a backhoe, covered the broken earth with artificial turf, and placed the casket next to the grave. But when the funeral cortege arrives, there are no workers to be seen. A short graveside committal service follows: "ashes to ashes, dust to dust." Laborers then lower the casket into the ground, typically with the feet pointing east. Friends and family may awkwardly sprinkle some soil into the grave before departing for food and drink at the home of the bereaved or at a favorite restaurant, but the bulk of the remaining labor is left to memorial park workers, who plant sod after filling the grave. In the months and years that follow, family members may be contacted by a "grief counselor" representing the funeral director. They may return to the cemetery to pray, to cry, to leave flowers, and to have a word with the departed. Or they may not, which would not be at all improper, since in the United States the care due the dead typically ceases the moment the corpse is committed to the earth. Such is the most common American way of death.

But there is now an alternative: the American way of cremation. This path may include many of the elements of a typical burial. A funeral director may be called. The body may be embalmed. It may be placed in a casket. There may be a visitation and perhaps a funeral, again either in the funeral home chapel or in a church, synagogue, or temple. The cremains, as the ashes and crushed bone fragments are called, may even be buried. But this precise scenario is unlikely, since the American way of cremation is not yet as routinized as the American way of burial. Far more than burial, cremation remains subject to the whims and idiosyncrasies of the relatives of the dead. Options are the order of the day, and customization and personalization are the emerging traditions.

Bereaved families might, for example, bypass the funeral home entirely, opting to hire a direct cremation provider. Disparaged by some funeral directors as "burn and scatter" or "bake and shake" outfits, these firms pick up a corpse, cremate it without fanfare, and return the cremains, often in a plain plastic or cardboard box and always for a nominal fee. It is then up to family members to do something meaningful with the contents. They might hold a memorial service, with or without the ashes present. They might hold a committal ceremony at the place where the ashes are to be buried, placed, or scattered. They might buy an urn to display in the living room or to tuck away in a safe-deposit box. Or

they might do some combination of these things, since cremated remains, unlike corpses, can easily be divided—a little for the son's mantel
here, some for the daughter's azaleas there, with the remainder reserved,
perhaps, for urn burial in the family cemetery plot.

These two competing American ways of death—burial and cremation—both accomplish what anthropologists have long recognized as
the key tasks of funeral rites. They assist the dead in their otherworld
journeys, and they help the living find their way back to everyday life.
They accomplish these tasks, however, in very different ways. Consider
the rotting corpse. Anthropologists have long understood that "decay is
the justification for all funeral rites." A dead body represents at least
two forms of decay (each of them dangerous): the material decay of the
corpse itself and the societal decay caused by the withdrawal of the deceased from social life (the mother from her family, the president from
the public life of the nation, or the clean-up hitter from the baseball
team). Both burial and cremation as practiced in the contemporary
United States respond to decay by forbidding it, via either embalming or
incineration (or both). But these two methods of holding decay at bay
are quite different.[1]

The American way of burial deals with the decay of the material
body via preservation. Embalmed, coffined, and buried, the preserved
dead are said to be merely sleeping, patiently awaiting a future bodily
resurrection, perhaps in a coffin designed to provide eternal protection
from the elements. U.S. burial traditions deal with the decay of the social body by preservation too—by maintaining significant ties between
the living and the dead. The dead, in other words, remain a part of society, interacting with the living. This interaction is plain in the Roman
Catholic tradition, where the living say prayers for the dead and deceased saints are said to answer the prayers of the living. Among Protestants in much of the American South, cemeteries continue to be places
of recreation, providing opportunities for couples and families to commune with the dead and with one another. These and other byways in
the American way of burial orient practitioners to the past, sustaining
in them a reverence for tradition, family, and community. If, as anthropologists believe, funeral rites always express both attraction to the
dead and revulsion from them, the U.S. burial-and-embalming regime
tilts the balance toward attraction—by beautifying and romanticizing
death.

The American way of cremation confronts decay very differently.
This way, too, shields mourners from the rotting corpse. But it deals

with decay by accelerating, not arresting, it. Rather than preserving the corpse through embalming, cremationists annihilate it through inciner- ation. Confident that the true self is spiritual rather than material, they welcome the swift fragmentation of the body into ashes. Cremationists respond to the threat of social decay with similarly surgical precision— by banishing the dead from society. Families choosing cremation for their relatives do not typically pray to the dead or expect the dead to contact them. At least in those cases where cremated remains are scat- tered from a boat or airplane, there is no place for the living to visit the dead and thus no memorial site for the living to maintain, perpetually or otherwise. The earth, after all, is for the living, not the dead. U.S. cremation rites, therefore, orient practitioners to the present and future rather than the past, inspiring reverence not for tradition but for prog- ress. In the dance between attraction to and revulsion from the dead, cremation tilts toward revulsion. By destroying the dead through the tonic of fire, cremationists inoculate the living from the dangers of death and decay.

Whether to bury or to burn is, therefore, no trivial matter. It touches on issues as important as perceptions of the self, attitudes toward the body, views of history, styles of ritual, and beliefs in God and the after- life. In other words, it amounts to a choice of worlds to inhabit. Do we owe our principle allegiance to the dead, to the living, or to the not-yet- born? Do the deceased play a significant part in social life or no part at all? Is ritual indispensable or useless? Is the body a temple or a tomb? Am I my mind? My body? Or a messy mix of the two? Is there an af- terlife? If so, is it for bodies or for souls? Or for both? And does it begin in all its glory immediately upon death or at some future moment of apocalypse, resurrection, or judgment?

Ancient Cremation

Americans are not the first people to have asked these questions, to have confronted the choice between earth and fire. Homer's *Iliad* describes cremation, as do the writings of Pliny, Pindar, Virgil, Tacitus, Ovid, and the Jewish, Hindu, and Buddhist scriptures. In fact, with the notable ex- ceptions of the Egyptians, the Chinese, and the Hebrews, cremation seems to have been the standard practice of the ancients.

We do not know where or why cremation was first introduced. Some trace it to sun worship, others to fear of the dead. Still others cite sani- tary considerations or practical matters such as the need to carry home the remains of fallen warriors. We know cremation was widely practiced in ancient India. The Vedas, Hinduism's earliest scriptures, contain cremation hymns from the late second millennium BCE. The priests who sang those hymns expected the soul to survive its fiery ordeal, then to fly birdlike to the world of the ancestors or the world of the gods. Later Hindu scriptures, principally the Upanishads (texts from the middle of the first millennium BCE that popularized concepts such as reincarnation and karma), describe cremation as a purification process in which burning the body cleanses the soul, preparing it for rebirth. The ancient Greeks also preferred cremation to burial. Convinced that fire separated the pure soul from the impure body and freed it to ascend, phoenixlike, from its altar of flames to the heavens, the Greeks, like the Hindus, found metaphysical and mythical reasons to cremate. When Hercules mounted the cremation pyre and immolated himself, Zeus proclaimed that the fire would burn off his humanity and invest him with the immortality of the gods. By the time Homer wrote the *Iliad*, cremation was for the Greeks the leading mode of disposal of the dead.

Toward the end of the Republic the Romans turned away from burial and practiced cremation too. Julius Caesar was cremated, as were Antonius, Brutus, Octavius, Augustus, Tiberius, Nero, Tacitus, and Caligula. The ancient Assyrians, Babylonians, Persians, Thracians, Egyptians, and Israelites also practiced cremation. But while Romans and Greeks saw incineration as an honorific act reserved for persons of high social standing, the Israelites (who like the ancient Chinese overwhelmingly preferred burial or entombment) viewed it as an abomination befitting only the despicable. There are numerous references to cremation in the Hebrew Bible—in Isaiah 30:33 "the breath of the Lord" is said to stoke a funeral pyre—and none of them praise the practice. Yet nowhere in that scripture is cremation unequivocally condemned. On whether to bury or to burn, both the Hebrew and the Christian scriptures are largely silent.[2]

Nonetheless, the dominance of cremation in the West came to an end around the time of Christianity's rise. Early Christians, citing the Jewish tradition of burial and the precedent of Jesus' entombment, supplanted cremation with burial. By the first century CE burial was widespread, and by late in the fourth century cremation had been effectively uprooted in most of the Christian West. In 789 the emperor Charlemagne declared cremation a capital offense, though it persisted into the Middle Ages among the Celts, Germans, Scandinavians, and Anglo-Saxons. Motivating the Christians' preference for burial was their sectarian desire to differentiate themselves from their pagan neighbors, and behind this desire were sociological, metaphysical, and theological concerns.

Popular opinion notwithstanding, the early Christians were no body haters. Unlike the Greeks, who disdained the body as a prison, Christians celebrated it as the temple of the Holy Ghost. The Greeks saw the person as a soul, and the drama of Greek life and death centered around efforts by that once-pure soul to escape from the pollution of the body back to its original perfection in the world of forms. The Christian person was more messy and, in many respects, far more intriguing. For Christians the human being was, in the words of Aquinas, an entity in which "soul and body are one being." Like the Greek drama, the Christian drama centered around a return to original perfection. But it was the whole person, understood as a body/soul amalgamation, that was to go back to that the Edenic state. And that miraculous return could be accomplished only through the resurrection of the body. After raising the body from the grave, God would reunite body and soul, recreating the person as a psychosomatic being. Reincarnation and the transmigration of the soul—ideas that commended themselves to Greek thinkers of no less stature than Plato—were roundly rejected by the early Christians, who insisted that a person had but one life to live.[3]

Both the Greeks and the Christians had metaphysical reasons for their methods of disposal of the dead; or, equally to the point, both had ritual reasons for their metaphysical views. Greeks lived by a myth of liberation in which the person, understood as an immortal soul, was freed by death and cremation from the bondage of the body to the liberty of eternal life. Christians, on the other hand, lived by a myth of integrity in which the person, fragmented by sin and death into body and soul and then by the unimaginables of interment into a myriad of bodily parts, would be made a whole person by the miracle of the bodily resurrection. Whereas the Greek myth climaxed at the moment of cremation, the Christian story put off the climax until the end times, when Jesus would return and summon the sleeping corpse out of its grave for judgment. To Greeks schooled in texts such as Virgil's *Aeneid,* Homer's *Iliad,* and Plato's *Phaedrus,* such a reunion of body and soul would have been not simply unimaginable but repugnant. What self-respecting soul would *want* to return to a body?[4]

Of course, the Christian myth triumphed in the West and burial came to enjoy a near monopoly over the disposal of the dead for roughly 1500 years. But there were tensions from the start in the Christian way of death. Those tensions arose largely from the early Christian assumption that the Second Coming of Jesus was imminent—that the end of time was to arrive very, very soon. Confused when some of their Christian brothers and sisters began to die before Jesus' promised return, early church members wrote to the Apostle Paul for answers. Paul, we are told, wrote back. But rather than overturning the expectation of Jesus' swift return, the epistles attributed to Paul reinforced that expectation. The end was fast approaching, but the dead, he affirmed, would rise first. Soon Christians were referring to death as a temporary slumber and to burial sites as sleeping places. This resolution served its purpose for a time, but in the Middle Ages Christians began to worry about the cognitive dissonance between this official theology, which seemed to imply that heaven is populated until the apocalypse only by souls (and not by wholly human beings), and an unofficial yet powerful folk conviction that the saints were already resting not simply in their graves but also in the bosom of the Lord. The doctrine of purgatory, officially proclaimed in 1274, tried to make sense of that contradiction by providing a place for souls to go between the moment of personal death and the end of time. It also gave those souls something to do after death to merit heaven and gave the living incentives to work to transport those souls from purgatory's trials to heaven's glories.

In the sixteenth century the Protestant Reformation revolutionized Christian deathways (or ways of dealing with death). Reformers like Martin Luther rejected not only the doctrine of purgatory but most Catholic rites of the dead (from last rites, to reverence for saints and their relics, to prayers for the dead). By emphasizing the drama of the individual soul at the expense of the story of the collective rising of the church at the end of time, by supplanting the relatively clear authority of tradition with the more ambiguous authority of scripture, by edging the Christian world in the direction of a conception of the self as wholly spiritual, and by nudging the modern world in the direction of reverence for individual conscience, the Protestant Reformers contributed, albeit unwittingly, to the legitimization of cremation in modern times.

Modern Cremation

Cremation's legitimization came to the United States via Europe. In 1658 the English physician Sir Thomas Browne responded to a find of ancient cremation urns by writing *Hydriotaphia, Urne-Buriall*, the first modern book on cremation. More than a century later, during the first few years of the French Republic, revolutionaries attempted to dechristianize funeral rites by promoting cremation. In 1794, the corpse of Beauvais, a physician and member of the National Assembly, was cremated and his ashes deposited in an urn in the national archives; and in 1799 the Seine Department passed legislation favoring cremation. In 1822 the English poet Percy Bysshe Shelley, whose body had washed ashore in Italy after a shipwreck, was cremated in the open air on a pyre constructed out of driftwood by his friend, poet Lord Byron. *La Cremation,* a Parisian journal, began publication in 1856.

Despite these and other efforts, the European cremation movement did not really get underway until the late nineteenth century. In 1869 in Florence an international congress of medical experts denounced burial as unhygienic and championed cremation "in the name of public health and of civilization."[5] At the Vienna Exposition of 1873 Professor Brunetti of Padua, Italy, exhibited a glass box containing roughly four pounds of cremated human ashes. "Vermibus erepti, puro consumimur igni," the exhibit sign read: "Saved from the worms, we are consumed by the flames." Soon cremation was the talk of Europe. In 1874 that talk crossed the English Channel. Advocates founded the Cremation Society of England, and Sir Henry Thompson, Queen Victoria's personal surgeon, wrote the most influential pro-cremation work of the century, "The Treatment of the Body after Death." From England the cremation impulse leapt across the Atlantic to the United States, where it sparked the American cremation movement.

Modern cremation was, from the beginning, a transatlantic concern. The most influential text in U.S. cremationism was Sir Henry Thompson's work. Americans read *Die Flamme,* a cremationist organ from Berlin (in German and in English translation), and integrated Italian and German engineering into U.S. cremation furnaces. Cremation bibliographies published in the United States included not only American and English texts but also works from Germany, Austria, Switzerland, Italy, Belgium, Holland, Sweden, and Denmark. Cremationists in Italy, France, and England, in turn, were inspired by the successes of the U.S. movement, which quickly outpaced its European counterparts.

Like cremation in Europe, cremation came to the United States as renaissance rather than revolution. A number of North American Indian groups had practiced cremation for centuries, and at least one notable non-Indian was cremated in the colonial period. Colonel Henry Laurens, a prominent merchant-planter from South Carolina and president of the Continental Congress, was the first Caucasian cremated in the United States. A classics scholar, Laurens learned of cremation through his studies of Greece and Rome. But unlike Pliny's Greek warriors, who cremated in order to prevent the desecration of fallen comrades by enemy forces, Laurens chose cremation out of a fear of being buried alive. His daughter had been pronounced dead after being stricken with smallpox and was close to being interred when she suddenly sprang back to life. Laurens directed in his will that his corpse should be burned, and he threatened to withhold his considerable estate if his kin insisted on burial. Whether his children were motivated by respect for their father's wishes or by a pecuniary interest in his estate is not known, but they did not bury their father, who was cremated in the open air at his Charleston estate in 1792.[6]

The U.S. cremation movement is a historian's delight. Cremationists agitated for their cause in three periodicals—*The Columbarium* of Philadelphia, *The Urn* of New York, and *Modern Crematist* of Lancaster, Pennsylvania—and in countless books, pamphlets, sermons, lectures, articles, and poems. These sources multiplied so quickly that as early as 1874 the Boston Public Library was able to publish a substantial bibliography of cremation-related publications.[7] Cremation was also widely covered in American newspapers, which from the movement's inception rightly recognized this new way of death as scandalously good copy.

Contemporary scholars, by contrast, have neglected American cremation almost entirely. Historians of medieval and modern Europe have for decades shown keen interest in studying death,[8] but writing about cremation remains something of a historiographic taboo in the United States.[9] There are now abundant reasons to overturn this taboo. One is cremation's popularity. Although rare in the nineteenth century, cremation boomed at the end of the twentieth century. Liturgies grew up around the practice, which was accepted by the vast majority of Protestant denominations and a growing number of Catholics. (Jews continued to resist the innovation, in large measure because of memories of the Nazi death camp crematories of the Holocaust.) In 1999, 25 percent of deaths in the United States were followed by cremation; that figure was up sharply from just under 4 percent in 1963. In some states, moreover, cremation overcame burial as the most common method for disposing of the dead. Such figures lagged far behind those for England, where cremation rates at the end of the millennium stood at approximately 70 percent, but they represented a significant overturning of what was until the late nineteenth century a virtual monopoly of earth burials in the United States.[10]

This book tells the story of cremation in modern America and attempts in the process to explore the shifting beliefs and practices of this new American way of death. It is neither an exposé of the funeral industry nor a manual on how to die well. Books in both of those genres abound, and I see no reason to add to the stock here. My goal instead is to steer clear of both sarcasm and sermonizing and to stick instead to interpreting the historical record. Another historian interested in the development of religion in the modern West has observed that crucial to history are its fractures, "the significant *breaks*—where old lines of thought are disrupted, older constellations displaced, and elements, old and new, are regrouped around a different set of premises and themes."[11] This book attempts to narrate the story of one such shift in premises and themes.

Some will be surprised to find that the break I have in mind is not secularization: the alleged shift from the dripping religiosity of premodern times to the dry secularity of modernity. Social scientists have been saying for decades that America is rapidly becoming secularized. "God is dead," they would have us believe, and at least some cite as evidence changes in the care of the dead. In the good old days, the argument goes, families cared for their own dying and their own dead. The sick died in their own bedrooms, not hospital wards. Brothers, sisters, mothers, fathers, uncles, aunts, and cousins would come by the home to help care for the dead—and for the caretakers. The corpse would be washed, dressed, and set out in the parlor for viewing, often in a home-made coffin. A cleric would officiate at the funeral in the home. Brothers and sons would carry the body to the horse-drawn hearse for transport to the graveyard. After the local clergyman shared some uplifting words (at least a few aimed at evangelizing the assembly by conjuring up the Day of Judgment and the horrors of hell), the coffin would be lowered into a grave. Kinfolk would fill the grave with earth, dirtying their fingernails with soil and decay. And in the ensuing months and years they would return to the cemetery to commune with the dead and to care for their graves.[12]

Clearly something has changed. But that change is not secularization. Many steps in the American way of death have been taken out of the hands of family members and clerics and taken over by death professionals. In the process, both death and dying have become privatized and commercialized. But death and its processes still demand ritual and stimulate meaning-making. So does cremation. In fact, the U.S. cremation movement can appropriately be viewed as an attempt to make the experience of mourning more, rather than less, ritually dense and spiritually meaningful. Cremation allows families to customize death rites—to memorialize their dead by displaying their cremains in a living room shrine, depositing them under a favorite tree, or scattering them to the wind at a place sacred to the deceased. These improvised rites need not employ undertakers and clerics, but as a rule they are spiritually charged. In fact, in many cases they seem to provoke deeper spiritual experiences in participants than traditional wakes, funerals, and graveside committals. The tensions that have marked the century-old relationships between cremationists and funeral directors, on the one hand, and cremationists and the clergy, on the other, are rooted, at least in part, in efforts by ordinary Americans to take back authority over the rites of death from professionals (undertakers and clergy included) and to reinvest those rites with meaning and purpose. Careful observers will not mistake that reinvestment with the demise of either religion or ritualization.

The early American battle between burial and cremation was not waged, for the most part, between Christian believers and non-Christian skeptics. It was, on the contrary, largely an intra-Christian affair. Moreover, the non-Christians in the cremationist ranks were rarely secularizers. Most aimed to translate America's deathways into new spiritual idioms, and their efforts only intensified as cremation moved into the 1960s and looked forward to the twenty-first century. The break explored in this book, therefore, is a shift not from religion to irreligion but from certain religious beliefs and metaphors (most of them Christian) to alternatives (some Asian, some New Age, and some more modern versions of Christianity). Accompanying this shift were a series of subtle but significant transformations in the theology of everyday life—from viewing fire as punishing to viewing fire as purifying, from seeing the person as an amalgamation of body and soul to seeing the person as soul-only, and from viewing hell as a real and present danger to viewing hell as an antiquated relic of nastier times. And as theology changed, ritualization also gradually but inexorably migrated from routinization to improvisation, from formality to informality, from ostentation to simplicity.

In the nineteenth century some cremation advocates boldly predicted that all Americans were fated to become cremationists. That may or may not prove to be true. But as the twentieth century yielded to the twenty-first, all Americans had a choice when it came to disposing of their dead. While the American way of burial persisted, an alternative, the way of cremation, had emerged. And in that emergence lies a fascinating tale.

PART ONE

Birth
1874–1896

1

The Cremation of Baron De Palm

ON DECEMBER 6, 1876, IN THE SMALL town of Washington, Pennsylvania, the corpse of Baron Joseph Henry Louis Charles De Palm went up in flames in an event billed as the first cremation in modern America. Supporters hailed the event, the first cremation in modern America, as a harbinger of a new age of scientific progress and ritual simplicity. Opponents denounced it as Satan's errand. Reporters too were divided. Some wrote up the story as a tragedy, others as a comedy. Either way, the event was a grand triumph for the U.S. cremation movement.

Although it is difficult to fix the precise moment of origination for any movement, there are good reasons to date U.S. cremation from 1874. Assorted writings on the topic appeared earlier, but interest boomed that year. The cremation vogue that followed was a transatlantic phenomenon set off by two European events: a display at the Vienna Exposition in 1873 that incorporated both a cremating furnace and the remains of an incinerated body, and the publication of Sir Henry Thompson's "Cremation: The Treatment of the Body after Death" in the *Contemporary Review* in January 1874. Together those events created a plausible case for what was coming to be known as modern and scientific cremation. While the exposition display proved the technological feasibility of the practice, Thompson's article trumpeted it as a sanitary necessity.[1]

Seizing on the cremation debate in the European media, American newspapers and magazines began in 1874 to cover the topic eagerly.

The *World*, a New York daily dubbed "[T]he apostle of cremation/To an unwilling generation," supported the reform most vigorously. In January it republished Thompson's *Contemporary Review* essay, and every Sunday for the next three months it devoted multiple-column stories (typically on the front page) plus an editorial to the question. The *New York Times* maintained more editorial distance, but it too covered the subject thoroughly. After publishing only one article on cremation in 1873, it published seventeen in 1874, noting in one that support for the reform was growing "suddenly and spontaneously." A *Philadelphia Medical Times* editorial, also from 1874, reported "a great deal of discussion" on the subject and speculated that "the ceremony of burning the dead might actually be introduced among us." A *Harper's New Monthly Magazine* piece from that same year described "the sudden interest in cremation" as "one of the striking events of the time." Before the year was up, the *Boston Globe*, the *Albany Evening Times*, the *Louisville Commercial*, the *St. Louis Globe*, the *Sacramento Record*, the *Jewish Times*, and even *Turf, Field and Farm* had lent their support to the cause. In an effort to determine whether there was any good science underlying all the puff, the State Board of Health of Massachusetts surveyed medical doctors on the cremation question. The Boston Public Library started putting together America's first bibliography on cremation. A group of cosmopolitans from New York City organized the New York Cremation Society. An enterprising gentleman from Philadelphia filed for and received a patent for a cremation urn. It was, in short, a time of near-millennial excitement for cremation partisans. As an ebullient medical student at the University of Pennsylvania put it, soon the "barbarous and injurious practice" of burial would step aside, uniting the whole world "in the one universal practice of disposing of the dead by 'cremation,' and persons will wonder and seem surprised that they ever conformed to the old system."[2]

All that and more might have come to pass under more auspicious circumstances, but neither economy nor society cooperated with the prophesies of this doctor-in-training. Traditional Christianity was strong. The preacher/singer team of Dwight Moody and Ira Sankey would soon bring revivals to major American cities. The depression that had hit when the banking house of Jay Cooke and Company failed on September 18, 1873, still gripped the country. Capital was scarce, and no one who had it was foolish enough to risk it on a venture as speculative as a crematory. But newsprint was cheap and the spoken word free, and cremationists used both liberally in an effort to attract reason and money to their cause.

Burial Pollutes, Cremation Purifies

America's Gilded Age, the period of rapid social and intellectual change spanning the years from the end of the Civil War in 1865 to the 1890s, has been called an age of debate. Lincoln traded barbs with Douglas. Robert Ingersoll, America's most famous agnostic, took on clergymen of all stripes. Should women be allowed to vote? Should baseball games be played on Sundays? Was Darwin right? The Bible true? Each of these topics was vigorously debated on the rostrum and the editorial page. So, too, was whether to bury or to burn.

In the burial versus cremation debate the cremationists bore the burden of proof. They were trying to overturn the time-honored tradition of burial, so it was their job to advance arguments and rebut critics. Two cremationists who took up this challenge in 1874 were Persifor Frazer, Jr., and the Reverend Octavius B. Frothingham. Frazer read "The Merits of Cremation" before the Social Science Association of Philadelphia on April 24, and Frothingham delivered a sermon titled "The Disposal of Our Dead" in New York City on May 3. Together these texts illustrate how America's early cremationists utilized the idioms of both theology and sanitary science, merging the ancient queen of the sciences and one of the newest modes of scientific inquiry into one overarching argument. According to these two men, a sanitarian and a preacher, burial presented both a danger to public health and a threat to the spiritual life of the nation. Cremation, by contrast, promised not only a more hygienic but also a more spiritual America.

Frazer began his social scientific argument by noting that his aim was to determine which of the many methods for disposing of the dead would serve "to make the dead harmless to the living." Drawing on the popular theory that diseases, especially urban epidemics such as cholera, were caused by "miasma" (dangerous gaseous emissions from decaying organic matter), Frazer claimed that burial failed to safeguard the living from the toxins of the dead. Bodies buried in graves emitted "poisonous exhalations," which polluted both water and air, he argued, resulting in "injurious effects," including fever, diarrhea, and, in some cases, death. Cremation, on the other hand, was the "safest" of methods. It resulted in "no horrid exhumations and mangling of remains; no poisoning of wells; no generation of low fevers" and restored "to nature most expeditiously the little store of her materials held in trust for a few years."[3]

Such was the sanitary argument. But theology too was at stake in the cremation debate. Was cremation an affront to the doctrine of the resurrection of the body? Absolutely not, insisted Frazer. God was as capable of raising a burned body as He was of raising a buried one. Or, as the Bishop of Manchester, England, had put it: "Could...it...be more impossible for God to raise up a body at the resurrection, if needs be, out of elementary particles which had been liberated by the burning, than it would be to raise up a body from dust, and from the elements of bodies which had passed into the structure of worms? The omnipotence of God is not limited, and He would raise the dead whether He had to raise our bodies out of church-yards, or whether He had to call our remains...out of an urn."[4]

The Reverend O. B. Frothingham's "The Disposal of Our Dead," delivered at Lyric Hall in New York City, was probably the first pro-cremation sermon in the United States. Although a number of prominent clerics would eventually support cremation, most steered clear of the controversy in the 1870s. But Frothingham was not like most Christian clerics. Though earlier in his career he had endorsed conservative Unitarianism and Christian Transcendentalism, Frothingham had long since moved beyond Christianity into the camp of free religion. He served as the first president of the Free Religious Association (founded in 1867 to provide "scientific theists" with an organizational home); and the appearance of his *Religion of Humanity* (1872) had transformed him into the most visible American spokesperson for radical religion. Frothingham's sermon, therefore, symbolized the link—a link opponents of cremation would later exploit—between the cremation movement and unorthodox religion.

Frothingham argued, first, against earth burial and, second, for cremation. His attack on burial, like Frazer's effort, began with an attempt to undercut the sentiment of eternal sleep in the restful grave with arguments from the budding field of sanitary science. Deriding the sentiment of everlasting peace in the cemetery as an illusion, Frothingham argued that "Nature...seizes at once the cast-off body, and with occult chemistry and slow burning decomposes and consumes it." This decomposition, he continued, disturbs not only the peace of the dead but also the health of the living. The grave was "a laboratory where are manufactured the poisons that waste the fair places of existence, and very likely smite to the heart their own lovers."[5]

Frothingham then took an strange tack for a sermon, attempting to divorce his subject from religious considerations. "There are many who feel that it is a case of religion against religion," he said, but "the practice of burning the dead can be reconciled with any creed." "The reform concerns us as men—not as believers in any particular dogma." Apparently Frothingham did not take this admonition seriously enough to heed it himself, since he devoted much of his sermon to answering religious objections to cremation. Was this "a pagan custom" practiced in the "heathen" Orient? Yes, the ancient Greeks and Romans had practiced cremation and Hindus continued to do so, Frothingham said, but those people were hardly heathens. On the contrary, they were "as intelligent, refined, and worshipful" as the most genteel Americans, and their funerary practices were "associated with feelings of the noblest kind, with veneration and tenderness, and regard to moral obligations." Frothingham added that while pagans burned, they also buried, "so that if there is any reproach in the paganism it must be shared by the custom of interment." On the resurrection question, Frothingham said that the body eventually met the same end in burial as it met in cremation. The only substantial difference between the methods was the time it took for the body to decompose. Neither nature nor God discriminated between cremation and burial. "A moment's reflection suggests," Frothingham concluded, "[that] to recover a shape from a heap of ashes can be no more difficult than to recover it from a mound of dust."[6]

After dismissing the religious arguments against cremation, Frothingham turned to sanitation, economics, and aesthetics. His sanitary and economic arguments were straightforward. Cremation, he claimed, was both more hygienic and less expensive than burial. The aesthetic argument was more fully developed. The swiftness of the process of incineration was "a relief to the mind" when compared with "the slow and distressing" decay of inhumation, Frothingham said, while "the graceful urn" was more beautiful than "the shapeless mound" and "white ashes" were preferable to "the mass of corruption" lying in the grave. Frothingham was also comforted by the fact that relatives could keep the cremated remains of the deceased in their homes or gardens and even carry them with them should they be called away to other locations. Finally, cremation presented "a sweeter field of contemplation" for the mourner, since "the thoughts instead of going downward into the damp, cold ground, go upwards towards the clear blue of the skies."[7]

These two orations provide an excellent overview of the early cremationist attack on burial. Cremation, these two men argued, was superior to burial on sanitary, economic, social, aesthetic, and religious grounds. In the world according to these early cremationists, it was more hygienic, more beautiful, more utilitarian, more refined, more egalitarian, more economical, more ritually auspicious, and more theologically correct to burn than to bury. Of all these types of arguments, however, the sanitary and the spiritual loomed largest. Many early cremationists believed the death rites debate should be settled on sanitary grounds alone. But even the most committed sanitarians typically found themselves merging the arguments of science and utility with those of theology and ritual.

While Frazer and Frothingham spoke from different perspectives, they arrived at one core claim: that burial polluted while cremation purified. Cremationists understood this stock thesis in two ways. From the perspective of sanitary science, it meant that burial caused epidemics while cremation prevented them. But it also meant that cremation articulated a more spiritual view of self, body, and afterlife and produced more refined death rites than the vulgar rites of burial. What is important about the foundational argument is how closely it intertwined the sanitary and the spiritual, which became in many respects two sides of the same coin.

Whether understood in sanitary or spiritual terms or both, the claim that cremation would purify a polluted America was also socially and politically charged. Cremationists were, by and large, genteel elites, and their cause was a genteel endeavor. The movement was most popular among white, well-educated, middle-class ladies and gentlemen from the Northeast and Midwest. Physicians and sanitarians were well represented in the ranks, as were newspapermen, lawyers, university professors, and ministers. Pro-cremation ministers typically came from liberal Protestant denominations such as Unitarianism and Episcopalianism, and from more radical religious groups such as the Free Religious Association and the Society for Ethical Culture (an organization established in 1876 and devoted to redirecting Christianity and Judaism away from belief in the supernatural and toward ethical action). Women's rights supporters—among them Julia Ward Howe, Margaret Fuller, Kate Field, Margaret Deland, Lucy Stone, Elizabeth Cady Stanton, Grace Greenwood, and Frances Willard—were also friendly to the movement.

The Gilded Age cremation movement participated in even as it contributed to a process historian Richard Bushman has referred to as "the refinement of America." During the Gilded Age genteel reformers feared that the urban and immigrant masses were plunging the country into chaos. They responded to that threat by working to cultivate taste and delicacy in those "dangerous classes" through vehicles as various as sentimental fiction, public parks, etiquette books, penmanship lessons, and liberal Protestant sermons. Motivating this refinement process— "the mission of teaching men how to behave"—was a strange combination of republican and aristocratic impulses. On the one hand, genteel elites drew sharp distinctions between the "washed" (themselves) and the "unwashed" (everyone else). On the other hand, they believed that all could aspire to gentility—that "every laborer [was] a possible gentleman." And so they took it as their sacred duty to work to "uplift" him to refinement. If, however, the laborer persisted in his ungentlemanly ways, genteel elites could justifiably scorn him for spreading the dual scourge of vulgarity and disease.[8]

Like other genteel reformers, cremationists saw themselves as educators and elevators of all classes of society. Cremation would not only make America more pure, it would make purer Americans. Toward the urban and immigrant masses, who were a main target of their disinterested benevolence, cremation reformers evinced an intriguing double-mindedness. On the one hand, the cremation cause provided ways for genteel cremationists to articulate differences between themselves and other Americans. ("We cremate; they bury." "We are educated and cosmopolitan; they are uneducated and parochial.") On the other hand, cremationists took it as their duty to attempt to raise the masses up to a supposedly higher level of culture. When the masses resisted that education to refinement, however, cremationists felt justified in judging them "stupid, ignorant, narrow-minded, contemptible." ("It is a pity," *Modern Cremationist* wrote, "that our neighbors do not know as well as we do what is best for them.")[9]

The cremation cause did not simply pit the polluting grave against the purifying fire. It pitted the cultivated class against the working class. And it reflected not only a hope for a more sanitary and more spiritual America but also a desire for a more homogenous society. In *The Invention of Tradition,* social historian Eric Hobsbawm observed that in the late-nineteenth-century United States there arose a host of new practices masquerading as time-honored traditions. One purpose of those invented traditions was to differentiate native-born citizens from not-yet-American immigrants. "Americans had to be made," argued Hobsbawm, and one way they were made was through new rituals. Hobsbawm does not mention the cremation movement, but cremation too was an invented tradition aimed at Americanizing immigrants. The cremation

movement seized on the metaphors of speed and progress appropriate
to the modern age of railroads and cities and machines, but it incorporated nonetheless a desire for simpler times when the country was less
ethnically pluralistic, when genteel elites were truly in charge. The effort
by cremationists to "uplift" the urban and immigrant masses by incul-
cating in them a compulsion to burn their dead was, among other
things, a strategy for constructing in the United States both the purity
and the order that historians have for some time understood as a preoccupation of Gilded Age reformers.[10]

Most Americans turned a deaf ear to the cremationists' call to refinement. But there is some evidence that at least a few began to aspire to
this new marker of gentility. In 1874, the landmark year for cremation,
one of the nation's most popular weeklies, *Frank Leslie's Illustrated
Newspaper,* put a cremation story under its masthead and accompanied
it with lurid illustrations. At least one newspaper spoofed (in iambic
pentameter) what it called "incineration for dead wits." And second-
year students at Princeton College conducted a mock cremation of the
remains of one "Brig. Gen. Joseph Bocher," which included a ballad
sung to these lyrics:

> Come one and all good Sophomores,
>   And drop a doleful tear;
> For he is dead—Bocher is dead,
>   And lies upon this bier.
> His reader is all bustified,
>   His grammar is all torn,
> His lifeless form is muchly mourned,
>   By Sophomores forlorn.

In sure testimony to the practice's cachet, urban legends spread of
fathers cremating sons in basement furnaces in Pennsylvania and of cremationists coming together to form clandestine societies as far south as
Georgia.[11]

Perhaps the strongest evidence for cremation's surging public presence was a minstrel show called *Cremation: An Ethiopian Sketch,*
which debuted on Broadway at the Olympic Theatre on October 12,
1874. The play starred an "eccentric" and single-minded reformer by
the name of Solomon Muggins, Esq., who by his own admission would
"not listen to anything at present on any other subject but cremation."
Unlike friends who long for the lively body of a rich lover, he pines for
the dead body of a poor man. "What benefit," Muggins is asked by his
sidekick, Henry, "will you ever derive from the burning of dead

bodies?" Putting on a cremation, Muggins replies, will make him "one of the greatest of public benefactors" because cremation is cheaper and faster than burial. The reform, says Muggins, will also decrease the problem of premature burial, since "by my system the very moment the fire strikes the body, if there is any life in it at all, pop goes the weasel." Muggins wants to determine how long it will take to reduce a human body to ashes in his new patent furnace, so he asks Henry to procure him a body and promises his friend his daughter's hand in marriage if he is successful. Henry heads off to a local medical college to steal a body slated for dissection, but along the way he encounters a gang of thieves. Happily, none has ever heard of cremation, so he is able to convince one of the boys (for $200 cash) "to appear as a dead body for a short time." Returning with an all-too-warm body, Henry is given Muggins' blessing to "go and get married as soon as you can" but is instructed, in a logic believable only in a show of this sort, to "be sure to be back in time for the great experiment." When that time comes, Henry is nowhere to be found and the boys, who turn out to know something about cremation after all, pull a switch on Muggins, placing a dummy in the furnace and walking off $200 richer.[12]

There are many morals to this story. The one worth underscoring here is that in 1874 cremation was not only on the docket of America's genteel reformers; it was also striking a public chord and producing popular resistance.

The First Modern and Scientific Cremation

While cremationists had plenty of arguments in 1874 for the superiority of cremation to burial, they lacked a suitable crematory. This would not have been a formidable obstacle if they had been willing to follow the ancient tradition of cremation on an open-air pyre. Despite their interest in restoring to America the grandeur that was Greece and the glory that was India, however, cremationists were reformers to the core and, as such, were determined to find a better, more modern, and more scientific way.

Cremationists went to great lengths in the nineteenth century to distinguish modern cremation from its ancient manifestations. They preferred the former over the latter for at least four reasons. First, whereas ancient cremation—and cremation among nineteenth-century Native Americans and "Hindoos" was included in this category—took place publicly on a crude outdoor pyre, modern cremation took place indoors in private in a state-of-the-art furnace. Modern witnesses were spared, therefore, the gory sights, sounds, and smells of the older procedure, which had the additional defect of taking far more time. Modern witnesses were also spared the noxious by-products of the affair, since the corpse's dangerous gases and liquids were destroyed by the "purifying fire" of the furnace. Second, in ancient cremation the body was literally burned, conjuring up negative associations, at least among Christians, of hell. But in the modern procedure flames never actually touched the corpse, which was consumed (at least in theory) by heat alone. Third, in modern cremation the ashes of the deceased were not mixed, as they were in the ancient rite, with what cremationists referred to as "foreign matter." Finally, in pyre cremation the body was only partially destroyed, while in a modern crematory the body was reduced entirely to its constituent elements. Like the philosophes of the eighteenth-century Enlightenment, cremationists looked to the ancients with both reverence and disdain. Surely, they were proud to be carrying on ancient traditions, but they were also determined to carry those traditions onward and upward. Their reform was part and parcel, therefore, of the nineteenth-century march toward progress. Given the aim of nineteenth-century American cremationists to marry an ancient rite with up-to-date technology, it is appropriate that the *New York Times* described the first modern cremation in America as "a form of burial at once ancient and modern." It was, in short, a modern revival.[13]

Cremation's migration from ancient India to modern America was made possible by the efforts of a few strong-willed pioneers. The man who made it technologically feasible was Dr. Francis Julius LeMoyne, a retired physician who constructed the first New World crematory on his estate in Washington, a small college town about thirty miles southwest of Pittsburgh in rural western Pennsylvania. The man who organized the rite was Colonel Henry Steel Olcott of New York City. And the man whose death made it all possible was the Baron De Palm. LeMoyne, Olcott, and De Palm were all "advanced thinkers," thoroughly modern men whose unorthodox religious beliefs and behaviors fueled the anticremationists' suspicion—a suspicion that would not be shaken, at least among Catholic leaders, until the 1960s—that cremation was an anti-Christian rite inextricably tied to Freemasonry, agnosticism, Theosophy, heathenism, Buddhism, and other forms of radical religion. All three were also genteel reformers, committed to uplifting the immigrant masses to an ostensibly higher level of culture and civilization (namely their own).

Dr. LeMoyne, "the *doyen* of incinerarians in our land," was the sort of character who inspires wildly divergent assessments. A wealthy and philanthropic physician of French Huguenot ancestry and "a life-long radical," LeMoyne was, according to one source, a person of "exceptional force, high culture, and broad humanity." According to another, however, he was simply a "fool." More objective biographers have noted that LeMoyne was an advocate of scientific farming and educational reform and an outspoken critic of slavery. Long before his estate was notorious for housing the first American crematory, it reportedly served as a stop on the Underground Railroad. Although LeMoyne declined a Liberty Party nomination to run for vice president of the United States in 1840, he did run for governor of Pennsylvania on an abolitionist ticket. (In fact, he ran for governor repeatedly—in 1841, 1844, and again in 1847.) And though he considered himself a Christian, he was reportedly thrown out of his Presbyterian church for his political views. Because of his strong belief in the moral value of education, LeMoyne gave money to a number of schools and colleges, including a normal school for freed Blacks in Memphis, Tennessee. He also paid for a new "Citizens' Library" in Washington on the theory that "it would tend to withdraw out young men and boys from questionable places of resort during their unoccupied hours." All were to be admitted to the library, LeMoyne insisted, "on equal terms without any distinction whatever, except that every person will be held to decorous and orderly conduct and personal cleanliness." LeMoyne's social and religious radicalism earned him at least a few outspoken enemies. One dismissed him as "a filthy old man in bad clothes." That slander concerned not sexual peccadilloes but hygiene, since among LeMoyne's odd convictions was reportedly the belief "that the human body was never intended by its Creator to come in contact with water."[14]

Like LeMoyne, Olcott was a middle-class gentleman attracted to social reform and unorthodox religion. Also raised a Presbyterian, Olcott turned as a young man to Spiritualism, or the practice of communicating with the dead through ritual experts called mediums. He pursued careers in scientific farming, military administration, and journalism before being admitted to the New York bar in 1868. In 1875 in New York City he cofounded the Theosophical Society with Russian occultist Helena Petrovna Blavatsky. For the rest of his life he would serve as that organization's president. Eventually he would move to India. On a trip to Ceylon (now Sri Lanka) in 1880 he would become the first American to convert formally to Buddhism on Asian soil. One of the grandest of

America's social reformers, Olcott's plate of reforms would eventually include, in addition to cremation, both temperance and women's rights.[15]

Among the early members of the Theosophical Society was Baron De Palm, an Austrian-born nobleman who, according to the *New York Tribune,* was fated to become "principally famous as a corpse." Upon his arrival in New York in the winter of 1875, De Palm befriended Olcott and joined the Theosophical Society. He fell ill shortly thereafter, however, and died on May 20, 1876. Although the Theosophists portrayed De Palm during his lifetime as someone of means and importance, the report that he was a "poor, friendless foreigner" was closer to the truth. His estate, once thought to be vast, turned out to be worthless. During his illness De Palm instructed Olcott (his executor) to arrange a funeral "in a fashion that would illustrate the Eastern notions of death and immortality" and then to have his body cremated. There is no record of exactly why the baron chose cremation, but he did express "a horror of burial" rooted in the fact that he had once known a woman who was buried alive. Olcott, knowing it would take some time to procure a suitable crematory, initially had the body embalmed. He then orchestrated what the New York City media billed as a "pagan funeral" on Sunday, May 28, 1876, at the Masonic Temple of none other than the Reverend O. B. Frothingham.[16]

This event, which preceded the cremation-to-come by roughly half a year, filled the 2,000-seat hall to overflowing. And it was very much a Theosophical affair—a coming-out party of sorts for the newly formed society and for Olcott as "Theosophic high-priest." In keeping with the Theosophists' interests in merging East and West, religion and science, and ancient and modern, the liturgy included references to fire worship, Darwin's evolutionary theory, Egyptian mystery cults, Spiritualism, the Nile goddess Isis, the Hindu scriptures, and American Transcendentalism. It also incorporated a credo affirming, among other things, that the body is nothing more than a "temporary envelope of the soul" and that "there is no death" because "the soul of man is immortal." Incense burning in an urn just to the side of the plain coffin foreshadowed the baron's impending incineration.[17]

Reviewers were not kind. A Boston-based critic described the proceedings as "another exemplification of the wickedness of the metropolis," seeing in the rite one more reason to be glad he did not live in Gotham. The Theosophical Society he dismissed as "a body of gentlemen who get rid of their spare change in importing Indian fakirs and organizing raids into the domains of necromancy and the supernatural." The *Tribune* took a similar tack. After professing that "there are immortal absurdities as well as immortal truths," it wondered, "Why should any one discard Christianity...and adopt a hodge-podge of notions, a mixture of guess-work and jugglery, of elixirs and pentagons, of charms and conjurations?" Months before the cremation for which he is now remembered, the baron was already more famous in death than in life.[18]

De Palm's idiosyncratic funeral brought notoriety to Olcott and his Theosophical Society, but complicated De Palm's cremation. When the New York Cremation Society was organized in April 1874, Olcott was in its ranks. After hearing of De Palm's wishes, he promised De Palm's corpse to that society for cremation. Initially, many agreed to coordinate the event. But after plans for the funeral were made public, members got cold feet, and Olcott was left to see to his friend's cremation himself. Now in retreat, the New York Cremation Society would not reemerge until the early 1880s.

The Cradle of American Cremation

LeMoyne's hometown was not the most auspicious place to hold cremation's coming-out party. A "dry" town of 4,000 to 5,000 inhabitants nestled into the lower foothills of the Allegheny Mountains, Washington was dominated, in the words of a *Times* newspaperman, by "old-fashioned Presbyterians, who regard the waltz as an invention of Satan and a game of cards as sure destruction." A *Tribune* writer emphasized ethnicity rather than religion, but his point was the same. Washington's citizens, he wrote, "belong, as a rule, to ancient Scotch Irish clans, who make a god of precedent and walk in the narrow but excellent path of their fathers from the cradle to their death-bed...they will not be likely to fling themselves out of that bed into a heterodox furnace." Though these reports were surely written to tickle the cosmopolitan prejudices of New York City readers, Washington was indeed both rural and provincial. Locals called their township "Little Washington," presumably to distinguish it from the nation's capital, but no one who had stepped foot outside of town was liable to confuse this Washington with the vast metropolis designed by Pierre L'Enfant. "Little Washington" was a sleepy place, largely lacking in the sorts of "advanced thinkers" who enlivened faddish salons in more cosmopolitan settings. Here cremation was, according to the *Times*, "rank heresy." "No good church member within

1000 miles of Washington would give his body to be burned any sooner than he would sell his soul to Beelzebub."[19]

Dr. LeMoyne had initially attempted to construct his crematory on the grounds of the local cemetery, but local officials rebuffed him. So he turned to his own estate. Located about one mile from town, his crematory stood atop a knoll known locally as "Gallows Hill" because it had previously served as a county site for executions by hanging. As a doctor who had witnessed the decay of dissected and exhumed corpses, LeMoyne endorsed cremation for reasons of public health. But he was also attracted to cremation's simplicity and economy, and his crematory reflected his highbrow conviction that extravagant burial rites were indecorous and immoral. A slight one-story red-brick building approximately thirty feet by twenty feet, the crematory roughly resembled a country schoolhouse. Faced with zinc, topped with a corrugated iron roof, and equipped with three chimneys, it reportedly cost $1500.

Inside were two bare chambers. One was a reception room, furnished with a number of ill-matching chairs and tables, a catafalque to display a body, and a makeshift columbarium, which according to one observer looked no more sacred than an ordinary bookcase. On the other side of a central door was the furnace room, built of brick and equipped with a coke-fired clay retort. The furnace was specially designed to prevent fire from touching the corpse, which theoretically would be consumed by heat alone. More than a few were scandalized by the crematory's appearance. Reporters judged it an architectural disaster. One called it an ugly "brick parallelogram" and described the furnace as "loathesomely [sic] cheap and plain for its purpose." Another said the building looked like a "large cigar box." Even Olcott described the facility as "very plain, repulsively so...as unaesthetic as a bake-oven."[20]

LeMoyne had built the crematory for his own use. But Olcott, after reading in the *Tribune* of the crematory's construction, had written LeMoyne, asking whether he might be willing to let De Palm christen his facility in order to demonstrate the legality, utility, and technological feasibility of modern cremation. Eventually the physician agreed. Olcott, drawing on his legal training and his New York City social connections, investigated applicable laws, obtained the necessary permits, and arranged for a panel of theological, economic, sanitary, and technological experts to present the cremationist case. He also gathered a slightly less committed cadre of scientists, clergymen, educators, and journalists to witness the spectacle to determine, in his words, "(a) Whether cremation was really a scientific method of sepulture; (b) Whether it was cheaper than burial; (c) Whether it offered any repugnant features; (d) How long it would take to incinerate a human body."[21]

A Ghastly Sight

The corpse of Baron De Palm had been injected with arsenic as a preservative before his May funeral, but as the search for a crematory dragged on it was determined that stronger stuff would be necessary if the corpse was to keep until the cremation. Mr. August Buckhorst, an undertaker from Roosevelt Hospital (where the baron had died), was called in to embalm. "A big, burly, red-faced, heavy mostached [sic] German," Buckhorst was the sort of man who would have been considered a live wire if he had not earned his keep as an undertaker, and he took on his historic task with what might be described as glee daubed with only a thin veneer of professionalism. One newspaper report claimed the embalming was performed "in the Egyptian fashion," but Buckhorst's efforts were far more haphazard than the techniques of the mummifiers of the Nile.[22]

Embalming had received a boost in the United States during the Civil War as battlefield medics on both sides of the Mason-Dixon line experimented with various techniques to preserve the war dead long enough to ship them back to their families for burial. By 1876, however, the practice was not yet routinized, so Buckhorst was free to freelance. And freelance he did. After extracting the guts out of the body, he packed the cavity and covered the skin with his own concoction of potter's clay and crystallized carbolic acid—"the best way to keep the old man," he said. He then had the embalmed corpse placed in a rosewood casket and deposited in a vault in a Lutheran cemetery in Williamsburg, New York.[23]

The tincture apparently did the trick. Four months later, in late November, a proud Buckhorst led a group of reporters to the vault to inspect the body, which was now slated to be cremated during the first week of December. One journalist called it "a ghastly sight," but all agreed the embalming was a success. Despite some shrinking and discoloration, the baron's distinctive visage remained recognizable, his dapper whiskers were wonderfully preserved, and his eyes displayed "an appearance of life." Neither corpse nor coffin, moreover, emitted bad odors. At one point in the inspection Buckhorst rapped the deceased on the head, proclaiming him "as tough as sole leather." "He ain't as dry as he ought to be," he concluded, "But I guess he'll burn nicely."[24]

He almost didn't. After being placed, coffin and all, into a plain wooden box for shipping, the baron's remains were transported on the evening of December 4 via a series of ferries and other conveyances to the Pennsylvania Railroad depot at Jersey City. There they were met by Colonel Olcott and a slate of Theosophists, hospital representatives, health officials, doctors, lawyers, and journalists assembled for the pilgrimage. On the sleeping car that evening Olcott played the charming host, winning over to the cremation cause at least two elderly women and one cub journalist. Olcott's arguments, one said, were persuasive enough "to convert the most stubborn lover of graveyard flowers...to an inveterate cremationist." The next morning, his two female converts at his side, Olcott prophesied (incorrectly, it would turn out) that the "fair sex" would soon become the cause's most passionate advocates, "for with them the preservation of their beauty was the supreme, as it was the last thought of their lives; and they could not bear to think of their own beautiful forms having to be subjected to the hideous process of slow putrefaction." When the train pulled into Pittsburgh, however, this bucolic scene veered sharply in the direction of farce.[25]

Mr. Buckhorst was the first to pronounce the body missing. "How can we have a cremation without a corpse?" he exclaimed as baggage handlers, in a macabre game of hide-and-seek, frantically searched for cargo that had somehow failed to board the Washington-bound train. Just as the undertaker was beginning to suspect theft at the hands of a pro-burial zealot, the body magically reappeared. Buckhorst breathed a sigh of relief, then lamented that the hunt had caused him to miss his breakfast. Around noon on December 5 the train pulled into the "Little Washington" depot, with the star of the show now securely on board.[26]

There the body was transferred to "a woefully shabby hearse" while "a crowd of dirty boys and rural yokels...almost stared their eyes out." Some townsfolk were shocked to see the coffin arrive in one piece, since rumor had it that the baggage car had caught fire just before Pittsburgh and prematurely cremated the remains. But such rich irony was not to be. After a bumpy ride from depot to crematory, the rough wooden box was given over to James Wolfe, a local fireman charged with stoking the furnace. Soon the reception room was filled with unofficial onlookers, some cracking crude jokes. But local gapers were not the only people in attendance. Journalists were, according to one eyewitness, "thick as blackberries," and scores of scientists and medical folk further crowded the scene.[27]

Olcott officiated at the opening of the coffin on the afternoon of December 5. But this impromptu viewing lasted only long enough for the assembly to arrive at a conclusion far different from the one drawn a week earlier at the cemetery. In fact, just a peek at De Palm's shriveled torso made it plain to all present that "the embalming process had not been so successful." It is probably an exaggeration to claim, as did a melodramatic *World* reporter, that "no spectacle more horrible was ever shown to mortal eyes." But the body, which had shrunk from 175 to as little as 92 pounds, did present "a painful and repulsive appearance." After seeing "some pretty, buxom, chubby-faced laughing girls" crowding around and staring at De Palm's "ghastly, grinning skull," a horrified Olcott commanded that the coffin be closed.[28]

Later, in private and under cover of night, attendants took the corpse out of the coffin, wrapped it in a white linen shroud, slathered it with aromatic herbs and spices, and placed it onto an cradle-shaped iron frame. The purpose of this transfer was to prevent any untoward mixing of the sacred remains of the baron with the profane charcoal of his coffin. But Buckhorst might also have made a few last-minute adjustments, because on the following day reporters who viewed the body reported it rather well preserved.

Making a Rite

On December 6, 1876, Olcott and LeMoyne awoke to the sort of bleak morning that can depress even the most uplifted soul. The day was unusually cold and windy, even for a Pennsylvania winter, and dirty snow clung to the ground. It was, in short, an inauspicious beginning for a movement that would hitch its fortunes to metaphors of sun, light, warmth, and purity.

About a week earlier Olcott had received some unsolicited advice from an editorial writer at the *Tribune*. The masses are moved far more by habit than by argument, that writer had warned. "It may be a fact that crowded cemeteries are breeding-places of malaria and typhus... but in the public eye they are valleys of peace, God's acre, in which sleep the sacred dust of our beloved, awaiting a future resurrection." The dire warnings of sanitarians would do little to convert ordinary folks to cremation. What was needed was a cremation rite as solemn and sacred as

the pageantry of burial. "If one or two cremations should take place...
without charlatanry, but with impressive and solemn ceremonies, they
would do much to soften the public prejudice" against cremation.
"[H]uman nature will insist upon shrouding its last state with some
kind of poetic pomp and meaning," so Olcott would be well-advised to
"not give to [this] experiment too much of the air of an ordinary baking."[29] How closely the organizers would follow this sage advice would
soon become a matter of no small contention.

Though Olcott and LeMoyne might have wished for better weather,
they could not have dreamed of a better turnout. Thanks to Olcott's
public relations efforts (which had begun with convincing Dr. LeMoyne
that the event should be open to the public) the cremation was well attended. Journalists arrived from as far away as England, France, and
Germany, and the health boards of Massachusetts, Pittsburgh, and
Brooklyn sent official observers.[30] Along with mourners and officiants,
this group brought the official guest list to about forty eyewitnesses assembled inside the crematory. But the publicity surrounding the event
also attracted a less genteel audience, many of them local residents
staunchly opposed to incineration. They lent to the occasion the rau-
cous air of a prizefight or an execution.

Inside the reception room friends and relatives meditated on the life
of the deceased while reporters jotted down notes. The uninvited
conducted themselves with less propriety, forming a "noisy, pushing
crowd" outside. "They were," according the *Times,* "coarse in their
ideas and conduct, and many a brutal joke concerning the dead man
went through the crowd, to the disgust of the more respectable visitors." A few journalists assigned to the story took the event no more seriously than did the crowds, poking fun at, among other things, the vulgar utilitarian arguments of a few radical cremationists and their need
for funerary speed. "Why cremate when there is still so much waste
land in which to bury?" a reporter for the *New York Daily Graphic*
asked facetiously. "[Long Island] soil needs burials, especially of that
practical race of people who, wishing to be of utility to mankind after
their demise, are willing through decomposition and consequent en-
richment of the soil to promote the growth of cauliflower and pota-
toes." The author even went so far as to suggest dynamiting the dead as
"a more speedy method of getting rid of human remains." Another reporter stepped farther over the line, surreptitiously lifting the sheet covering the baron to sneak a peek at his private parts.[31]

Unfortunately, no one did much to discourage either the bawdiness of the reporters or the raucousness of the crowds, according to a clearly disappointed *Times* newsman who objected that there were "no religious services, no addresses, no music, no climax, such as would have thrown great solemnity over the occasion. There was not one iota of ceremony. Everything was as businesslike as possible." Neither Olcott nor LeMoyne would have been surprised by this assessment, since both promoted the event as an utterly secular exercise. In fact, LeMoyne had written to Olcott that he "never intended or expected that our programme should include any kind of religious service, but should be a strictly scientific and sanitary experiment." But the occasion was lacking in neither ritualization nor spiritual significance.[32]

After Mr. Wolfe, the fireman who had started feeding the furnace with coke at two o'clock in the morning, declared the machinery ready, the guests took one last look at the body. Someone pulled the sheet down a bit, exposing a face with a horribly pained countenance. After this final, grotesque viewing, Olcott, LeMoyne, and two other men appointed to usher the body into the furnace took off their hats, as if to signal that whatever reverence might be mustered should be expended forthwith. Members of the impromptu congregation dutifully removed their bowlers. Then the body was lifted and "solemnly borne" across the threshold of the two-room crematory into the furnace room, and cremation's rite of passage to America was underway. Olcott, in his capacity as high priest, soaked the white sheet covering the corpse with water saturated in alum in an effort to prevent both the body's immediate blazing and any further public display of the baron's nakedness. In a nod to the Asian origins of cremation and the Theosophist's love of Mother India, someone placed a simple clay urn—"the present of a friend in the East"—atop the furnace. Olcott then sprinkled the body with spices, including cassia, cinnamon, cloves, frankincense, and myrrh. According to one confused reporter, the Theosophist was "following the Egyptian ceremonials, with a touch of the Indian, Greek and Roman customs." But he was also bequeathing to the occasion a vaguely Christian air—playing the Wise Man bringing spices from the East. Finally, Olcott placed on the corpse a collection of roses, smilax, primroses, and palms, as well as evergreens as a symbol, he announced, of the immortality of the soul. Recalling perhaps the Christian tradition of burying lay people with their heads to the west so they could look to the east for the Second Coming, Olcott and LeMoyne debated whether it was more auspicious to place the body into the furnace head-first or feet-first. The fireman and the crematory's builder then joined the procession, forming a coterie of six pallbearers, as in a traditional burial. At approximately 8:30 A.M. they slid the baron's body into the retort head-first.[33]

Spiritual Phenomena

There was a momentary sizzle and a bit of smoke. But soon the door was cemented shut and the furnace made airtight. The evergreens and the hair around the head caught on fire, and "the flames formed," according to the *Times* reporter, "a crown of glory for the dead man." At first witnesses were repelled by the smell of burning flesh, but soon the sweeter aromas of flowers and spices banished foul odors from the room. Witnesses who peered through a peephole in the side of the furnace noted that the flowers were almost miraculously reduced to ash without losing their "individual forms." About an hour into the proceedings a rose-colored mist enveloped the body. Later the mist turned to gold. Meanwhile, the corpse became red-hot and then transparent and luminous. All these effects lent to the retort "the appearance of a radient [*sic*] solar disk of a very warm...color." After some time yet another intimation of immortality pressed itself on the witnesses: "the palm boughs...stood up as naturally as though they were living portions of a tree." Then the left hand of the baron rose up and three of his fingers pointed skyward. The scientists present later attributed this incident to involuntary muscular contractions, but others saw in it something of a spiritual phenomenon. The main event concluded officially at 11:12 A.M., when Dr. Folsom, secretary of the Massachusetts Board of Health, formally pronounced the incineration complete. All that remained of the body had fallen lifelessly to the bottom of the retort, but the ashes of a few sprigs of evergreen remained, seemingly suspended in air above the iron cradle. Cremationists interpreted this too as a propitious sign.[34]

    In the afternoon interested parties gathered at the town hall to listen to pro-cremation speeches, including an address by the Reverend George P. Hays, president of Washington and Jefferson College, on cremation in light of the Bible. The next day, after the furnace had cooled, Colonel Olcott collected the ashes. From the first firing of the furnace to this denouement the De Palm cremation had exhausted nearly two full days. After sprinkling the ashes with perfume, Olcott reportedly placed them in a Hindu-style urn for transport to New York. One critic, disgusted over how the cremation had mutated into a carnival, suggested it would be most appropriate to toss the cremated remains into the surf off Coney Island. Instead they were deposited into the safekeeping of Theosophical Society headquarters in New York City. A few years later, before he departed for a new life in India, Olcott scattered the ashes "over the waters of New York Harbour with an appropriate, yet simple, ceremony."[35] But Olcott may not have strewed all of the baron's cremated remains. Some bone fragments were reportedly saved in a makeshift reliquary: a bottle in Dr. LeMoyne's office. Other bits of the baron were reportedly given away to gawkers as souvenirs.

Those who were not lucky enough to acquire such relics were not left without any means to remember the baron. Not long after the furnace's fire had cooled, Mr. Wolfe the fireman fanned the flames of public opposition when he wrote, directed, and produced a play that cost him his job moonlighting at the crematory. A satirical look at the De Palm cremation, Wolfe's production climaxed with "the shoving in and blazing up of the body." Its local success testifies to the fact that the residents of Washington and its environs were repulsed yet titillated by cremation. The new death rite of Gallows Hill, though as entertaining as a good old-fashioned hanging, was apparently of less redeeming social value. According to one estimate published shortly after the cremation, ninetenths of the citizens of Washington were opposed to the reform. That was surely an understatement. Before LeMoyne's crematory would be shut down, forty-two people would be cremated there, but LeMoyne himself would be the only resident of "Little Washington" to make use of the facilities.[36]

Part Folly, Part Farce

The De Palm cremation was big news across the country. Virtually every major paper reported on it, and many editorialized. The event might have received even more attention, but on the same day a fire at New York City's Brooklyn Theater killed over 200 people and, as Olcott later wrote in his diary, "the greater cremation weakened public interest in the lesser." Still, assessments of the "lesser" event made their way into print. Most reviews came in somewhere between mildly critical and utterly hostile, which is to say that journalists interpreted the cremation in the same light as the townspeople of "Little Washington." Even the *World* judged cremation "objectionable." "Ridiculous," wrote the *Daily Graphic*. Part "folly," part "farce," concluded the *Herald*.[37]

Assessing the event as theater, ritual, and science, reviewers came to
negative conclusions on the first two grounds. As theater, the December
cremation fared about as well as De Palm's May funeral, which the
Tribune had panned as a "dire disappointment." The cremation was
"weird" and "strange"—that is to say, either too thinly packed with
meaning or too avant-garde to be understood. And the main character
in the drama was "revolting" and "repulsive." As ritual, the cremation
was, in anthropological parlance, undercooked—far too quotidian to
count as a proper funerary rite. Too much ribaldry and not enough
emotion, the ritual critics concluded. It was, one wrote, a "desecration." "For all the ceremony that was observed," complained another,
"one might have supposed that the company had been assembled to
have a good time over roast pig." A different source compared the cremation to coarser fare, skewering the roasting as akin to "the barbeque
of an ox." A few reviewers were perceptive enough to place the blame
on the crowds and other journalists rather than with Olcott and his
charges. After all, it was not Olcott who had sneaked a peek at the
baron's private parts or made jokes about his anatomy. In fact, in many
reports Olcott comes off as a tragic figure, a would-be minister in the
midst of a three-ring circus, dutifully yet futilely attempting to bring
some measure of dignity to a sordid and comic affair. The *Times,* for example, noted that the officiants "displayed all proper respect for the
dead." And the writer who likened the event to a pig roast specifically
absolved Olcott and his minions from charges of ritual impropriety.[38]

From the perspective of science, most reviewers admitted that at least
as an experiment in "scientific roasting," the cremation was a success—
"the first careful and inodorous baking of a human being in an oven."
The body had been successfully reduced to ashes, and in decent time
and at minimal expense. But one editor dissented even on that score,
claiming that because of the embalming and shrinkage of the corpse it
was not a fair test. "Not one scientific purpose was served," he complained, except to prove "that a mummy could be burned." And that,
he said, "was known before."[39]

Echoing these sentiments were the decrees of a number of clerics and
other scions of society, who did little to hide their revulsion over burning the dead. William Bacon Stevens, an Episcopalian bishop, called
cremation "the freak of a disordered brain," and added that he had "little fear that a Bible-loving people will ever become advocates of cremation." Mayor William Stokley of Philadelphia denounced the practice as
"a relic of a less civilized age, a custom of pagan nations." The Catho-

lic Archbishop James Wood, also of Philadelphia, after being told they were going to burn De Palm's body, bandied back, "And his soul will be burning in the other world." Cremation, he said, was "a natural outgrowth of the spirit of rebellion against the government of Christ."[40]

Even some converts expressed reservations. A handful of sanitarians who favored cremation on hygienic grounds had to admit after December 6, 1876, that they too now shrank in horror from the method. Others, following the *World,* worried that De Palm's rites had forever tainted cremation with a laundry list of negative associations. The practice, they said, was now fated to be linked to radical social theories, irreverent humor, heathen religions, vulgar utilitarian ethics, shabby architecture, social misfits, strange theories of the body, ghastly corpses, bad weather, and sexual innuendo. It would be decades before cremation would be judged on its merits.

Long before the baron was committed to the furnace, a newsman who described cremation as "thoroughly respectable" had warned advocates against proceeding with their plans. "It would be a pity to see the whole business turned into a ghastly joke by carting across the mountains the remains of a man dead and embalmed months ago over whom a grotesque parody on a burial service was long since performed," he had written. "If cremation is advocated on the ground of the public health, this performance is far more likely to prejudice than promote it; if on the ground of good taste, the cremationists ought to raise a subscription to get this scheme abandoned."[41]

After the cremation, many concluded that the rite had indeed degenerated into farce. In fact, if there was a media consensus it was this: that the De Palm cremation, while a scientific success, was a ritual failure. Writer after writer predicted that the events of the day would only hasten cremation's demise. One said it was hard to imagine "anything more devoid of sentiment and essentially business-like than the conduct of this affair" and concluded that cremation had a rocky road ahead of it in the pious United States. Opposition was chiefly sentimental, he noted, but in such matters sentiment was king. "The mausoleum, the cemetery, made a charming spot by both nature and art, the quiet village churchyard where the grass grows rank, all interspersed with daisies, have grown into the traditions, the literature and the affections of our Anglo-Saxon race," he argued. "There will linger in the hearts of most a reverential preference for the spot upon which the sun shines and the rains fall, over which the flowers of spring blossom, and the birds of air sing their summer songs." Another prognosticator asserted that cremation would not prosper until it pressed beyond scientific experiment to religious practice, until it addressed hearts as well as minds. "Grief, reverence, delicacy, religion" were, in his view, all missing from the De Palm incineration. "No matter how many arguments are brought in favor of a funeral in which these are wanting, humanity will not be convinced of its fitness," he wrote. "Until something of the pious care that watches over human dust is bestowed upon human ashes, cremation will not be popular.... The philosophers must learn a little reverence if they would advance their theories."[42]

Reading the Rite

There are many things to say about this pioneering cremation. The first and most obvious is that its organizers were social reformers. Their movement was an effort to improve society by substituting for the pollution of burial the purity of cremation. More precisely, early cremationists were just the sort of enlightened ladies and gentlemen whom historians have seen as central to the tradition of genteel reform. Colonel Olcott was a lawyer and Dr. LeMoyne a physician. De Palm was a foreign-born baron and, if we are to believe *Frank Leslie's Illustrated Newspaper,* also a high-ranking Mason—"Grand Cross Commander of the Sovereign Order of the Holy Sepulchre at Jerusalem, Knight of St. John at Malta, Prince of the Roman Empire, late Chamberlain to His Majesty the King of Bavaria." Soon the movement would attract an even more impressive list of genteel elites: capitalist William Waldorf Astor, temperance advocate Kate Field, Harvard president Charles William Eliot, newspaper editor Charles A. Dana, educator Elisabeth P. Peabody, philanthropist Andrew Carnegie, abolitionist Cassius Clay, Senator Charles Sumner, Buddhist sympathizer Moncure Conway, ethical culture leader Felix Adler, Unitarian minister Jenkin Lloyd Jones, Episcopalian bishop Phillips Brooks, and Transcendentalist Thomas Wentworth Higginson, to name only a few.[43]

Cremation was to these reformers a method for cultivating individuals and improving society. Not simply a way to make a better nation, it was a way to make better citizens—by uplifting the vulgar to refinement. Individuals who resisted cremation were, by this logic, resisting both the betterment of society and the cultivation of their own virtues. America's pioneering cremationists, like other genteel reformers, were egalitarians insofar as they believed that even the most lowly American was capable of being raised up to a higher level of culture and civilization. But each was also determined to rank Americans on a continuum from unwashed to washed and thus to preserve the time-honored distinction between uncultivated and cultivated souls: the lowly who needed to be lifted up and those, like themselves, who would do the heavy lifting. Such was the logic of this under-studied aspect of the "refinement of America."[44]

Early cremation reformers may have stood near the center of genteel society, but they were largely religious outsiders, frequently aligning themselves with alternatives to both mainline Protestantism and traditional Catholicism. Later, cremation's popularizers would heed the advice of editorial writers and begin to distance their cause from religious dissent, but at least in its infancy cremation was closely tied to unorthodox spirituality, including Spiritualism, Theosophy, and Asian religions. Many leading cremationists were eccentric in religion as well as temperament. LeMoyne was, according to his friends, nearly as radical religiously as he was politically. Olcott was a Spiritualist turned Theosophist well on his way to becoming a Buddhist. De Palm was, in Olcott's words, "a Voltairean with a gloss of Spiritualism," and, if we are to believe the *Tribune,* a Rosicrucian and dabbler in "occult sciences" to boot.[45] The "pagan funeral" that Olcott had conducted in May 1876 was as replete with references to Egyptian religious traditions as it was lacking in references to Christianity. And the De Palm cremation in December 1876 was attended, as the *Times* lamented, by nothing that resembled traditional Christian funerary rites.

Witnesses to De Palm's cremation clearly associated the practice with the "heathen," but exactly which "heathen" isn't clear. Both defenders and detractors wrote repeatedly about cremation as an Asian import, and reinforcing that view were a variety of articles about cremation in Japan and India published in the popular press. Most reports echoed Olcott in describing the receptacle used for the baron's ashes as a "Hindoo cremation urn...decorated with Hindoo characters and devices," but one *Times* reporter indicated that the urn was designed "after the manner practiced by the ancient Greeks and Romans." This confusion is telling, since America's early cremationists linked cremation with what they saw as the great civilizations of Greece, Rome, and India, and Americans in general were not yet aware of the differences among the traditions they lumped together as "heathenism."[46]

Though organizers linked the De Palm cremation with the antique glories of Greco-Roman civilization and the ancient grandeur of India, cremation was a peculiar revival. Early cremationists may have been reviving an ancient rite, but they were modernists to the core. As such, they were determined to improve on ancient precedents, to adapt them to modern, scientific contingencies, and thus to evolve out of a crude, ancient ritual a new and improved practice that was as scientific as it was modern. By drawing a sharp distinction between ancient and modern cremation, American cremationists were able to be true to both their colonial and their anticolonial impulses. Their cosmopolitanism led them to laud India as a cradle of cremation (and to flatter themselves for exhibiting religious and cultural tolerance). But their ethnocentrism led them to view ancient cremation (even as it was practiced at the time in India or among Native Americans) as badly in need of modern improvements. This distinction between ancient and modern cremation was not lost on the folks at *Frank Leslie's Illustrated Newspaper,* who published illustrations accompanying a front-page story on cremation that contrasted "The Ancient Grecian Method" of cremation with the high-tech modern Western one (and noted the superiority of the latter along the way). The same distinction was underscored repeatedly by Olcott, who despite his attraction to the religions of India took pride in the fact that the baron's cremation represented a vast improvement over traditional Hindu practices. Because the body was disposed of in a closed furnace instead of an open pyre, Olcott wrote, "there could be none of that horror of roasting human flesh and bursting entrails which makes one shudder at an open-air pyre-burning....There was none of that unpleasant odour that sometimes sickens one who drives past an Indian burning-ghat."[47]

In part because of the association of cremation with modernity, genteel reform, and unorthodox and Asian religions, the efforts of America's nineteenth-century cremationists did little in the years immediately following the De Palm cremation to sway ungenteel Americans, who like the citizens of Washington continued to overwhelmingly prefer burial, largely on religious grounds. When they were not either ridiculing or ignoring the rite, these traditionalists argued that cremation was a heathen, pagan, and therefore anti-Christian practice: it overturned nearly 2,000 years of the Christian custom of burial, it demonstrated a lack of respect for the sanctity of the body (which was the temple of the Holy Ghost), and it flew in the face of the Christian doctrine of the resurrection of the body.

This verdict notwithstanding, early cremationists were as a group neither areligious nor inattentive to ritual. Neither De Palm's May funeral nor his December cremation were overtly Christian. But neither was secular either. Each was a creole rite that creatively combined Christian and non-Christian, Eastern and Western elements. Virtually every step in each process, moreover, was endowed with spiritual and ritual significance. The baron's Masonic Temple funeral was, no doubt, post-Christian, but it aimed to "illustrate the Eastern notions of death and immortality" via hymns, creeds, prayers, and a myriad of religious symbols.[48] No cremationist involved in the events surrounding the cremation of Baron De Palm believed that his corpse was simply profane material to be dispensed with this way or that. All, in fact, were convinced that there was a right and a wrong way to perform the new cremation rites they were in the process of inventing. De Palm's death rites, in short, demonstrated dechristianization without secularization. What they rejected was not religion per se but traditional Christianity.[49]

Ritual studies expert Catherine Bell has contended that to act ritually is to act in ways that distinguish what you are doing from more ordinary activities. Rituals do not need to be formal or repetitive. In fact, they can be informal and improvised. But they need to distinguish themselves from more mundane practices. Jonathan Z. Smith has made much the same point: "Ritual is, above all, an assertion of difference." From this perspective, Olcott and his charges were clearly acting ritually. The same *Times* reporter who lamented that "there were no religious services...not one iota of ceremony" at the De Palm cremation also reported that Olcott and his fellow cremationists evinced "all proper respect for the dead," that the corpse was "lovingly showered" with flowers and evergreens "as an emblem of immortality," that the flames of the burning evergreen formed "a crown of glory for the dead man," and that some witnesses saw the gradual uplifting of the left hand and the pointing upward of three of its fingers as a miraculous message of sorts. The reporter (who compared the rite with "the fiery ordeal through which Shadrach, Meshach, and Abednego passed" in the Hebrew Bible) also noted that officiants preoccupied themselves with all sorts of fine details that together served to distinguish the rite they were constructing from more commonplace activities. They emptied the corpse of fluids in order to prevent an unseemly explosion, wrapped it in a pure white shroud, draped it in an alum-soaked sheet in an effort to prevent any display of nakedness, and dressed it with incense. After some debate, they purposefully placed the body into the furnace head-first. They took pains to take the baron out of his coffin prior to the cremation in order to avoid mixing his ashes with foreign remains (and thus confusing sacred relics with profane fuel). They acted, in short, like priests conducting a solemn ritual. Yes, they were promoting a sanitary technology, but they were also performing a purification rite. It would not have been the least bit out of character if at the end of this rite Olcott and his cofficiants had prayed, as one newsman did: "peace to his ashes."[50]

Cremation after De Palm

The De Palm cremation spread the good news of cremation, but likely set the cremation movement back rather than propelling it forward. Still, in the years that followed that landmark event a slow but steady stream of the dead lined up to follow him into the fire. On July 31, 1877, Dr. Charles F. Winslow, formerly of Boston, Massachusetts, became the second person to be cremated in modern America when his corpse was reduced to ashes in a furnace in Salt Lake City, Utah.[51] A few months later, in November 1877, Julius Kircher, a German-American Lutheran, caused a stir in New York City when, after arguing with his Jewish wife about whether their dead eight-day-old son should be interred in a Lutheran or a Jewish cemetery, he cremated the infant in a furnace in his paint factory.[52] On February 15, 1878, Mrs. Benjamin Pitman of Cincinnati became the first woman to be cremated in modern America and the second person to make use of the facilities at Dr. LeMoyne's crematory.[53] On October 16, 1879, Dr. LeMoyne himself was cremated.[54] Each of these death rites followed to a remarkable extent the precedent of the Baron De Palm.

Like De Palm, Dr. Winslow was a well-traveled and European-educated religious eccentric who was cremated amid religious conservatives (in Winslow's case, Mormons). But Winslow was no secularist. He believed that "what of him was immaterial...returned unto the God who gave it." Like LeMoyne, he was a physician who was attracted to cremation because of unpleasant encounters with exhumed human remains. And his cremation, too, stirred controversy; nearly 1,000 people were said to have witnessed his fiery end. Like De Palm, he was embalmed and wrapped in a white linen sheet. Flowers and evergreens adorned his body. And he was carried lovingly and solemnly by pallbearers to the furnace door. Although "no prayer was uttered, no sermon preached, no funeral anthem sung," organizers went to great lengths to assure the purity of his ashes. After iron chips from the apparatus flaked off into the doctor's remains, they were removed one by one before the remains were inurned, shipped to Mount Auburn Cemetery in Cambridge, Massachusetts, and buried alongside his wife's grave—the first cremated remains known to have been interred in Massachusetts. Predictably, editors at the *Salt Lake City Daily Tribune* responded to Winslow's rite by denouncing cremation as a "cold science" and waxing nostalgic about the heartwarming practice of cemetery visitation.[55]

Mrs. Benjamin Pitman was a professional woman renowned in the field of shorthand. A well-educated but "somewhat eccentric" ex-Swedenborgian who belonged to "the school of advanced thinkers," she was "a woman of more than ordinary refinement" who adhered not to secularism but to the "creed of the beautiful." Constitutionally optimistic, Mrs. Pitman ran a cheerful home where "there was never a thought of gloom." Although only an occasional churchgoer, she "felt confident," according to her husband, "of a life beyond the grave" and, as a result, believed that death should be greeted with gaiety, not sorrow. Her husband apparently agreed not only with Mrs. Pitman's belief in the soul's immortality but also with her scorn for funerary extravagances. In a clear breach of Victorian mourning codes, he refused to allow the customary black crape of death to mark his home's door. Like the De Palm incineration reporters, most newsmen covering Mrs. Pitman's cremation complained that the ritual was scandalously underdone. Under the headline "An Unceremonious Rite," a *Times* reporter said the task was performed "heartlessly"—"there were no religious exercises whatever." "Not a prayer was uttered; not a sigh was heard," the reporter lamented, "not a tear-drop moistened the winding-sheet of the woman who for thirty years had been the beloved wife of Mr. Ben Pitman." These conclusions were not entirely unsubstantiated; Mrs. Pitman's will had directed her survivors that there were to be "no religious observations of any kind." However, the reporter's own writing contains ample evidence of the violation of those directions. Mrs. Pitman's body had been displayed at her Cincinnati home in a beautiful cherry and mahogany casket—an elegant example, custom-carved with the monogram "P" at the foot and a large cross at the head. On the cross sat a wreath of fresh flowers, and the catafalque supporting the coffin was dressed in light blue silk. At an informal service at her home, an address was read and a poem recited. For the trip to the LeMoyne crematory the coffin was draped with black cloth. The corpse was displayed in the crematory's reception room, where observers noted that the pure white satin interior of the coffin perfectly matched the purity of her white satin dress. At the crematory Mrs. Pitman was eulogized, and an original poem was read in lieu of a prayer. The body was taken out of the coffin, wrapped in a white, alum-soaked shroud, covered with flowers, and placed on the catafalque. Attendants then committed the corpse, head-first once again, to the furnace. Later, Mr. Pitman was said to be considering strewing the ashes around the base of Mrs. Pitman's favorite rose bush, "that the blooming and fragrant rose may bring brightly before [her husband's] mind the memory of his loved and faithful wife." In this way, Pitman had added, this believer in the "creed of the beautiful" might be born again as a rose.[56]

Dr. LeMoyne's cremation was more high church. Although painted in the press as a secularist, LeMoyne remained a Christian his whole life. He endowed two chairs at Washington and Jefferson College, an evangelical Protestant school. He said the cremation treatise he drafted just before his death was written "from a Christian stand-point." It included references to "the great Creator" and called Jesus "Savior" and the Bible "the revealed will of God." At a private funeral service at his home, attended by two Protestant ministers, scripture passages were read and a prayer offered. And at the crematory a benediction was recited. Like Mrs. Pitman, LeMoyne reportedly instructed his family to scatter his ashes in a rose bed, "so that the queen of flowers might seek sustenance in his cinerary remains and scent the air with her message of beauty and fragrance." Once again, reporters took offense. Echoing the *Tribune*'s complaint that the De Palm cremation had degenerated into "a charlatan advertisement of a heathen society," the *Philadelphia Inquirer* concluded that "the great difficulty [with] this reform...has been the impracticable character of those persons who have been foremost in urging its adoption.... Then the theory of cremation had the misfortune of being taken up by a body of mystics who rejoiced in the learned title of Theosophists, and in whom every vestige of common sense was obliterated.... They were the very last class of men and women who should have been picked out to introduce a reform of any kind among a sober and intelligent people, and more especially a reform which, to most minds, seems barbarous and inhuman."[57]

Newspapermen at the *Tribune* and the *Inquirer* mistook these pioneers as irreligious and unceremonious because they wrongly equated mainline Protestantism with religion, and traditional rituals with ritualizing itself. Anthropologist Mary Douglas has argued that societies in which social order is emphasized and pressure on the individual to conform to social norms is high tend to be ritualistic. Their rituals, moreover, tend toward the formal. One classic example of this type of society, which Douglas terms "high grid, high group," was Victorian America. In the United States in the 1870s, non-Christians were often denounced as heathens, and rebels against fixed and formal rites were seen not as advocates of new rituals but as opponents of ritualization itself. It should not be surprising, therefore, that eyewitnesses judged early American cremations as unceremonious and sacrilegious. But rather than taking them at their word, we should interpret their judgments as evidence of a historic shift in American ritualization. The Gilded Age is now widely recognized by historians of American religion as an era that, by bringing Buddhism and Hinduism to the United States, nudged the country away from its Protestant past toward a new era of religious pluralism. But it was also an age in which the country began to step, however haltingly, away from ritual formalism and extravagance toward a new era of ritual improvisation and simplicity. At the time, critics dismissed the idiosyncratic rituals invented by the cremationists as unceremonious and areligious. More neutral observers will discern, however, that they were neither. Surely the cremations of De Palm, Pitman, Winslow, and LeMoyne strayed from the standard ritual formula of Gilded Age Americans. While the unwritten rules of ritual propriety dictated a reverence for tradition, those rites celebrated innovation. But however improvised and personalized, they were rites nonetheless. The careful observer will see in them neither an end of religion nor an end of ritual, but a desire for new wine and new wineskins. In the events of December 6, 1876, and beyond we see evidence for a new diversity in American religion. We also glimpse the beginnings of a revolution in American ritual life that would come to fruition in the creative cremation rites of the 1960s through 1990s.[58]

2

Sanitary Reform

AROUND THE MIDDLE OF NINETEENTH century cleanliness sidled up to godliness, and the sanitarian movement was born. Although this movement did not draw as much attention as the efforts to abolish slavery or to win the vote for women, its advocates were no less passionate. Speaking at an early convention of sanitarians, as these evangelists called themselves, Dr. Jacob Bigelow of Boston said that the sanitary crusade was "one of the greatest reforms that this country has ever entered upon." According to most accounts, the sanitarians were remarkably successful, instilling in everyday Americans in the years immediately following the Civil War "a national obsession with contamination and, alternatively, with sanitation."[1]

Like other U.S. social reforms, sanitarianism was viewed as a battle against a grave social problem. In this case the enemy was dirt. Or, put another way, the problem was the jarring disjunction between the view that America was progressing onward and upward to something approaching the kingdom of God and the fact that America's cities were hotbeds of squalor and disease. During the 1840s and 1850s, immigrants from Ireland and Germany flooded into U.S. urban areas. So did rural folks from across the country. After the Civil War, Southern Blacks joined the march to the cities, and they were accompanied in the late nineteenth century by a new immigrant wave from Eastern Europe. All were attracted by prospects of work and advancement in a rapidly industrializing America, but what greeted them was in some cases worse than what they had left.

Living and working in the midst of filth, these "dangerous classes" became scapegoats for the social and intellectual chaos wrought by rapid industrialization and urbanization. Among the ills they were charged with spreading was the epidemic. Cholera, yellow fever, typhoid, diphtheria, smallpox, and other infectious diseases plagued the country throughout the nineteenth century. Cholera struck hard in 1832, 1849, and 1866. In colonial times epidemics had been interpreted as judgments of God on an immoral people. The prescription was prayer and fasting. In the nineteenth century Americans increasingly responded to these outbreaks with naturalistic rather than supernaturalistic theories. Some blamed immigrants. The Irish, for example, were charged with bringing the scourge of cholera and the Italians with importing polio. Others pinpointed more scientific sources. The "old sanitarians," as early sanitary reformers are called, believed contagious diseases were caused by "miasma," a mysterious but noxious gas emitted from fermenting organic matter. Eliminate the filth, the theory went, and you eliminate the air-borne contagion. So, in addition to recommending the quarantine of already-infected individuals (a public health strategy that had been around since the seventeenth century), the old sanitarians called for a thorough cleanup of the urban environment—garbage collecting, street sweeping, improved sewage, inspections of city markets and slaughterhouses, and household cleaning. Their efforts were institutionalized in the Metropolitan Board of Health in New York City (established 1866) and the Massachusetts Board of Health (established 1869).[2]

Quarantining the Dead

Many pioneering sanitarians also fixed their sights on another form of miasma-causing waste: the decaying underground corpse. Convinced that urban graveyards, too, represented a threat to public health, sanitarians agitated for changes in the American way of burial. In the process, the dead joined immigrants as scapegoats for urban perils, and burial was added to the agenda of the "body reformers." As early as 1806, public health officials in New York City, decrying "a vast mass of decaying animal matter" in urban churchyards as "hot-beds of miasmata," recommended "that the interments of dead bodies within the city ought to be prohibited." This concern persisted throughout the century. In 1866, as cholera was ravaging Europe, a U.S. author rightly noted that "the subject of interments has occupied the public attention for more than fifty years."[3]

The rural cemetery movement translated this concern into action. The goal of the rural cemeterians was to do with the dead what public health officials were doing with the sick. Mimicking the quarantine strategy, these reformers separated the dead from the living by banishing graveyards from the cities to suburban areas. Mount Auburn Cemetery, established outside Boston in 1831, was America's first suburban burial ground. Universally acclaimed to be as sanitary as it was beautiful, Mount Auburn had by 1850 spawned imitations in Philadelphia, Baltimore, New York, Cincinnati, Pittsburgh, Providence, Washington, D.C., St. Louis, Detroit, Milwaukee, Atlanta, and a number of smaller cities. Each of these rural cemeteries married a concern about sanitary reform to new aesthetic and theological convictions. To be more precise, Romanticism lent the rural cemeteries beauty and Arminianism (the view that individuals could cooperate with God in effecting their own salvation) lent them hope. Suburban cemeteries like Harmony Grove in Salem, Massachusetts, and Mount Hope in Rochester, New York, boasted not only idyllic monikers but also open vistas, meandering lanes, cultivated landscapes, and elegantly carved family monuments. They also symbolized a new, post-Calvinist optimism about the afterlife. While the fear of hell fire and damnation hovered like the plague over old urban graveyards, these new rural cemeteries were places to celebrate life on earth and rest in the assurance of eternal life in heaven. As they became popular, the "graveyard" was rechristened the "cemetery" (literally, "sleeping chamber"), and gloomy death's heads on gravestones gave way to willows, oaks, and acorns—naturalistic images of life, hope, resurrection, and immortality. By the time of the first shot at Sumter's Ferry, the rural cemetery had effectively replaced the urban graveyard, traditionalists were wringing their hands about the declining belief in hell, and things were looking up for the dead.[4]

The success of these cemeteries produced at least one rich irony. While initially designed as a way to isolate the dead from the living, they inexorably drew the living to them. Instantly de rigueur, the new rural cemeteries became tourist attractions. Some drew over 100,000 visitors a year. And many stayed, building homes on nearby land with views of the meadows and lakes of these picturesque abodes of the dead. The rural cemetery movement might have been able to manage this influx, but it could not survive the swift expansion of America's cities. As cities swelled, cemeteries became as overcrowded as the urban graveyards they had replaced. Suburban cemeteries became urban, swallowed up by the cities they had fled. New construction—of buildings, roads, railways, trolley lines, and subways—unearthed old graves, waking the sleeping dead not with Gabriel's trumpet but with shovels and pickaxes. The system of quarantining the dead was breaking down. Meanwhile, mortality and morbidity rates continued to rise, and the Civil War brought the issue of death front and center. Once again, the problem of what to do with the dead was on the national agenda.

After 1865 sanitarians continued to speak of the perils of decaying organic matter, dead bodies included. And they still blamed immigrants for spreading epidemics. But by the 1870s miasma theory was beginning to be challenged by a new hypothesis, which posited that infectious diseases were carried not by miasma but by microorganisms, or "germs." While these microbes could travel by air, they could also be transmitted through ground, water, and food. Germ theory had been around in one form or another since ancient times, but it got a big boost from the invention of the compound microscope in the 1820s and was effectively proven in the laboratory in the 1880s. In that decade scientists isolated the organisms that caused cholera, diphtheria, tuberculosis, and typhoid—the great killers of the nineteenth century. In the 1890s lab tests detected these killers, and an antitoxin against diphtheria became the first major application of germ theory to American medicine. By this decade the bacteriological revolution, which one historian has termed "the major medical breakthrough of the nineteenth century, and possibly of all time," was well underway.[5]

As the theory of miasma yielded to germ theory and talk of disease and death flooded the nation after the storm of the Civil War, the sanitary movement entered a new phase. The "new sanitarians," as the sanitary reformers aligned with germ theory are called, shifted their sights from the public to the private realm. They continued to be preoccupied with cleanliness, but that preoccupation no longer focused on the filthy environment. Instead, it targeted personal hygiene. "Wash your hands," these new sanitarians told America's dangerous classes. "Cover your mouth when you cough." "Use a handkerchief when you blow your nose." "And don't spit." Convinced that epidemics were spread by bad habits that might be reduced or eliminated through proper education, sanitarians transformed themselves into preachers of etiquette and guardians of manners. Gradually, bad hygiene became not only un-healthful but unvirtuous. "Public health ever goes hand in hand with true liberty," the *Journal of the American Medical Association* editorial-ized in 1883, "and is the companion of orderly habits and pure morals." The sanitary movement was now in the genteel business of the cultiva-tion of individual character. Cleanliness had taken its seat next to god-liness.[6]

The paradigm shift from miasma theory to germ theory did nothing to diminish fears concerning the dead, who along with the immigrants and the poor continued to be blamed for the nation's plagues. The new sanitarians no doubt worried less than their predecessors about corpse-caused miasma, but they worried more about corpse-borne germs. In fact, the bacteriological revolution, at least in its infancy, only reinforced the perception that the putrefying bodies of the dead threatened the health of the living. In books, tracts, articles, papers, and lectures, sani-tary scientists attacked the tradition of earth burial as unclean, unsafe, unsanitary, and impure. It had become "impossible to give any serious consideration to the question of public health without meeting at the outset this matter of the disposal of the dead." How to dispose of corpses had become "one of the important sanitary questions" of the day.[7]

Burial Reform

Mark Twain, whose book *The Gilded Age* helped to shape popular per-ception of the era as gilt with pretense and hypocrisy, took on the issue of burial in his own indomitable fashion in *Life on the Mississippi* (1883). Of the cemeteries of New Orleans he wrote, "It is all grotesque, ghastly, horrible." His concern was sanitation. "Graveyards may have been justifiable in the bygone ages, when nobody knew that for every dead body put into the ground to glut the earth and the plant-roots and the air with disease-germs, five or fifty, or maybe a hundred, persons must die before their proper time," he complained, "but they are hardly justifiable now, when even the children know that a dead saint enters upon a century-long career of assassination the moment the earth closes over his corpse."[8]

In the decades after the Civil War a growing vanguard of reformers denounced these saintly assassinations. Doctor after doctor cited studies by scientists as distinguished as Pasteur, Koch, and Darwin. Each physician seemed to have a favorite anecdote (most of them from

Europe): an English village decimated when topsoil removed from an old churchyard was scattered over nearby gardens; three grave diggers who died from noxious fumes at a Parisian graveyard; nuns ravaged by disease for a dozen years by a corpse buried under their convent floor.[9] The moral of these stories? Corpses are poison. Burial is unsanitary. "History teems with proof of epidemics caused by decomposing human bodies."[10]

Such dangers were not confined to the old urban graveyards; the new rural cemeteries were also a threat. God's suburban acres were themselves becoming overcrowded, and the sanitarians knew from experience in city slums that overcrowding could be hazardous to health. Moreover, as cities encroached on suburban cemeteries, even seemingly isolated cemeteries were believed to pose hazards. Some feared that "the breezes that blow from Greenwood, Mount Auburn, and Laurel Hill" were "laden with germs which propagate the diseases which have already slain our kindred." In addition to polluting air, cemeteries were said to pollute water. Effluvia from some suburban cemeteries, it was thought, drained into reservoirs. According to one doctor, the waters of Philadelphia's Schuylkill River were "loaded with sure death" by drainage from beloved Laurel Hill Cemetery: "When you drink Schuylkill water you are sampling your grandfather."[11]

Having looked at burial and judged it unhealthful, reformers cast about for an alternative. Their opponents cited the popularity of burial and asked, "Why change?" But the reformers followed a less parochial strategy: surveying the options across time and cultures and determining which of the methods was best. "Shall we throw out the dead into the Ganges, or more conveniently into the Ohio?" one asked. "Shall we expose our dead, West Indian fashion, in the fork of a tree, or East Indian fashion, as do the Parsees, on the grated platform of a tall tower, for vultures to pick to pieces? Shall we be embalmed...mummified?"[12] The answer to each of these questions was no. These authors were, after all, forward-looking Americans, and among them there was little interest in reviving the supposedly barbarous customs of "heathens" (ancient or modern). They were committed instead to finding a modern, scientific way.

Two popular alternatives called for limited modifications to the American way of burial. The first, which was supported most forcefully by Mr. Seymour Haden of England but gained a hearing in the United States, was the "earth-to-earth system." The dead were buried in perishable wicker enclosures, which allowed soil to break down the corpse (and its contagions) quickly. To prevent contamination to the living, this system called for deeper burial than usual, typically ten rather than six feet under.[13] The second option, also designed to hasten decomposition, was "quick-lime burial"—covering the underground corpse with caustic lime.[14]

Also proposed were new and improved tombs—airtight mausoleums that would not allow disease-causing agents to escape—and equally impervious coffins or "air-tight metal cases." Colin T. Martin, a former sanitary commissioner in Bombay, India, supported a modification on the secure coffin. His brainstorm, later taken up by American colleagues, was to construct "air-tight and durable coffins" fitted with "subterranean ventilating tubes with shafts rising high above the ground to carry off the putrid gases." Other suggestions included "deep sea burial" in metal coffins designed to corrode, "desiccation" or a thorough drying of the body followed by "pulverization," and "cementation" or the encasing of the body in cement. Perhaps the most gruesome alternative was a form of electrocution in which the body, placed between large copper plates and acting the part of "the filament in an incandescent lamp," was "instantly carbonized." Yet another possibility, dubbed "metallic burial," was to convert corpses into "statues of gold, silver, and copper by electro-plating them" for display in "domestic galleries."[15]

While most of these practices were proposed in all seriousness, some critics found them laughable. After blasting the proposal to electroplate the dead as "purely eccentric and grotesque," one writer took a jab at a French proposal to convert corpses to stone via "petrification." "In a thousand years time if persons will only preserve their relations and friends," he mused, "they will be able to build a house with them, and thus live in residences surrounded by their ancestors." This same writer, however, went on to propose "calcification, or cretafaction"—chemically transforming the body into stone and them pummeling it into powder for preservation or scattering.[16]

Incinerating Sanitarians

Of all the alternatives to burial proposed in the Gilded Age, the most popular was cremation. In waging their war for cremation, which one overzealous advocate dubbed "the greatest reform movement of the century," cremationists attacked burial on all sides. Their method, they said, was superior to burial on sanitary, economic, aesthetic, social, political, historical, practical, ethical, theological, and ritualistic grounds. Of all these types of arguments, however, cremationists focused first and foremost on sanitary claims. In fact, sanitary considerations were so important to Gilded Age cremationists that many claimed the debate between the torch and the tomb should be decided on sanitary evidence alone.[17]

Sanitary arguments for cremation were made most often and most persuasively by physicians, who during the last quarter of the nineteenth century were beginning to emerge as professionals. In publications like the *Journal of the American Medical Association* and in more specialized mouthpieces for sanitary science, medical experts weighed the relative merits of burial and cremation. They determined that burial was a sanitary evil and cremation a boon to public health. Sanitary arguments for cremation nearly always began with a rehearsal of the evils of burial. Studies were cited and anecdotes rehashed; inevitably, Sir Henry Thompson's work on cremation was summoned to the bar. "No dead body is ever placed in the soil without polluting the earth, the air, and the water above and about it," Thompson had written. And an American admirer added, "No human body can pass through the cheering glow of the cinerary furnace and come out in the purified and utterly inoffensive form of white ashes, without contributing substantially to the liberation of earth, water and air from this dreaded pollution."[18]

This much was inevitable, the argument went: the corpse was going to be resolved into water, acid, ammonia, lime, and assorted minerals. Nature demanded as much. But how and where would that decomposition occur? How long would it take? And what havoc would the fermenting corpse wreak in the meantime? All that was up to the public, and the public's health hung in the balance:

> The question for this hour is, Shall this be done in sixty minutes or less, through the influence of, and with all the grandeur, and beauty, and brilliancy, of the cumulative heat of an imprisoned and condensed sunbeam, with harmless and beneficial results; or shall it through a period of fifteen or twenty years moulder in the earth, polluting everything with which it comes in contact—earth, air, and water—offering habitat and pabulum to the universal scavengers which feed and fatten by the millions on the feculent matter, and therefrom exhale mephitic gases, with which to load the air, and be wafted to the lungs of the living and troubled survivors?[19]

It was not much of a choice. From the onset of death to the cessation of decay, a cadaver was poison. So why allow it to fester longer than necessary? Rather than impeding the laws of nature via embalming or

metal caskets, why not give Mother Nature a technological boost—
especially when from the viewpoint of science even burial was a form of
combustion?

Advocates initially yoked sanitary arguments for cremation to the
miasma theory of the old sanitarians. From this perspective the prime
public health dangers were the noxious gases emitted by decomposing
organic matter—what one sanitarian, in a marvelous fit of rhetorical
excess, called "the noxious exhalations and mephitic gases evolved
from a reeking, putrefying, mouldering mass of flesh." The main repos-
itories for those gases and that flesh were cemeteries, especially ones
with shallow and overcrowded graves. Here statistics were frequently
marshaled. Given 25,000 dying per year in New York City and an average weight of only 100 pounds each, *Frank Leslie's Illustrated Newspaper* calculated that local cemeteries were filled each year "with two
and a half million pounds of animal matter to poison the air and water
which we breathe and drink." Additional proof for what *Leslie's* described as "the deadly vapors rising from the ground" was the stench of
death, which the nostrils of medical men, fine-tuned at dissecting tables,
could reportedly detect in the cemetery. Contagious diseases were quite
literally in the air; ghosts were not the only dangers wafting through the
graveyards.[20]

Early cremationists were especially fond of telling stories about individuals felled by the vapors of the dead—Pisto the grave digger who
"met with instantaneous death" after "inhaling graveyard gases" on an
errand into a vault to steal a corpse's shoes; or the four French monks
who descended to remove a stinking cadaver from under a monastery,
only to die (all of them) by suffocation. (Even dogs, cats, and birds
brought into contact with the deadly "mephitic gas" of the monastery
died within minutes after violent convulsions!) The dead, the cremationists concluded, can and do kill the living. Cemeteries were fertile
farms in which diseases were planted, then sown; burial was kin to murder. It was high time, therefore, for "clean, pure, and undangerous" cremation to replace burial—time for "God's acre" to "become a thing of
the past."[21]

In addition to telling lurid stories and marshaling scientific theories,
sanitary-minded cremationists conjured the Biblical metaphor of the
body as seed. In 1 Corinthians 15, Paul attempts to explain how the
identity of the buried person can be the same as the identity of the person raised from the dead at the end of time. His explanation hinges on
two metaphors: the corrupt corpse as seed sown and the incorruptible

resurrection body as wheat harvested. For Paul, these are metaphors of hope. Burial is the sowing of the mundane "natural body," resurrection the reaping of the glorified "spiritual body." Cremationists borrowed from Paul images of seeds, crops, planting, harvesting, and fertility, but described a far more dangerous yield. Buried bodies were "seeds of pestilence and ghastly horrors" that brought forth "a terrible crop of pollution, disease germs, and death." Cemeteries were not hopeful sites for resurrection but "nurseries of disease" and "beds of pestilence." "By burying in the ground a body dead of any zymotic disease," one wrote, "we are planting for our descendants, seed, sure, sooner or later, to bring forth a horrible crop of pestilence and death!" In this way, the cremationists turned cremation into a moral as well as a sanitary crusade. To bury was, by this logic, to murder.[22]

As the bacteriological revolution set in, the "incinerating sanitarians" were forced to rework their metaphors and retool their claims. They continued to agitate by anecdote, but between the 1870s, when germ theory was first seriously debated, and the 1890s, when the bacteriological revolution was well underway, they often hedged their bets, drawing on the idioms of both theories. Buried corpses threaten the public health, one advocate wrote, by "giving off noxious gases and disease germs." Burial remained a crime against the living, but cremation was now promoted as "the great purifier," "the greatest of all disinfectants," and "the only true germicide." Whether expressed in the idiom of miasma or the idiom of germs, the crux of the sanitary argument remained the same: burial was polluting and cremation purifying. Incineration was the cleanest way to dispose of the dead, and the crematory the "greatest of sanitary institutions."[23]

In 1878, in one of the earliest writings plainly linking cremation and germ theory, Dr. LeMoyne noted that with the assistance of the microscope "the germ theory of disease has become more and more popular with scientific investigators." It had been proven, he argued, that burying the bodies of victims of infectious diseases amounted to "loading the atmosphere, and polluting the waters... with the *specific* germs of the diseases from which death resulted." Unlike the earth, which failed to act as an effective destroyer of those germs, the crematory furnace was a fail-safe germ killer. Three years later a paper read before the American Public Health Association claimed that recent studies had proved the theory that typhoid, cholera, yellow fever, and perhaps diphtheria were all caused "by the direct reception into the body of a particular and specific disease germ."[24]

By the mid-1880s cremationists had largely shifted the focus of their fears from miasma to germs. In "Cremation as a Safeguard against Epidemics," an 1884 paper also read before the American Public Health Association, the Reverend John D. Beugless, U.S. Navy chaplain and president of the New York Cremation Society, posed this question: "How then shall we best avoid epidemics of contagion?" Quarantine had not worked, and neither had disinfectants. "The crematory," he concluded, "is the only never-failing germicide." His pro-cremation rhetoric, the art of a zealous convert, lit on both sanitary and spiritual themes: "Instead, therefore, of putting our beloved dead into a damp dark hole in the ground, there in the companionship of loathsome bacteria to putrefy, and thence to send forth the poisonous and deadly exhalations and emanations of the grave to seize upon the tenderly ministering survivors and drag them into the loathsome caverns where disease and death hold carnival, let us purify the material of their bodies from every defiling and corrupting agency, and translate them decorously and reverentially, but expeditiously, into the elements of all new and beauteous life."[25]

While most cremationists were content to campaign for cremation as an option, a number of medical experts saw it as a sanitary necessity, at least during epidemics. Claiming that germs could lie dormant in buried corpses for years, only to spawn outbreaks after being surfaced by earthworms or exhumation, some sanitarians argued for compulsory cremation in the case of victims of contagious diseases. We burn the clothes and personal effects of victims of epidemics, they noted, why not burn their bodies, which are more saturated with germs? "The objector should be compelled to submit," one doctor wrote, "when the public health is in danger." One crusading sanitarian went even farther, borrowing from the language of the antislavery movement to argue for the "entire abolition" of the evil of burial.[26]

Scapegoating the Dead

Like other public health crusades of the time, the Gilded Age cremation movement was an effort to purify America, and that effort had social as well as spiritual and sanitary import. When confronted with the problems associated with rapid immigration and urbanization, cremationists, like other reformers of their time, found a group to blame. But rather than focusing on cleansing America of sinners or Blacks, cremationists focused on cleansing the nation of the dead. On the face of it, this analysis is not particularly troubling. After all, there are far worse ways to exercise what French theorist René Girard claims is a universal human tendency to scapegoat outsiders during times of social chaos. But there was a dark side to the cremation movement's purity quest, namely, the tendency of many cremationists to draw close associations between the dead and immigrants. Journals such as *The Urn* and *Modern Crematist* repeatedly reinforced the theory, popular among sanitarians, that infectious diseases were imported rather than homegrown. They also spread the view that those imported diseases survived and thrived in America largely because of the filthy habits of unsanitary immigrants. One issue of *The Urn* included a lead story called "Spring Cleaning" and another article entitled "Keep the Destroyer Out." The first story predicted that, in the absence of new immigration restrictions, the spring would bring cholera to U.S. shores. In the second article the destroyer seems to be both cholera and the immigrant himself.[27]

The tendency of cremationists to scapegoat the "dangerous classes" along with the dead became plain during a 1880s campaign to construct crematories for immigrants and the poor. In his 1884 paper on "Cremation as a Safeguard against Epidemics," the Reverend Beugless recommended establishing "a crematory at every quarantine station and in connection with every public hospital and in every Potter's Field" to facilitate the incineration of the poor and of immigrants struck down on U.S.-bound ships. "But we should not stop here," he said. City garbage too should be "purified" by crematory-style furnaces. A later article on "Cremation and Its Importance in Cholera" listed the main sources of the century's most feared epidemic disease as "immigrants, mechandise [*sic*], clothing, excretions, water, earth-corpses, and insects." In this way Beugless and his contemporaries laid bare the tendency of genteel reformers to associate immigrants and the poor with dirt, disease, and death. Beugless did not get his wish for a vast national network of crematories for immigrants and the poor, but in 1889 New York City did replace a crowded potter's field (a cemetery for the poor) with a crematory next to the Quarantine Hospital on Swinburne Island. The country's first publicly run crematory, this facility was designed to cremate immigrants who had died of infectious diseases.[28]

Surely the Gilded Age cremation movement as a whole should not be reduced to a cultural artifact of an age of purity or dismissed out of hand as nativistic. Most early cremationists were cosmopolitans. Some, like LeMoyne, were abolitionists. But it is probably not a coincidence that the movement arose as Anglo-Saxonism was at its height. The last two decades of the nineteenth century witnessed the rise of Jim Crow laws, increased anti-Semitism, the passage of anti-Chinese immigration legislation, the formation of the anti-Catholic American Protective Association, and the publication of perhaps the most influential tract in American nativism, Josiah Strong's *Our Country* (1885). All across America in the 1880s and 1890s, genteel Americans were working hard to purify America, feverishly separating themselves from what pollutes. The U.S. cremation movement capitalized on and contributed to those cultural preoccupations.

Sanitary Skepticism and the AMA

The *Medical Record* exaggerated when it claimed in 1886 that "no one has dared to oppose [cremation] on scientific grounds." So did the *New York Tribune* when it reported two years later that "every medical and sanitary expert favors cremation." Nevertheless, support for cremation among medical professionals was widespread. When Dr. Adams of the newly formed Massachusetts State Board of Health surveyed 133 physicians and chemists in Massachusetts in 1874, only about a third preferred cremation over earth burial. A decade and a half later reporters from the *Medical and Surgical Reporter* interviewed nearly as many physicians from cities across the Northeast and Midwest. Of those who had a clear preference, nearly 80 percent cast a vote for cremation. During the last two decades of the nineteenth century, committees of the American Public Health Association, the Society of Medical Jurisprudence and State Medicine of New York, the Boston Homeopathic Medical Society, and even the American Medical Association (AMA) concluded that cremation was a sanitary necessity. Apparently the views of these elites trickled down at least to a few newspaper men. In 1880 a *New York Tribune* editorial admitted "it would unquestionably be a good thing for the public health if this way of cremation should become popular."[29]

Of all the endorsements, the most controversial was the AMA's. The occasion was the reading of a cremation committee report at the annual meeting of the AMA in St. Louis on May 6, 1886. Turning Paul's seed metaphor on its head, the committee likened burial to "the planting of the seeds" that "propagate the germs of disease and death, and spread desolation and pestilence over the human race." The report concluded: "God's half-acre must become a thing of the past. The grave-yard must be abandoned...[since] the earth was made for the living and not for the dead, and...pure air, pure water, and pure soil are absolutely necessary for perfect health." After this report was read, the AMA adopted a resolution, by a vote of 159 to 106, recommending cremation as "a sanitary necessity in populous cities." But a dissenting hand shot up, and a motion to reconsider was on the table. After some discussion that motion carried, and the matter was referred to another committee for further consideration. In 1887 the cremation committee issued another report, whose recommendations were again shuffled elsewhere, buried forever in internal AMA machinations.[30]

Shortly after the AMA's 1886 annual meeting the *Medical Record* denounced the initial pro-cremation vote as a "hasty and careless action," adding that "cremationists have not yet been able to trace a disease, much less an epidemic, to the suburban graveyards of our populous cities." Also in 1886, Dr. Frank H. Hamilton, president of the New York Society of Medical Jurisprudence and State Medicine, opposed a resolution urging the state of New York to pass a law mandating cremation for both victims of infectious diseases and the indigent. According to Hamilton, cremationists had "greatly over-estimated" the dangers of burial, which could be eliminated merely by burying bodies four to six feet underground and avoiding cemetery overcrowding. Writing at a time when miasma theory had not yet been totally routed, Hamilton admitted that decaying organic matter emitted noxious gases that, under certain circumstances, could cause illness and death. But he insisted that those gases ceased to be formed two months after interment and that in the interim the earth disinfected them well. Hamilton then turned to some stories of his own. Chicago's ascent to its status as the world's slaughterhouse had not been accompanied by a decline in the general health of the city, he said, and the keeper of New York's morgue hadn't missed a day of work in nineteen years.[31]

Hamilton's arguments recapitulated the earlier work of other medical skeptics, who had denounced cremationists as "sanitary Jeremiahs" and their cause as "humbug." In 1875 Dr. Adams of Massachusetts had concluded that cremation was not a hygienic necessity in the United States. Adams admitted that urban graveyards had in the past "repeatedly proved injurious to the health of the community" and he recommended their "complete abolition." But he insisted that the modern practice of interment in rural cemeteries was perfectly safe. Dr. A. Otterson, who was dispatched by the Brooklyn Board of Health to witness the De Palm incineration, was also unconvinced "of the necessity or adaptability of the process to our times and country." Later in the century a number of physicians interviewed on the subject also expressed skepticism. "The dangers of earth burial are all fanciful. No serious epidemic has ever been started by a cemetery, and very slight precautions will make all cemeteries safe," said one. "I do not believe that pathogenic germs ever escape from the ordinary grave," affirmed another. Hygienic objections to burial were for the sanitary skeptics "as baseless as the ghosts that were supposed to infest the graveyards."[32]

Some commentators admitted to minor sanitary problems with burial but insisted that those problems paled in comparison with more serious public health dangers. In a letter to the editor of the *Detroit Commercial Advertiser,* one concerned citizen asked, "Are not more lives poisoned by the fumes of tobacco and alcohol, than by the malaria that eminates [*sic*] from grave-yards?...Before we erect crematories in every town...my hope is that the saloon, the flood gate of disease and death, will be closed." Dr. T. DeWitt Talmage also believed that the living were more dangerous than the dead. In a quotation later reprinted in *Modern Cemetery*, he told *Ladies' Home Journal* readers that "Greenwood is healthier than Broadway...Pere la Chaise than Champs Elysees." The anti-cremation rhetoric of Dr. D. W. Cathell of Baltimore was more florid. In twenty-five years of practicing medicine in the vicinity of Baltimore's cemeteries, Cathell testified, he had not seen a single case of sickness attributable to them. There were in his view far more dangerous sources of miasma and germs to worry about:

> With stinking garbage boxes in every yard; with our germ-producing sewers and our cesspool exhalations; our filthy gutters, our stable effluvia and our market-house debris; with our suburbs alive with disease-breeding slaughter-houses, dumps, pig-styes, manure piles, night-soil-using truck farms; with fertilizer factories, carcasses, weeds, gullies, stagnant pools and hundreds of other unsanitary foci staring us in the face, with dangers as much greater than inhumation as a camel is larger than a mote, the gain by cremation would be very small. Let us continue to bury our dead, with increased precautions against their affecting the living, and leave cremation to its dreamy partisans and Pagan history.[33]

The sanitary claims of the cremationists were also resisted by some cemetery officials, who apparently weighed the threat of burial to both public health and personal wealth. A paper read before the Association of American Cemetery Superintendents proposed that the earth, which the author described as "nature's depository and deodorizer," was as effective a disinfectant of germs as the crematory furnace. Others claimed that the ornamental trees and bushes in the lawn-park cemeteries of the late nineteenth century acted as "fresh air reservoirs" that scrubbed urban air clean.[34]

Such skepticism produced no groundswell of resistance to cremation among medical professionals. At least in the nineteenth century, cremationists won the sanitary argument. But the contest between burial and cremation would not be decided on sanitary grounds alone.

Iron-Hearted Progress

While sanitation loomed large in the minds of cremationists, matters of taste were crucial to their opponents. In fact, just as cremationists often dismissed aesthetics as mere sentimentality, partisans of burial brushed off sanitary science by arguing that in some matters sentiment alone should rule. One critic even disqualified doctors from the debate. "A question as important as what is to become of our mortal remains should not be left to those who make so light of the remains of others," he argued. "Men who are in the habit of handling the remains of others as though they were sticks of cord-wood and only worth the amount of fuel there is in them, are hardly proper judges where the feelings of others are concerned." Another skeptic dismissed the "humbuggery and charlatanry" of the sanitarians as so many cries from Chicken Little. "Doctorcraft," he complained, "has taken the place of priest-craft."[35]

Perhaps cremation's critics should not have discounted so severely the opinions of physicians. When reporters quizzed Gilded Age doctors about cremation, virtually all admitted its sanitary benefits, but many conceded the facts reluctantly, noting that they were personally partial to burial. Dr. V. P. Gibney's divided mind was representative. "If I divested myself of sentiment and took a purely scientific view of the matter, I should of course say that cremation was the best mode of disposal of the dead," he said, "but there is something about a well-kept cemetery that appeals to my sentiment. Time and again I find myself envying those who lie buried amid these beautiful surroundings." Aesthetics weighed heavily for Dr. George Strawbridge too. He knew that cremation was "unquestionably the only fit and hygienic method for the disposal of the dead," but "sentimentally speaking" he did not like "the idea of being baked in an oven."[36]

Many commentators on both sides of the question said they recoiled instinctively from the mere thought of cremation, so it is fair to conclude that one of the main objections to the practice was "the feeling of

repugnance, and even of horror, which is naturally excited in the minds
of the majority of civilized people, by the idea of doing violence to the
remains of the beloved dead." Prophesies that the question would be
"decided by individual sentiment" alone would prove to be incorrect;
aesthetic considerations were never paramount in the nineteenth-
century cremation debate. But those considerations never went away
either. For partisans of burial, moreover, that was all for the good, since
in the arena of sentiment, burial clearly had the upper hand. "The place
of the grave in the affections, literature and history of mankind," one
editor noted, was not about to be "ceded at once to an urn of ashes."[37]

The aesthetic argument against cremation typically began with what
is now called visualization. "Think of the horrors," one critic wrote, "of
the crisping, crackling, roasting, steaming, shriveling, blazing features
and hands that yesterday were your soul's delight." Think of exploding
cadavers. Think of the stench of burning flesh and hair. Think of the
smoke. Think of bubbling brains. Then you will be gripped by "paralyz-
ing horror" at even the thought of "submitting the remains of...dear
departed relatives to its sizzling process." Cremation was, in a word, repulsive: "There is nothing beautiful in being shoved into an oven, and
scientifically barbecued by a patented furnace."[38]

This, of course, had been the main objection to the De Palm cremation. The crematory was said to be offensively unattractive, its rooms
cheap and insufficiently furnished, the crowds coarse, and the journalists uncouth. Critics had described the De Palm cremation itself as more
barbeque than rite. The body was in their view ghastly and the odor of
sizzling flesh (at least in some accounts) pervasive. Even the publicity
surrounding that event was said to be vulgar. "There may be a class of
surviving relatives, who consider it a flattering attention to have the
world advised of the appearance of their dead while in various stages of
consumption by the Le Moyne oven," one newspaper man wrote of a
later cremation in Washington. "But then there are others who might
resent this well-meant service as a profanation of the privacy of their
grief."[39]

If crematories were to the skeptics all sizzle and horror, graveyards
were but splendor and grass. Partisans of burial conjured up "a myriad
tender associations" of the cemetery. Green grass. Cooling shade.
Heartfelt monuments. Family strolls. Pleasant memories. The old,
crowded churchyards may have been eyesores, but the new rural cemeteries were "valleys of peace, God's acre, in which [sleep] the sacred
dust of our beloved, awaiting a blessed resurrection." On the aesthetic

question no less a literary light than Walt Whitman weighed in for burial. America's poet conceded in the *Philadelphia Inquirer* that "we had better burn our dead, if preserving the corpse underground is going to wither us all," but he was no fan of cremation:

> God's acre won't be watered with tears or blooming in flowers any more if the grim old furnace stands there and the white ashes are blown by the winds.... No, I don't believe in it, and I don't want to see the practice become general. It makes a fellow tremble to think of the iron-hearted progress of the age.... The body with life in it is a beautiful thing. I don't think we do right, St. Paul and the rest of us, in deriding its warmth of appetite and the passions that attend upon the flesh. And when the life is gone out of it I rather respect the old shell for all it has been, as well as for all it has contained.

The body electric was too beautiful to be burned.[40]

A Beautiful Art

The aesthete's love affair with the cemetery did not go unchallenged. Cremationists knew their reform ran the risk of being associated too closely with calculating manliness. They worried about the stereotype of the cremationist as an all-too-rational gentleman who valued head over heart. And they knew their movement would never become truly popular if they limited their appeals to reason and common sense. "Unless [cremation] is shown to have inherent excellence and inherent attractiveness, unless it moves us by its 'sweetness and its light,' unless it builds above the grave a trellis-work of thought and hope upon which sorrowing love may train its clinging vines and seek its sweetest flowers," one conceded, "it cannot take the place of those familiar methods which are dear and venerable from age." And so cremationists argued that their method was as aesthetically pure as it was hygienically necessary—"a beautiful art."[41]

Secure in the knowledge that women were the final arbiters of beauty if not truth, cremationists published cremation accounts by female eyewitnesses won over after learning firsthand of cremation's aesthetic virtues. While burialists recoiled at the thought of cremating a loved one, these converts seemed to relish the idea. Mary B. Comyns of the Massachusetts Cremation Society, for example, contended that the corpse she saw cremated was "absolutely undisturbed" by the fire. Heat alone transformed it, first, into a "beautiful rosy color," later to a "beautiful white" and finally to "pure ashes." All was "tenderly done,"

she concluded, with "neither carelessness nor levity." Another eyewitness, Alice N. Lincoln, wrote that as "we stood in silence watching the
rosy glow which played over the white surface of the retort, a feeling
came to me of awe, certainly, but also of peace and rest. There was
something so spiritual, so elevating, in the absolute purity of the intense
heat, that it seemed to all of us who stood there far less appalling or de-
pressing than the blackness of an open grave." Another women argued
that a crematory visit converted her too. Initially she was reluctant to
accede to her husband's wishes to be cremated. But when "I saw the
door of the crematory taken down, its rosy light shine forth, and his
peaceful form, clad in white, laid there at rest amid a loveliness that
was simply fascinating to the eye, and without a glimpse of flames, or
fire, or coals, or smoke, I said, and say so still, this method, beyond all
methods I have seen, is the most pleasing to the senses, the most charming to the imagination, and the most grateful to the memory."[42]

Cremationists concerned about pleasing the senses tried to distance
their modern, scientific method from its ancient, unscientific kin. "The
system of the Hindoos and of the North American Indians will bear no
sort of comparison with it," one advocate wrote, while another said the
modern method was "as far in advance" of ancient burning "as is the
telephone of the trumpet...or the brilliant electric light of the fitful
torch." Among the supposed advantages of modern, scientific cremation was the fact that it took place privately in a modern furnace, while
the ancient rite took place publicly on a pyre in the open air. Modern
cremation, advocates insisted, had "altogether evolved away from the
customs of Indian Gaikhwars." It had also progressed beyond burial,
which despite efforts to create Jim Crow cemeteries segregated by race,
class, and ethnicity, still allowed for the scandalous mixing of the bodily
fluids of blacks and whites, rich and poor, Irish and German, clean and
unclean. Cremation, on the other hand, by scrupulously attending to
one body at a time and then depositing the individual ashes safely in a
secure urn, offended neither the sensibilities nor the prejudices of genteel Americans.[43]

As eagerly as they lavished praise on cremation its supporters lashed
out at "the abominations of the grave." Burial, they said, was "unclean
and repulsive" and the cemetery barbaric and unrefined. While their opponents associated cremation with heathens in Greece and Asia, cremationists likened the burying public to Parsees. "It is about as disgusting
to think of our departed friends rotting in the ground," one com-

plained, "as to know them to be devoured by carrion-eating vultures."
"True and refined sentiment," another said, "is in favor of cremation."[44]

In an effort to sustain the claim that the grave "presents the most terrible spectacle" imaginable, cremationists, too, urged Americans to en-
gage in visualization. See the water oozing into the coffin and effluvia
oozing out. Smell the stench of decaying flesh. Tremble at the darkness.
See the brain "fallen out of its bony case, a shapeless, unctuous, stinking mass, abhorred even by the worms which so ravenously seize upon
the flesh, the heart, the lungs, and especially the intestines." Then ask
yourself, "Why in the name of a merciful God, should we subject ourselves, and those we love, to so dreadful a condition?" Which method
of disposal of the dead was really most vile?[45]

One sanitarian urged his listeners to visualize their hometown of Buffalo, New York:

> Every city has its shadow. There is a Buffalo over and a Buffalo under-
> ground. There is a Buffalo with fine houses and daylight and sunshine and
> pure air and populous streets. There is a Buffalo with narrower, peopleless
> streets, with coldness and darkness and silent cells, with still inhabitants, and
> an atmosphere which is the breath of pestilence. Visitors go there from the
> brighter city, but return not. The Buffalo above ground grows, but the un-
> derground city grows faster. If reverence be really due the dead, let them go
> not there. Let us lift this shadowy city into the sunshine. Let the elements go,
> if need be, by fire, purely and speedily into the sunlight whence they came.[46]

This "tale of two cities" illustrates wonderfully the battle of metaphors
that was the aesthetic debate. From the cremationists' perspective, it
was a choice between light and darkness, warmth and cold, sunshine
and shadow, purity and pollution. (Who wouldn't flee a shower of
worms for "a bath of rosy light"?) But at least a few aesthetic arguments for cremation veered toward the theological. One cremationist
confessed in an article published in *The Urn* that he saw fire not as
something demonic but as "something sacred." It reminded him of
heaven, not hell. "Its power, its purity, its beauty, make me understand
how it was anciently used as an image of the attributes of the divine."[47]

Here, as in most cremationist writing, nontheological concerns were
closely tied to spiritual convictions. Cremationists were, to be sure, sanitary reformers. Sanitarians were prominent in the movement from the
start, and cremation was a frequent topic in journals such as *The Sanitarian* and *Medical and Surgical Reporter.* But cremationists were also
religious and ritual reformers. Although many cremationists tried to

argue that the cremation versus burial debate should be settled on sanitary grounds alone, hardly anyone was able to get through a procremation speech or article without referring to theology. Some tried to crown sanitary science king, while others tried to do the same to theology. But for the most part, sanitary, spiritual, and aesthetic concerns worked together to build the case for cremation.

In considering the connection between godliness and cleanliness across human cultures, some have tried to reduce ritualization to hygiene by arguing that certain religious rites are essentially hygienic codes. It is commonplace, at least in some circles, to affirm that Muslim rites of bathing or Jewish codes against eating pork arose for purely hygienic reasons—because Muhammad was a good sanitarian or Moses "an enlightened public health administrator." But this position, dubbed "medical materialism" by psychologist William James, is unconvincing. After all, is it not equally plausible that behaviors commended by sanitarians because of their salubrious effects may actually be ritually motivated? Is it not possible that America's earliest cremationists embraced cremation for ritualistic reasons rather than for its public health benefits? That is not the line I am taking here. But I do want to resist the notion that cremationists were motivated wholly by sanitary considerations. As anthropologist Mary Douglas has written, "Our ideas of dirt also express symbolic systems."[48]

The cremation cause surely should be viewed as part of a broader movement for sanitary reform and part of the even broader social reform impulse in Gilded Age America. It must not be reduced, however, to either a scientific or a social impulse. In fact, the sanitary and social reform movements can themselves be viewed as ritual demonstrations—parts of a vast movement for the elimination of dirt evident in the cremation crusade and in contemporaneous campaigns for circumcision, hand washing, nail clipping, hair brushing, and bathing. Perhaps even social reforms like temperance can fruitfully be interpreted as purity rites of a sort—key moments in a history of American ritual life that still waits to be written.

3

Resurrection and the Resurrectionists

LATE IN THE SUMMER OF 1887, AS sun and steam conspired to make Boston unbearable in an era still awaiting air conditioning, human bones began to materialize on Boylston Street across from the Boston Public Library. The culprit was progress. Laborers digging a trench for Edison Electric Light Company had run into brick burial vaults. Soon pickaxes and shovels were prematurely resurrecting skeletons and ribald schoolboys were fiddling with bones hanging on the fence at Boston Commons. One skull was reportedly purchased by a Harvard medical student for fifty cents. Others disappeared without a story. A few years later on the same street, a subway demanded another sacrifice. Once again, human remains were pitched in the air by gangs of workers "with no more respect...than for so much stick and stone." "This settles it for me," declared an eyewitness. "No laborers shall toss my skull about like a football years hence." Cremation, he decided, was the way to go. Or at least that's how *The Urn* told the story.[1]

Such tales were regular features in the nineteenth-century cremationist literature. In fact, they were nearly as frequent as stories of grave diggers choked to death by the miasmic exhalations of the decaying dead. Scan the pro-cremation literature even haphazardly and you will find stories about buried bodies snatched for ransom, children stillborn in the tombs of prematurely buried mothers, worms chomping on corpses, snakes slithering into coffins, hungry dogs digging up human remains, burial vaults caving in, and floods washing coffins downstream.

Other postmortem misadventures read like outlines for Edgar Allen Poe short stories: the body of a white woman is disinterred in Vossburg, Mississippi, by three black men intent on procuring "'conjure' bones'" to be used for dice; enterprising students from a medical school in Kansas City are arrested for masterminding a lucrative grave robbing ring supplying cadavers to professors; Brooklyn schoolchildren raid an abandoned burial ground at recess, using unearthed bones as playground swords; an exhumed coffin in Dayton, Ohio, yields a girl who tore out most of her hair and bit off parts of her fingers as she struggled to free herself from premature interment; the spring waters of the upper Delaware River flood through an old graveyard, leaving skeletons "dangling from trees"; and salacious young men satisfy their animal instincts "by outraging the fresh corpses of young and pretty women." Even the doggerel of cremationists hammered home the Gothic horrors:

> I laid my loved form in the grave—
>   The grave so deep, and damp and dark;
> My cheeks were wet with bitter tears
>   That he should be Death's chosen mark.
>
> I fondly thought the grave would be
>   To him a quiet, peaceful place,
> Where he might rest his weary limbs,
>   Free, at last, from Life's toilsome race.
>
> Mistaken thought—why veil the truth,
>   When knowledge, free from doubt, confirms
> The fact that in a few short months,
>   His flesh will be "chawed up" by worms?[2]

Some tried to bring to this barrage of poetry and prose a semblance of quantitative analysis. Body snatchings were an "almost *daily* occurrence," attested one source, while another calculated that "not one entombed body in a hundred remains undisturbed." An advertisement for "burglar proof grave vaults, made of steel" testified that no fewer than 40,000 dead bodies procured by midnight ghouls were "mutilated every year on dissecting tables in medical colleges in the United States."[3]

Grave profanations were not, as *The Urn* admitted, "the strongest argument in favor of the [cremation] cause," but they were an excellent backup, at least for practical folks more worried about the postmortem hazards facing their own flesh and bones than about refinement or public health. Like the stories of Pisto the grave digger, these lurid narratives were morality tales, and the moral was clear: Don't allow yourself to be buried unless you want your skull to be kicked around like a football or your heart dissected over the sputtering wisecracks of a medical student. No grave was safe from the outrages of the resurrectionists (as body snatchers were called in the Gilded Age), to say nothing of the dangers of heavy rains and other natural and cultural disasters. There was only one way to avoid "the embarrassing prospect of a premature burial, the cheerful chances of being boiled by the janitor of some medical college and our skeletons wired together and hung in a museum, and the opportunity if we escape the first two of being tipped out of our graves by a flood, earthquake, or act of the common council." That way was cremation.[4]

It is difficult to classify these appeals. They are, to be sure, horror stories. (*The Urn* offered its reports under the headline, "Our Chamber of Horrors.") As such, they both frightened and titillated. But they were also sermons of a sort, intended to change religious beliefs and behaviors. None of these stories constituted a theological argument per se. But all aimed to subvert the rites of burial by undermining assumptions, beliefs, attitudes, metaphors, and practices about death, the afterlife, the self, and the body that had been held dear for centuries in the Christian West. So while partisans of burial preferred to think of the cemetery as a "sleeping chamber," the grave as a bed, and death as a temporary rest before the great apocalyptic reawakening, the cremationists struggled to link burial instead with body snatchers and dissection tables. What would wake the buried dead? Not the trumpet but the pickax—not the resurrection but the resurrectionist.

Demythologizing the Grave

Students of New Testament scholarship will recognize these efforts as a sort of demythologization. In the nineteenth century pioneering New Testament critics worked to peel back layer upon layer of biblical myth and legend to uncover the historical Jesus underneath. Their method was to subject the Christian scripture to critical analysis. Anything that smacked of myth-making—the Virgin Birth, references to Jesus as "Son of God," or the miracle of the loaves and fishes—was thrown out as unreliable fiction. What remained was the "real" Jesus. The faithful, of course, were outraged.

What the cremationists were doing was equally outrageous. They too were trying to replace fiction with fact, myth with history, religious hope with scientific certainty. But rather than taking aim at Jesus, they set their sights on the traditional metaphors and narratives of burial.

Their goal was to unmask Americans' love affair with the cemetery as "false sentimentality." Consider the popular metaphor of death as sleep. Consider also the narrative that burial is followed first by rest in the coffin, later by bodily resurrection, and finally by the reconstitution of the person as a body-soul unity in heaven or hell. The obvious tension between this popular view—that the corpses of the Christian dead are lying in their graves awaiting Judgment Day—and the equally popular view that the faithful go to heaven immediately at death has never been fully worked out in Christian theology. But the metaphor of death as sleep and the narratives about the transition from life to death to burial to sleep to resurrection to judgment to eternal reward or punishment remained popular, inculcated in hymns, liturgies, Bible classes, and tombstones in the Judeo-Christian West.[5]

Aware of the power of this metaphor and these narratives, cremationists tried to demythologize both. The grave was not a pleasant place of sleep, they insisted, but a horrid site of ceaseless and gruesome activity. Time spent six feet under was anything but restful. There, change, not stasis, was the rule. Dr. Samuel D. Gross, one of America's most celebrated surgeons, knew in excruciating detail how decay afflicts the corpse. If ordinary Americans could only see exhumed and dissected bodies as medical doctors do, he said, they would recoil at the thought of burial. Or, as another doctor put it:

> If *they* would know what the physicians ken
>   And see but once the process of decay,
> No longer would they "plant" their dead in mud,
>   But would adopt the new and better way.[6]

Underground change was inevitable, the demythologizers insisted; the body was going to decay. "Shall we deceive ourselves with the idea that rest, eternal rest, for the body here begins?" asked one doctor. "No, not for one instant; never was there greater activity in the tissues of that still corpse than at [the moment of death]." Decomposition, not rest, is the rule of the grave. According to Felix Adler, whose spiritual journey led him from Reform Judaism into a radical alternative known as Ethical Culture, poets who say that the grave promotes rest and sleep are "throwing a false glamour over the hideous reality." "'He rests well,'" the critics concluded, "is a hideous mockery."[7]

In an effort to assist readers in imagining for themselves the postmortem horrors of the buried corpse, *The Urn* published gruesome photographs of exhumed bodies in varying states of decay. "Compare with these," it preached, "the pearly Ashes of the cinerary urn!" The literary equivalent of those images was a short piece called "Posthumous Revelations: From the Diary of a Corpse." Here a fictional diary writer, poor and in a coma, is taken for dead. Although he had told his wife he wanted to be cremated, a domineering aunt intervenes and he is buried—alive. After rattling around in his coffin while being ferried from ceremony to ceremony, he is deposited into an overcrowded metropolitan cemetery, "the second from the top in a tier of six." Later he hears resurrectionists stealing the corpse from the coffin above him. Worms attack next, boring through his coffin and then his body, mercifully killing him. After years and worms have reduced him to a skeleton, laborers dig him up to make room for a railroad. "Should I ever be reincarnated for another earth life," his tale concludes, "my arrangements for cremation will be ironclad."[8]

Like the testimonials of doctors about the body's postmortem transformations, "Posthumous Revelations" reminded Americans what ancient and medieval Christians had known but many modern Christians, in their determination to defy death, had forgotten: the corpse is a site of decay. Historian Carolyn Walker Bynum has referred to decay as "the fundamental religious and cultural problem." The traditional Christian resolution to that problem was the bodily resurrection. According to the faithful, this miracle would transform the grave from a site of decay into a site of fertility; out of that hallowed ground would spring a new body fit for heaven. Nineteenth-century cremationists offered a new resolution to the problem. Now postmortem decay would be overcome scientifically, not supernaturally. Through the miracle of modern technology cremation would resolve change into stasis, corruptibility into incorruptibility. Cremationists undermined the doctrine of the resurrection of the dead, therefore, not so much by refuting it as by threatening to render it obsolete. It is the soul that is immortal, their rite seemed to say, not the body. The real resurrection occurred at the moment of death, not at the end of time. And what emerged out of the corpse's decay was not a new body but a disembodied spirit.[9]

Premature Burial

Of all the efforts the cremationists made to demythologize the metaphor of death as sleep and the grave as a site of rest and reawakening, their hammering away at the possibility of premature burial may have been the most horrifying to most Americans. That premature burial was a

major fear of many Gilded Age Americans is undeniable. Even in the
late twentieth century it was not plain to doctors precisely when death
occurred; at the end of the nineteenth century things were far murkier.
Newspapers regularly featured stories of individuals, given up for dead,
waking up from trances just before being lowered underground. And
witnesses to exhumations testified repeatedly about finding corpses that
had turned on their sides, gouged out their eyes, and even fractured
their bones in what one medical encyclopedia termed "desperate strug-
gles for escape." Many Americans quivered at the prospect that they
might be buried prematurely. There is "a widespread fear on this subject," one citizen testified in 1880. "It is not talked about much, as it is
a subject attended with too many horrors for common conversation;
but once introduce it, and you will find every one has his or her fears."
In an effort to capitalize on those fears entrepreneurs patented a
number of devices designed to permit prematurely buried persons to
signal to the living that there was still life in them. There were designs
with bells, designs with breathing tubes, designs with alarms—all intended to avert what Poe characterized as "beyond question the most
terrific of all extremes which have ever fallen to the lot of mere mortality." A "Grave-Signal" patented in 1882 for the aptly named inventor
Albert Fearnaught raised a rescue flag as soon as the prematurely buried jiggled a hand (which was connected to the flag by a string).[10]

Premature burial could be avoided by cremation, argued advocates
of the practice. Why being burned alive would be preferable to premature burial was not always made plain, but some cremationists attempted to delineate the benefit. Theosophist Franz Hartmann contended in *Premature Burial* (1896) that being buried alive was far more
psychologically gruesome than being prematurely cremated. "At the
crematory: not even a breath, no movement, not a conscious thought,"
he wrote, "in the grave: the return to consciousness, the terrible effort
to escape, the fearful agony of a second death." Others also described
cremation's advantage as psychological. Both the prematurely buried
and the prematurely incinerated person would meet horrific ends, but
those who awoke six feet under would suffer untold psychological torment for days or weeks, not seconds. Again, cremation was promoted
as a quicker alternative.[11]

Concerns about premature burial likely contributed to cremation's
diffusion. But the effect of the premature burial argument should not be
measured simply by the number of converts it garnered (Henry Laurens
and Baron De Palm among them). More than other Gothic tales of

burial's horrors, stories of premature burial destabilized popular perceptions of the grave as a place of stasis and rest. Like the cremation movement as a whole, they nudged American popular theology toward new views of body and soul, death and immortality.

A Detestable Abuse

While cremationists busied themselves with spreading tales of premature burial and grave desecrations, burial partisans spoke of religion and the resurrection. Cremationists, in turn, attempted to deflect spiritual concerns entirely. Well aware that any debate about the religious merits of cremation, at least in Gilded Age America, would end in a victory for burial, cremationists insisted ad nauseam that "the whole question of the disposition of the dead...is a sanitary and not a religious one," "there is no relation between cremation and religion," "the question belongs to science rather than to theology."[12]

Listen only to these assertions and you might come away with the impression that the Gilded Age contest between cremation and burial was an utterly secular battle. America's pioneering cremationists insisted repeatedly that their reform was rooted exclusively in reason, science, utility, and common sense, and on this score they proudly distinguished themselves from their supposedly sentimental and superstitious foes. Still, it is difficult to find pro-cremation works that do not address theological and ritualistic concerns. More often than not, efforts to distance the cremation question from spiritual considerations served as prolegomena to extended discussions of theology and ritual. Many preachers used their rhetorical skills to promote cremation, and cremationists frequently published the names of preachers they had enlisted in their crusade (Episcopalians Phillips Brooks, George Hodges, and Henry Potter; Methodist Howard Henderson; and Unitarians Moncure Conway, Edward Everett Hale, and Jenkin Lloyd Jones, to name just a few). But even the medical experts championing cremation typically had something to say about God and the afterlife. Perhaps against their better judgment, cremationists as a group were religiously preoccupied.

One source of this preoccupation may have been the tendency of burial partisans to cast their arguments in religious terms. While cremationists tried to distance themselves from religious matters, anticremationists appealed to theological, ritualistic, liturgical, and hymnological concerns. To the traditionalists, cremation originated among "heathens" and "pagans" and was therefore anti-Christian: it flew in the face of the Christian tradition of burial, it violated scripture, it refused to recognize the sanctity of the body as "the temple of the Holy Ghost," and it shamelessly ridiculed the doctrine of the resurrection of the body. If the case for cremation was framed largely in sanitary terms, theology was the queen of the burying sciences.

At or near the top of this list of religious concerns was the worry that just as ancient cremation was promoted by "heathen" and "pagan" peoples, the modern cremation movement was led by freethinkers and other radicals who were intent not on reforming ritual but killing religion. This view was articulated most famously by a series of high-ranking Roman Catholic clerics, including Pope Leo XIII, who branded cremation "a detestable abuse." These Roman Catholic thinkers were convinced, as the editors of the *American Catholic Quarterly Review* wrote, that "the great army of cremationists in Europe is made up of Atheists and infidels, professed enemies of God and His revelation [who] re-echo the spirit, if not the words, of the Pagan crowds who burnt the martyrs." In 1886 the Vatican denounced the practice as unchristian and forbade Catholics from joining cremation societies or committing their bodies to be burned. This ruling was endorsed a year later by Cardinal James Gibbons of Baltimore. James P. Murphy contended in 1901 in "The Cremation Movement is Anti-Catholic" that "the attempt to introduce cremation in our time is primarily and above all things a blow aimed at the Catholic Church by the Freemasons" and other anti-clerical activists. Some critics went further, linking the cremation movement not merely with Freemasons and heathens but with Satan himself. "The Almighty," a letter to the editor stated, "did not command that his loved ones should be destroyed in the devil's furnace."[13]

There was some truth to this slander. It was not the case, as one pro-cremation Freemason proudly claimed, that "the advocates of cremation are generally freethinking foreigners—unbelievers in any kind of religion." But the more measured observation that "cremation has many warm friends among freemasons" was no doubt true. Freemasonry, which arose in America during the Enlightenment and drank deeply of the eighteenth-century philosophes' emphasis on reason (as opposed to revelation), heavily influenced cremation's radical wing. Both Olcott and De Palm were Freemasons. So was Dr. Hugo Erichsen, an influential early cremationist who would go on to form the Cremation Association of America in 1913. The cremation ranks also included a disproportionate number of so-called advanced thinkers—Unitarians, Theosophists, and even a few atheists (such as Orson S. Murray, whom the *New York Times* described after his 1885 incineration as an infidel who "believed that death ends all"). Moreover, the rhetoric of free thought colored much cremationist writing. *Modern Crematist* referred to God as "the Great Architect." The agnostic Robert Ingersoll was quoted liberally in the pro-cremation press, which also printed approvingly the aphorisms of the French materialist d'Holbach and the English deist Thomas Paine. Three-quarters of a century before the secular theology boom of the 1960s *The Urn* published an anonymous tract called "The Death of God."[14]

Free thought no doubt influenced at least a few radical cremationists. One in that camp responded with Paine-like sarcasm to the filing of a bill outlawing cremation in New York State: "What a free country this is fast becoming!...One set of fanatics tells us what we shall drink; another set forbids the use of tobacco; a third set wants God put in the Constitution when the place to put Him is in our hearts and daily lives; a fourth asks Congress to shut up the World's Fair on Sunday; a fifth would prohibit Sunday newspapers and traveling on the 'Lord's Day'; and now looms up a spokesman of a sixth set whose aim is to make cremation illegal in a state where population is densest and most rapidly increasing, and where, in consequence, earth burial is most pernicious." Another freethinking cremationist complained that "conservatism" was forever at war with science and progress. "It persecuted Copernicus, discredited Newton, terrorized Galileo and ridiculed Darwin. It burnt Bruno and Vanini. It poisoned Socrates. It crucified Christ...[and] today is the most potent obstacle" in the way of cremation. As these passages indicate, freethinking cremationists made little effort to hide their disdain for the Catholic Church and, by extension, America's Catholic immigrants. Some cremationists were openly nativistic, grounding their appeals in critiques of the empty rituals of priests and the superstitions of their blind followers. Augustus Cobb, president of the U.S. Cremation Company, exemplified this anti-clerical and anti-ritualistic position. His *Earth-Burial and Cremation* (1892), one of the most important early cremationist texts, blasted the Catholic Church as a doer of evil and purveyor of fanaticism, prejudice, superstition, and intolerance. According to Cobb's sacred history, burial was destined to give way to cremation just as surely as the "intellectual anaesthesia" of medieval Catholicism was fated to yield to the scientific knowledge of the Enlightenment.[15]

These anti-Catholic works may have won some church haters to the cause, but they also deepened the suspicions of Catholic leaders that cremationists were at the beck and call of infidels. And they did little to win over Catholic immigrants, who were cast as scapegoats rather than potential recruits. Ironically, Cobb-style anti-clericalism also alienated at least one Grand Master of Freemasonry, who rebuffed a request to place the cremated remains of a fraternity brother in his lodge. "A lodge room...is not a graveyard," he wrote in a letter penned, he noted, on Good Friday. "Burning the body to ashes is considered with us a disgrace, a penalty.... The practice is a relic of heathenism. Freemasonry is divine."[16]

The Poetry of the Grave

Religious thinkers—Catholic, Protestant, and Jewish—also rejected cremation on the basis that it would overrun long-standing Jewish and Christian traditions of burial and cemetery visitation. If cremation were to be generally adopted, one Catholic priest claimed, "the poetry of the grave, with its unbroken rest, and all its touching associations, would speedily vanish." Another Christian argued for burial on ritual grounds. "Cemeteries exert a good influence," he wrote. "The care of graves, the erection of monuments, the decoration of cemeteries with shrubs and flowers, are all humanizing and refining." The widespread adoption of cremation would hasten the end of a host of socially beneficial behaviors associated with cemetery visitation. "To visit the graves of our ancestors, near and remote; to perform those kindly offices which keep alive family feeling; to unite the scattered members of households at the grave," he wrote, "these...are social bonds. They are also moral ties, exerting upon youth an effect not easily overestimated."[17]

Some ritually minded traditionalists turned the tables on the cremationists' strategy of demythologization, contending that ashes tucked away in urns were no more secure than interred human remains. One female critic, noting that arsenic was sometimes mistaken for baking powder, wondered what was to prevent ashes kept at home from being mixed with buckwheat flour. "Further," she asked, "what is to hinder unscrupulous men from robbing a columbarium for the reward that would be offered for the ashes of a millionaire?...How can we know but rude hands would steal the urns, and scatter their contents to the wind?" Another skeptic worried about urns being knocked off mantels and swept into cinder boxes. At least one urban legend also worked to destabilize the argument that cremation purified. According to this story, "ashes of a wealthy and highly esteemed white man were mixed with those of a negro" at a New Orleans crematory. Clearly the cremationists were not alone in constructing their arguments on the foundation of the racist prejudices of white elites.[18]

Ritual criticisms of cremation came from all quarters. A rabbi, vowing that posterity would never judge the Jews "so vile, or so accursed," promised that "we will not change our resolve to stand by anti-cremationism." Catholics led the opposition, however, and their shrillest voice was Monseigneur Gaume's. His *The Christian Cemetery in the Nineteenth Century: or, The Last War-Cry of the Communists*, originally produced in France, was translated into English and published in New York in 1874. The book's working premise was that state entities hell-bent on mandating cremation might seize control of the cemetery from the Church. Gaume portrays the battle between burial and cremation in apocalyptic terms—right against wrong, good against evil, Christianity against infidelity, civilization against barbarism, Jesus against the devil, church against state. Cremationists are "modern pagans" who view the dead body as "but a soulless mass of rubbish" and the cemetery as "a rubbish-heap." In Gaume's screed the devil himself speaks for the cremationists. "Man must be burnt; for in thus annihilating him as much as possible," his devil says, "I will wipe out all knowledge of, and belief in, the dogma of the resurrection." The aim of the Satan's handmaids is nothing less than "the utter extermination of Christianity."[19]

Some Protestants also denounced cremation on theological grounds. In fact, it was an Episcopalian bishop, the Reverend Arthur Cleveland Coxe, who earned the title of America's "most violent opposer of cremation." In "Vulcan, or Mother Earth?" Coxe dismissed cremation as a "craze" as fleeting as the newfangled sports of roller-skating and bicycling. Cremationists, he wrote, were as mentally unbalanced as women's suffrage advocates. Turning the tables on the cremationists' genteel pretensions, Coxe branded cremation an affront to refinement. "To a people whose wives and daughters enjoyed a Roman holiday, enlivened by the butcheries and martyrdoms of the Coliseum, it was not uncongenial," he argued. But Christianity came as "a softener of manners," replacing this violent and vulgar practice with a more tender rite. According to Coxe, the cremation movement was promoting nothing less than "chaos and communism" by refusing to attend to the spirit of the deceased. "Mere Materialism is master of the situation in America."[20]

Congregationalist Henry Ward Beecher, the liberal pastor of Brooklyn's Plymouth Church and one of the nation's most celebrated preachers, lent his reputation to the religious critique of cremation. His 1884
sermon against the practice was all the more worrying to cremationists
because Beecher was no conservative. Widely respected as a champion
of women's rights, antislavery, and other social reforms, he was just the
sort of cleric cremationists hoped to win to their cause. Although
Beecher admitted that "there may be sanitary reasons for preferring cremation," he was convinced they were outweighed by the spiritual
benefits of burial. He reminded his congregation of the poetic and liturgical conventions surrounding the grave. He tarred cremation as a
"pagan custom." And he insisted that "reverence for the body afforded
a lasting resistance" to burning the corpse.[21]

More nativistic Protestants, critical of Catholic traditions of reverence for relics of the saints, contended that cremation would promote
idolatry: "Should we adopt cremation, how long would we have peaceful and happy families? Would there not soon be wrangling and discon-
tent as to who was to have grandfather's or grandmother's ashes?
'Twould be but a little while ere each and every family—yes, each and
every person—would have their own particular god." Another oppo-
nent wrote, "There is less danger of idolatry where the dead are placed
out of sight and the green grass creeps over the mounds, than when they
are kept ever convenient for bowed adoration."[22]

The Resurrection of the Body

Both Protestants and Catholics also condemned cremation on scriptural
grounds. Some tried to find commandments to bury both in Jesus'
words (Matthew 8:22: "let the dead bury their dead") and in the Hebrew Bible ("thou shalt surely bury him" [Deuteronomy 21:23]). But
most admitted there was no definitive "Thus saith the Lord" on the
burial versus cremation question. Nonetheless, there were scriptural
grounds for opposing cremation.

Traditionalists argued that the Old Testament regarded burial as nor-
mative. The Hebrew patriarchs bury their dead, and God praises them
for it. The last commandment of Jacob to his sons is that he should be
buried in Canaan. Only in exceptional cases (war, plague, or the death
of a criminal) is cremation performed. In the book of Amos, moreover,
God condemns Moab to death because he cremated the king of Edom
(Amos 2:1–3). In the New Testament, Paul describes the body as a

"temple of the Holy Ghost" (1 Corinthians 3:16; 6:19; 2 Corinthians 6:16). Those who prepare Jesus' body for burial are praised (Matthew 26:12 and John 19:38–42). Finally, Christian traditionalists noted that Jesus was buried instead of burned. If burial was good enough for Jesus, they reasoned, it should be good enough for you.

Of all the religiously based arguments against cremation, the most popular concerned the bodily resurrection. This objection was framed best by the Reverend Wordsworth, bishop of Lincoln, England. Recalling Julian the Apostate, who pointed to the pious practice of burial as a key factor in the spread of Christendom, Wordsworth argued from the pulpit of Westminster Abbey in 1874 that one of the "first fruits" of cremation "would be to undermine the faith of mankind in the doctrine of the resurrection of the body." On the other side of the Atlantic, Episcopalian Bishop William Bacon Stevens said cremation amounted to a covert effort by unbelievers "to discredit and undermine the doctrine of the resurrection, and throw us back on that old Saduccism which says 'there is no resurrection,' and which, if it prevails, would break down the whole system of the Christian religion." But how exactly would cremation undermine resurrection piety? Few traditionalists actually believed what one source attributed to them, namely, "that a body returned to ashes...cannot be raised at the call of Judgment Day." It would, after all, be blasphemy to state that an omnipotent God could not resurrect a cremated corpse. And most traditionalists freely admitted that scripture did not command burial.[23]

Resurrection-based objections to cremation were rooted instead in subtler concerns. Cremation was wrong, critics argued, because cremationists were motivated by "blasphemous intent." Like the persecutors of the early church, cremationists promoted their cause in order "to show that they could conquer God and destroy the resurrection of the bodies, saying, now let us see if they will rise." Opponents were no doubt also concerned that cremation would render less convincing the popular beliefs, behaviors, attitudes, and metaphors that created and sustained the credibility of the resurrection of the body—belief in the self as an amalgamation of body and soul, fear of hellfire, prayers for the dead, cemetery visitation, and the metaphors of death as sleep and body as temple. The widespread practice of cremation, they thought, might supplant the Jewish and Christian belief in the resurrection of the body with the Greek (and gnostic) belief in the immortality of the soul.[24]

According to the *American Catholic Quarterly Review,* Christianity had affirmed for centuries "that the body is an essential part of the man." Unfortunately, "unphilosophic Protestantism" had wrongly convinced itself that the human being was predominantly, perhaps entirely, made of soul. Forgetting that the body was the means through which God conveyed grace to the soul, Protestants radically de-ritualized Christianity, rejecting five of the seven sacraments. (Baptism and the Lord's Supper survived.) As part of a broader effort "to establish a purely spiritual system of religion for beings who have a mixed nature, a physical body as well as an immaterial soul connected with it," Protestants ignored the body and shunned the corpse. Gradually, they began to think of the afterlife in terms of the immortality of the soul rather than the resurrection of the body. But both scripture and natural law protested against this spiritualization of self and afterlife. "The whole man, not merely a part of him, is destined for eternity," this journal insisted, since "man is not complete without his body, either in this life or in the next." It was no coincidence that the modern revival of cremation was "due to pantheists, materialists and other unbelievers in the resurrection of the flesh."[25]

Although the *American Catholic Quarterly Review* was not as obsessed as France's Mgr. Gaume with the encroachment of legislative fiat on funerary rites and the cemetery, it was concerned "that the day will come when cremation will be forced upon unwilling peoples by law." Above all else, American Catholic leaders feared that in the United States, as in the France of Gaume's imagining, civil authorities would insist on desecrating consecrated burial grounds by interring or scattering cremated remains in them. What was at stake, therefore, was not only theology but authority. Who controls the bodies of the dead? The answer, at least from the Catholic camp, was unequivocal: "The Church claims the corpse." "It has once been a holy tabernacle of the body and blood of Jesus Christ. She orders the civil power away from the bier and the graveyard. The funeral and requiem mass are hers. Her jurisdiction over them is supreme." Burial of the dead was not merely a sacred obligation. It was a God-given right.[26]

Liberals and Radicals

Cremationists responded to Christian criticisms in two ways. One group, the radicals, dismissed their opponents' spiritual concerns as superstitious and unreasonable, while a second group, the liberals, eagerly joined the theological debate, trading Bible verse for Bible verse. Of these two groups, the liberal cremationists predominated. Although the cremation movement attracted religious radicals, most cremationists appear to have been committed Christians, and the bulk of the rest adhered to alternative religious traditions such as Swedenborgianism, Spiritualism, Buddhism, and/or Theosophy, rather than to no religion at all. The accusation that the cremation movement was run by infidels was false. The debate between cremation and burial was largely an intra-Christian affair. And it was by no means a secular one.[27]

Radical and liberal cremationists dealt very differently with the claim that their movement was dominated by Freemasons and freethinkers. Radicals responded to this charge with a mixture of bravado and anticlericalism. Hugo Erichsen (who would later liberalize his stance) freely acknowledged early in his cremationist career that he was a Mason, and he brashly termed Pope Leo XIII's claim that cremation and Freemasonry were in cahoots "a great compliment." Liberals took a different tack. Instead of criticizing Catholicism or Christianity, they contended that cremation was, in the words of the Right Reverend William Lawrence, Episcopal bishop of Massachusetts, fully "in harmony with Christian principles." The cremation movement, they added, was not the result of "the versatile brain of the crank, neither the progeny of free-thought ideas, or Spiritualism, or of infidelity."[28]

Liberal and radical cremationists also responded differently to charges that cremation was a heathen rite. Both camps contended that virtually everything that antedated Christianity originated in heathenism. If modern Americans were to reject cremation because of its heathen roots, they would "have to quit eating with knives and forks, stop wearing boots and pantaloons, and do away with surcoats and rings." Even the coffin and burial itself, they said, originated among heathens. John Storer Cobb, president of the New England Cremation Society and a leading Theosophist, argued that to refuse cremation on these grounds was as foolish as for heathens to shun the phonograph because it is Christian. What man in his right mind would practice polygamy just because Herbert Spencer professed monogamy?[29]

So far liberals and radicals agreed. But while liberals felt superior to the heathens, radicals praised them as equals (or superiors). According to the radicals, the "Indian mind" was "deeply tinged with religious and philosophic thought"; Rome and Greece were "the most cultured nations of antiquity." From this perspective, cremation's associations with India, Greece, and Rome were accounted as a credit rather than a debit. Or, as one radical succinctly put it, "The heathen were wiser than we."[30]

Liberal cremationists further distinguished themselves from radicals by referring in their arguments at least as much to the Bible as to reason. Some tried to argue that the Bible prescribed cremation by contending that the early Christians cremated their dead or that Jesus disparaged burial, but a more common strategy was to say that scripture mandated no method of disposition of the dead. Regarding the Old Testament, liberal cremationists said that while the Israelites buried in most cases, they practiced cremation in at least a few. Moreover, cremation in the Hebrew Bible was reserved for kings and dignitaries and was practiced as a mark of respect. For example, Saul, the king of Israel, was cremated (1 Samuel 31:12). Cremation also supposedly received at least indirect support in the New Testament—for example, when Paul wrote "and though I give my body to be burned, and have not charity: it profiteth me nothing" (1 Corinthians 13:3). Regarding the claim that cremation represented a desecration of the "temple of the Holy Ghost," liberal cremationists posed a rhetorical question. Which method is more of a desecration: giving the body up to the purifying fire or consigning it to pollution underground? Finally, liberals noted that Abraham, Isaac, and Jacob were not buried but sepulchred. And Jesus was entombed. Moreover, had Jesus not declared, God "is not the God of the dead, but of the living" (Matthew 22:32; Mark 12:27; and Luke 20:38)?

Far more than radicals, liberals were genuinely concerned about the potential demise of liturgical, poetic, and Biblical references to death as sleep and the cemetery as a place of rest. They suggested, however, that cremation would quickly gather its own tender associations, both scriptural and natural. Moses communing with God in the pillar of fire, Elijah's chariot of fire, the tongues of flame of the Pentecost, the germinating warmth of the sun—all were potential resources for these new associations. According to the liberals, soon the words of Tennyson:

> And from his ashes may be made
> The violet of his native land

and the lyrical lines of Pope:

> And heaven that every virtue bears in mind,
> E'en to the ashes of the just is kind

would be known and beloved by cremationists across America. And new rituals would no doubt arise, making sense once again of ancient liturgical formulations such as "Peace to his ashes" and "Ashes to ashes, dust to dust."

PLATE 1. "Tolkotin Cremation," in J. W. Powell's *First Annual Report of the Bureau of Ethnology, 1879–80* (1881). Long before the first modern American cremation in 1876 many Native American groups practiced cremation. This lithograph depicts an open-air cremation among the Tolkotins of Oregon.

PLATE 2. Henry Laurens by John Singleton Copley, oil on canvas painted in 1782. Laurens (1724–1792), a one-time president of the Continental Congress, was cremated in the open air on his South Carolina estate long before the U.S. cremation debate began. Courtesy of National Portrait Gallery, Smithsonian Institution, Washington, D.C.

PLATE 3. Sir Henry Thompson, surgeon to Queen Victoria and England's foremost advocate of cremation, as depicted in 1874 in the British weekly *Vanity Fair*. Thompson's groundbreaking essay, "Cremation: The Treatment of the Body after Death" (1874), was a core text in the American cremation movement.

PLATE 4. "Cremation—the Ancient Grecian Method of Burning the Dead," *Frank Leslie's Illustrated Newspaper* (1874). Early cremationists distinguished sharply between "primitive" cremation in India, Rome, and Greece and "scientific" cremation in modern America. In indoor crematory rites, one advocate noted, there was "none of that horror of roasting human flesh and bursting entrails which makes one shudder at an open-air pyre-burning."

PLATE 5. The birthplace of modern American cremation. This lithograph depicts the country's first crematory and its owner, Dr. Francis Julius LeMoyne. The landscape at the top is a view of Washington, Pennsylvania, from "Cremation Hill." Critics derided both the reception room on the left and the furnace room on the right as "loathsomely cheap and plain." Even supporters admitted the facility was "as unaesthetic as a bake-oven." Courtesy of Washington County Historical Society, Washington, Pennsylvania.

PLATES 6A AND 6B. America's first modern cremation took place on December 6, 1876, at the private crematory of Dr. Francis Julius LeMoyne in Washington, Pennsylvania. These woodcuts, both from *Frank Leslie's Illustrated Newspaper* (1876), depict the man whose corpse was cremated, Baron Joseph Henry Louis Charles De Palm, and the day's events at the crematory.

PLATE 7. Colonel Henry Steel Olcott (1832–1907), who organized the first cremation in modern America, typified some early cremationists in his interest in Asian religions. A cofounder, with Helena Petrovna Blavatsky, of the Theosophical Society, he moved to India in the winter of 1878–79 and formally converted to Buddhism in Ceylon (now Sri Lanka) in 1880. In this *Harper's Weekly* woodcut from March 5, 1887, he is standing in the center of the back row, surrounded by a variety of Indian religionists.

PLATE 8. Dr. Samuel D. Gross, one of the country's most distinguished surgeons, gave cremation a boost when he had
his corpse cremated in 1884. "A man who spends much of
his time in the dissecting-room, and looks at the horrible
features of the putrefying bodies as they lie before him
upon the tables," wrote Gross, "is not likely to hesitate between burial and cremation." Courtesy of Countway Medical Library, Harvard Library, Boston, Massachusetts.

PLATE 9. "A 'Bogus' Cremation for the Benefit of the 'Life-Long Democrats'" by Joseph Keppler, *Puck*, November 18, 1885. By the 1880s cremation was a familiar enough topic for parody. Here *Puck* magazine tells its readers that the Democrats are a bit premature in celebrating the death of the Mugwumps, the public moralists of the Gilded Age.

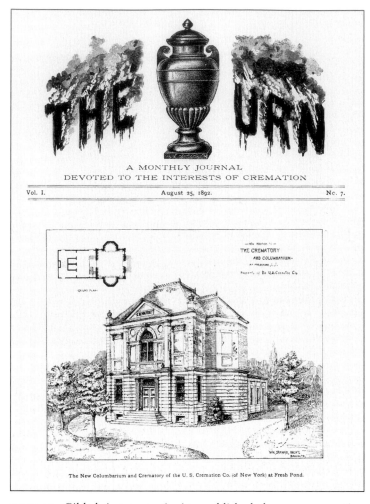

THE URN

A MONTHLY JOURNAL
DEVOTED TO THE INTERESTS OF CREMATION

Vol. I.   August 25, 1892.   No. 7.

The New Columbarium and Crematory of the U. S. Cremation Co. (of New York) at Fresh Pond.

PLATE 10. Gilded Age cremationists published three pro-cremation periodicals: *Modern Cremist*, *The Columbarium*, and *The Urn*. This August 25, 1892, cover of *The Urn* features an image of the U.S. Cremation Company's elegant columbarium and crematory at Fresh Pond, New York.

PLATES 11A AND 11B. Postcards of Earl Chapel and Crematory in Oakwood Cemetery, Troy, New York. Built by William S. Earl in memory of his son, this was the most extravagant crematory in the United States at its opening in 1890. In addition to five Tiffany stained glass windows, it boasted an elaborate mosaic floor, an onyx altar, carved bronze doors, and a marvelous view of the Hudson River.

PLATE 12. The San Francisco Columbarium. Thanks in large measure to its grand neoclassical columbarium, built in 1898, the Odd Fellows' crematory (established in 1895) became the busiest crematory in the country in the first decade of the twentieth century. The city banned cremations in 1910, but the San Francisco Columbarium, as the facility is now called, lived on. Courtesy Neptune Society of Northern California.

PLATE 13. Bigelow Chapel, Mount Auburn Cemetery. Rather than resisting cremation, cemetery managers embraced it, giving rise in the early twentieth century to the American model of the cemetery-based crematory. Mount Auburn, the country's foremost rural cemetery, helped legitimize cremation when it built a crematory in 1900. This photograph shows Mount Auburn's Bigelow Chapel as it appeared in 1970, shortly after the new crematory entrance on the left was built. Courtesy of Mount Auburn Cemetery, Cambridge, Massachusetts.

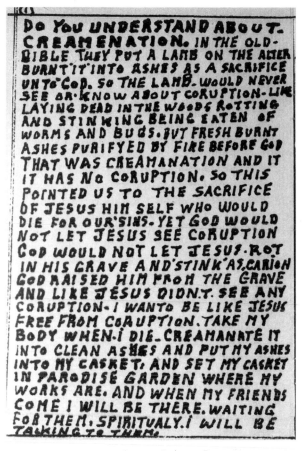

PLATE 14. "Do You Understand about Creamenation" by the Reverend Howard Finster. Here Finster, an outsider artist whose illustrations have been used on the cover of *Time* magazine and on an album cover for the rock band R.E.M., explains his support for cremation: "GOD WOULD NOT LET JESUS SEE CORUPTION GOD WOULD NOT LET JESUS ROT IN HIS GRAVE AND 'STINK' AS CARION GOD RAISED HIM FROM THE GRAVE AND LIKE JESUS DIDNT SEE ANY CORUPTION I WANTO BE LIKE JESUS FREE FROM CORUPTION. TAKE MY BODY WHEN I DIE. CREAMANATE IT INTO CLEAN ASHES."

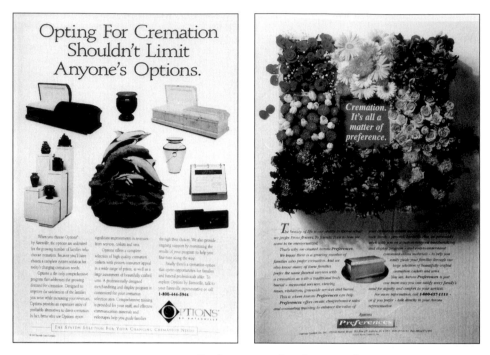

PLATES 15A AND 15B. In the 1990s advertisements for cremation products and services stressed individual choice. Here an
ad for the Batesville Casket Company reads, "Opting for cremation shouldn't limit anyone's options." Ad copy for the Au-
rora Casket Company says, "Cremation. It's all a matter of
preference."

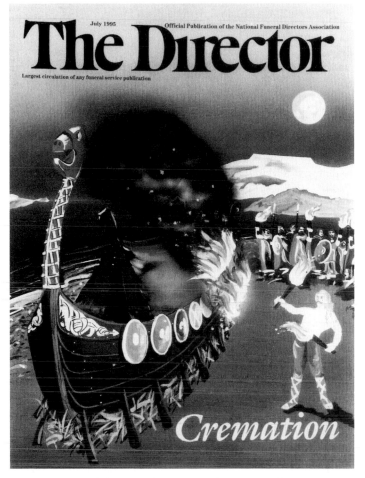

July 1995

Official Publication of the National Funeral Directors Association

The Director

Largest circulation of any funeral service publication

Cremation

PLATE 16. Funeral directors began to make peace with cremation as the millennium drew to a close. In July 1995 *The Director*, the official organ of the National Funeral Directors Association, put the topic on its cover.

PLATE 17. Manufacturers capitalized on a trend toward the personalization of cremation rites by making urns in all shapes and sizes. This golf bag urn, available through Kelco Supply Company, was designed to appeal to golfing enthusiasts.

Immortality of the Soul

Liberal and radical cremationists were also divided on the resurrection
of the body. Most radicals rejected any notion of the afterlife, and some
ridiculed the doctrine of the bodily resurrection. Recalling ancient objections to what has been called the particle theory of the bodily resurrection (in which God at the end of time gathers and then reassembles
the parts that had once constituted a body), one skeptic urged readers to
think of Union soldiers arising from unmarked graves in the South and
finding a new battle on their hands. "There will be a merry row on resurrection day," he mused, "particularly if old animosities should be re-
vived, over the ownership of those bones in which two or more persons
have held a life interest." Another satirist quoted a pro-resurrection
poem to demonstrate to the readers of the *World* the "aesthetic mon-
strosities" of materialistic views of the resurrection:

> Through the echoing sky
> Fragments of bodies in confusion fly
> The heads move on to meet
> The distant necks, the distant legs the feet.[31]

Liberals crafted two very different responses to the resurrection question. The first went like this: Assuming that the doctrine of the resurrection of the flesh is true, the fate of that flesh is substantially equivalent in
burial and in cremation. "In cremation and ordinary burial the ultimate
result is the same," an advocate said. "In one it is rapid, in the other
slow, combustion." At the end of times God will be confronted with substantially the same material in both the grave and the urn. And He will
not be frustrated in His efforts to transform the remains of both the buried and the cremated into new "spiritual bodies" fit for eternal life. A
Mormon cremationist put the matter concisely: "The same power that
can call forth from the tomb a body that has decayed and gone to dust
can quicken the dried ashes and draw from the elements the gases that
have been dispersed by the flames of the crematory....Belief in the resurrection implies belief in God, and with him all things are possible."[32]

This pro-cremation, pro-resurrection faith is best illustrated in a
piece called "The Resurrection of a Cremationist: Revelation XXI, 27."
Here a Christian author imagines what it will be like for his ashes to answer Gabriel's trumpet blast. As the earth's convulsions spill the author's remains out of a columbarium urn and a wild storm agitates the
atmosphere, "a million human bones are drawn up into the vortex of
the cyclone and madly whirled through space, together with the human

ashes, onward, upward." Then, "as the Scriptures predict," both ashes
and bones are miraculously transformed into "bodies, airy and luminous, not of the heavy earthly type" and ushered toward the "New Jerusalem." At heaven's gate, a man with an urn is told heaven is not open
to those who have chosen cremation. But saints whose bodies were
burned at the stake protest, asking: "Shall we also be deprived of our
rightful and promised inheritance?" After conferring with St. Peter, St.
Paul proclaims, "Whosoever has the resurrection body, that spiritual
body of which I preached, be it from bones or ashes, unto him the ritual is no law. You may enter the gates and take this man with the urn
along." The point? Describing cremation as a stumbling block to the
resurrection was a sacrilege tantamount to challenging the omnipotence
of God. Or, as Lord Shaftesbury of England put it in one of the most
frequently quoted passages in U.S. cremationist literature, "If burning
the body interfered with the resurrection, what would become of the
blessed martyrs?"[33]

A larger (and more successful) contingent of liberal cremationists
conceded that cremation was "at variance" with the old theology of
"the literal resurrection of the actual particles buried." But this contingent did not give up entirely on resurrection belief. Citing Paul's claim
that the dead will be raised not in their "physical" but in their "spiritual" bodies and his insistence "that flesh and blood cannot inherit the
kingdom of God" (1 Corinthians 15:50), they offered a more spiritual
interpretation of the resurrection. In the process they revisited ancient
debates about, among other things, the relationship between spirit and
matter, the nature of the body, and the possibility of the perseverance of
personal identity into the afterlife. Though in many respects these views
echoed the early theology of Augustine, who affirmed the immortality
of the soul but denied the resurrection of the material body, they also
provided good reasons for outraged Catholic critics to brand cremationists as heretics—revivers not only of pagan death rites but of the
early Christian heresy of docetism (a view that posited a stark dualism
between spirit and matter and argued that Jesus merely seemed to in-
carnate in human form).[34]

In his first letter to the Corinthians (just after his description of the
dead body as seed sown for a future harvest) Paul wrote of the resurrection of the dead: "What is sown is perishable, what is raised is im-
perishable. It is sown in dishonor, it is raised in glory. It is sown in weak-
ness, it is raised in power. It is sown a physical body, it is raised a
spiritual body. . . . I tell you this, brethren: flesh and flood cannot inherit

the kingdom of God, nor does the perishable inherit the perishable" (1 Corinthians 15:42–44, 50). These words, even if divinely inspired, hardly settle the matter. Tantalizingly enigmatic, they have inspired over the centuries a wide range of interpretations. What, after all, is a "spiritual body"? Is it, as those influenced by the Jewish tradition have asserted, a glorified soul-body amalgamation, a restored psychosomatic person? Or is it, as those influenced by the Greeks have claimed, a spiritual person—soul-only?

Most cremationists insisted on the latter reading. One liberal argued that "nobody now believes in the resurrection from the grave of the very matter, the gross flesh and bones of the body. . . . There is a spiritual body as well as a natural body. It is that spiritual body which shapes and molds the atoms of the natural body, and thus preserves our personal identity in this life. That spiritual body will come up out of the grave. We will know it is our body. Those who knew us on the earth will recognize us. And yet we will be free from all the grossness of matter." By so thoroughly spiritualizing the resurrection, cremationists inclined perilously in the direction of a modified docetism. While ancient docetists had been branded heretics for their conviction that Jesus only seemed to have a body, these cremationists implied that the bodies of ordinary humans, too, were more apparent than real. Or, to be more precise, just as ancient docetists saw Jesus' corporeality as inessential to his true self, these modern docetists saw the body as inessential to the real human being. The material body, one wrote, "is *mine*, not ME." Another added, "the spirit is the *man*." In this way cremationists turned the tables on Bishop Coxe, who had argued that the cremation movement provided yet more evidence for the fact that materialism was ruining America. "To fasten our affections on the bodies of our dear ones is 'carnal-mindedness,'" they insisted. "To fix them on the spiritual immortal self is alone Christian, and alone rational."[35]

Religious Materialism

Literary critic Harold Bloom contended in the early 1990s that the late-twentieth-century United States was "post-Christian" but thoroughly religious. American religion was Hellenistic religion, Bloom said. Americans did not know it, but they were taking their religious cues from an idiosyncratic palate of Greek sources, including Orphism and gnosticism. While other interpreters saw American religion as a tug-of-war between Christianity and the Enlightenment, Bloom saw the combatants as the Christians and the Greeks. And the Greeks, he said, were winning. Gradually Americans were ceasing to see themselves in traditional Jewish and Christian terms—as a messy mix of body and soul. Some secular humanists, admittedly, were seeing themselves as matter-only. But many more were constructing a Greek conception of the self—as immortal soul. If Bloom was correct, then the liberal cremationists were in the vanguard of this new American spirituality.[36]

Cremationists spoke out repeatedly against "making too much of the body." Consider, for example, the views of the Reverend George Hodges, an Episcopalian minister, dean of the Episcopal Theological School in Cambridge, Massachusetts, and a quintessential liberal cremationist. "The body which is put in the grave will never come out again," Hodges stated in an 1895 address to the New England Cremation Society. "The body is laid away in the earth and that is the end of it." So far Hodges sounded like the freethinking Ingersoll. What saved him from charges of agnosticism, however, was his certainty that the dead would rise spiritually. "When the soul leaves the body it leaves it forever," he explained. There was not to be any heavenly reunion of body and soul. For Hodges, Paul's "spiritual body" meant, in effect, the immortal soul. Why, Hodges asked, would any good Christian prefer burial over cremation? Burial focuses attention on the inessential body. "But personality is not in the body, it is in the soul," he said. In order to "get rid of this subtle materialistic temptation" to focus unduly on the body, we should cremate the dead. Cremation "agrees with the right idea of the resurrection of the body and it symbolizes the supremacy of the soul," Hodges concluded. "Cremation used to be called Pagan; but what can be more Christian?"[37]

On this point liberal cremationists again brought to the bar the words of an English cleric, this time the bishop of Manchester, who had concluded that "no intelligent faith can suppose that any Christian doctrine is affected by the manner in which or the time in which this mortal body of ours crumbles into dust....Christians should in mind dissociate the resurrection from all physical conditions." U.S. cremation advocates offered variations on this line of reasoning. Felix Adler wrote that "immortality for us cannot mean physical immortality." "If those whom we call the dead still live," he explained, "they do not live in the grave." To believe otherwise was to lapse into what one termed "religious materialism."[38]

Augustus Cobb pushed to the extremes the liberal critique of resurrection literalism. "It seems strange that in an enlightened age the cast-off emblem of mortality should be associated with a future spiritual state," he wrote, "for the blending of the material with the spiritual, by merging into a heavenly body the physical attributes of an earthly one, betray a gross conception of immortality and is worthy only of a savage race." This passage illustrates once again the preoccupation of Gilded Age cremationists with purity and pollution—a preoccupation that can only be understood as both spiritual and sanitary, both religious and ritualistic. What was "gross" about the traditional Jewish and Christian conception of the afterlife was that it mixed categories (body and soul) that should not be mixed. Whether they were talking about polluted chips from the iron cradle mixing with the pure ashes of the dead, "unwashed" immigrants mingling with the "washed" middle class, Union corpses cohabiting with Confederate corpses, the corrupt body entangling itself with the incorruptible soul, or the dead cavorting with the living, Gilded Age cremationists were deeply concerned about purity and pollution. "Purity is the best good," claimed one ardent cremationist, "and Fire is the purest of mundane things."[39]

Theosophists and Spiritualists

This spiritual perspective on the resurrection and the self was also held by some cremationists who were quite radical religiously. Theosophist Henry Olcott, for example, testified that he was "too firm a believer in the immortality of the soul, to view with patience the inconsistency of those who behave over the dead bodies of their friends as if the immortal part were being laid away in the ground." Other Theosophists as well as a number of Spiritualists pressed beyond Olcott by reviving the ancient Greek and Hindu conviction—a conviction Roman Catholic thinkers were quick to label superstitious—that cremation was in some sense spiritually efficacious. By burning away the corrupt body, they believed, cremation purified and released the soul. And by quickly freeing the soul from earthly restraints, cremation sped the true self on to its otherworldly journeys, or perhaps to a this-worldly reincarnation. For all of these thinkers cremation was a key rite of passage from this world to the next: "a last baptism by incandescent heat, a purification by fire, whereby the corrupt takes on incorruption." Like baptism, in which Christians took off sin and put on righteousness, cremation substituted the material cloak of the body for the spiritual garments of immortality.[40]

Some of the most intriguing arguments on this point came not from Theosophists or Spiritualists but from disembodied spirits of the dead conjured up at seances. One spirit quoted in *Banner of Light*, a Spiritualist publication from Boston, contended that cremation sped up the postmortem process of freeing the essential self, the spirit, from the inessential and polluting body: "Whatever tends to separate the particles and atoms of the physical, and to hasten the disintegration of the organic structure, such as the process of cremation will do, only assists in the work of more speedily releasing the spirit from its irksome contact with senseless clay." By this logic embalming was spiritually dangerous, since according to *Alcyone,* a Spiritualist journal from Springfield, Massachusetts, "all processes which arrest the disintegration of particles composing the body hinder, in a measure, the complete withdrawal of the finer properties which are made use of by the spirit." Theosophists advanced similar pro-cremation arguments, albeit in occult language. "It is a convenient and expeditious way of letting loose the astral body," contended one, who admitted that she was attracted to rather than repelled by the fact that Hindus practiced the rite.[41]

Of course, not all Theosophists and Spiritualists favored cremation. Some claimed that fire pained the spirit, while others thought the spirit learned invaluable lessons from the body in the three days between death and the moment of its liberation. There was good evidence, however, both for the claim that "spiritualists, as a class, endorse cremation" and for the boast that "theosophists everywhere are at one with us in the dogma of terrestrial purification by fire." Both groups saw the liberation of the spirit from the body as the true resurrection.[42]

In summary, cremationists took up three discernible positions on the doctrine of the bodily resurrection. Radicals said no to the resurrection and, in rare cases, to spirituality itself; more traditional Christians in the liberal ranks affirmed the bodily resurrection; while most liberals hoped only for the immortality of the soul. The cremationists clearly attempted to demythologize traditional Christian responses to death. If they had stopped there, they might rightly have been labeled secularizers. But they did not. Accompanying their demythologization of Christian stories and images was a new portfolio of myths, symbols, and rites. The slowly unfolding drama of the sleeping corpse awaiting its resurrection was roundly rejected by most. But in its place came the fast-paced drama of the fiery separation of pure soul from impure body and the freeing of that soul from earthly restraints. Cremation, wrote one theologically minded doctor, represented nothing less than the "spiritualization of the body."[43]

Omit the Flowers: Funeral Reform

Around the time of the birth of modern American cremation, a movement for funeral reform arose. Though not as far reaching as the sanitary crusade, it too gave cremation a boost. According to funeral reformers, Gilded Age obsequies had become "vulgar, unbecoming, ostentatious." "It costs more to die than to live," one complained. Americans ought to reject, therefore, "the costly casket, the hired conveyances...the expensive tombstone...the showy mourner."[44]

The impulse to simplify death rites had been around since colonial times. In 1721, 1724, and 1742 the Massachusetts Puritans passed legislation outlawing "Extraordinary Expense at Funerals," and in 1737 a letter in the *Boston Post* decried funeral extravagances as "pernicious and (to many) ruinating."[45] But not until the end of the nineteenth century did this impulse produce voluntary associations specifically devoted to the cause. Spearheaded by an odd coalition of Protestant ministers and cemetery managers, the funeral reform movement agitated for simpler death rites. In a few cases—for example, the Lancaster Cremation and Funeral Reform Society (established 1884)—the movements for cremation and funeral reform came together into one association. But more often they were less officially allied.

Like all social reforms, funeral reform began with a complaint—namely, that funerals had become both costly and vulgar. Undertakers had first banded together in 1882 to form the Funeral Directors' National Association of the United States (later renamed the National Funeral Directors Association, or NFDA), and their subsequent efforts at professionalization were quickly rewarded. To the delight of the nation's first generation of death professionals, social pressures stimulated strong demand for fancy caskets, hearse rentals, door crapes, floral set pieces, mourning garments, and embalming. Funerals too became more elaborate. Whereas early Puritan funerals had incorporated neither singing nor sermonizing and were often finished in a matter of minutes, Victorian funerals typically included lengthy homilies and a variety of prayers, hymns, and scripture readings. It was not uncommon for services to stretch beyond an hour.

Funeral reformers were not able to do much about funeral extravagance, but they did bring to the American funeral a new spirit of good cheer. In the late 1880s the gloomy spirit of the seventeenth-century best-seller, Michael Wigglesworth's *Day of Doom*, had been largely uprooted. Threats of hell had given way to promises of heaven. Nowhere was this new optimism more apparent than in the flower vogue of the 1880s and 1890s. Black remained the appropriate color for mourning, but reds, yellows, blues, and oranges now flooded the funeral with gaiety. The coming out party for this new style was the famous "flower funeral" of the Reverend Henry Ward Beecher in 1887. Certain that death was a promotion, as Beecher had affirmed, followers adorned his front door with a floral basket rather than the traditional black crape, and his church, too, was laden with flowers. Soon flowers were a funerary rage. Funeral parlors, churches, and homes across the country were weighed down at death with extravagant floral set pieces shaped like wreaths, crosses, anchors, harps, lambs, and broken columns. One favorite decoration, called Faith, Hope, and Charity, incorporated an anchor, a cross, and a heart in tribute to the deceased and to the new spirit of sweetness and light. In these ways the Victorians ushered in a new era in American ritualization—an era rich in pomp, circumstance, and good cheer that would last until the 1960s.

While funeral reformers applauded this cult of cheerfulness, they blasted costly indulgences (including overwrought bouquets) and their unscrupulous purveyors. Some even tarred the new Victorian funeral with the taint of "heathenism," denouncing hired mourners as an extravagance borrowed from Egypt and floral excesses as pagan. It was time, these genteel elites decided, to lead the masses back to good taste.

One way to make funerals both more simple and more affordable, the funeral reformers argued, was to make them more private. Like the floral arrangements that adorned them, Victorian funerals had become elaborate set pieces, theatrical productions staged for public effect rather than private grieving. The spectacle of the funeral was more dreaded by some families than death itself. "The entire system of public funerals is wrong," complained an advocate of family-only funerals. "It is even more indelicate than it would be to call into one's home a host of one's friends to witness a birth." One additional advantage of private interments was sanitary rather than ritualistic: They would expose fewer mourners to the health hazards of standing around an open grave in inclement weather. Perhaps the most florid critique of the Victorian funeral as public pageant, the following passage makes the Gilded Age case for the privatization of death rites. It merits quoting at some length:

> Public funerals, with their show of funeral paraphernalia, with their gathering in of curious, long-visaged, solemn people; with their wordy clergymen; with their doleful singers; with their crape decked pall bearers; with their

public procession from the chamber of mourning to the carriages in waiting; with their solemn journey to the church; with more heart rending words from the minister and more dole-begetting music; with more parading up and down the aisles of the church; with the slow journey to the burial ground; with another parade of the mourners about the open grave; with more saddening words from the men whose office is to comfort and not to torture the soul; with that barbarous, dreadful, blood curdling, outrageous rattle of gravel upon the coffin lid, to the atrocious accompaniment of "Earth to earth, ashes to ashes, dust to dust," that is an almost invariable portion of the horrid ceremonial at the grave; with the conventional standing of the mourners about the pit while the diggers shovel back the earth over the form of the one just laid away; with all this empty, useless, cruel and damnable ceremonial; public funerals are simply schemes of human torture, and the sooner the whole system is abolished the better.[46]

Prominent in the funeral reform movement were Unitarians, who since their genesis in the late 1700s had distinguished themselves not only from Catholics but also from other Protestants by their utter disdain for ritual. The Unitarian minister Jenkin Lloyd Jones of Chicago's All Soul's Church called burial a menace to public health and to the "spiritual well-being of the community." Convinced that—at least in death rites—less was more, he too urged parishioners to exorcize vulgarity from the funeral:

Let not the sacred privacy of life be disturbed in death; let there be a quiet, tender memorial half hour at home, where the family and their nearest friends will gather to listen to a few chosen selections from deathless writings, a breathing of sympathy and aspiration, a word of commemoration for the dead and of companionship with the living. There may be flowers, a few, if brought by loving hands and arranged in the simple, wholesome way of the home. Singing? Yes, if the dear, familiar things are sung by loving and familiar voices. No, if it means the professional quartet hired for the occasion. ...After this memorial half hour let the friends take loving leave, and go to their homes, leaving the bereaved with their dead. At another hour, sufficiently removed to effectually break up the temptation to stay and see, let the undertaker and necessary friends come and take the body away. Why should the family, in their overstrained condition, expose themselves to the profitless ride to the cemetery and prolong the added strain of the unsatisfactory leave-taking? But, if they go, will the minister go along? Shall we try to have another service at the grave?...I frankly urge the abandonment of the practice. It is so great an outlay of strength, time, and money for such poor results.[47]

Episcopalians were also prominent in funeral reform. After a two-year study of the funeral, Episcopalians from New York recommended a simplified and economized form: "plain hearses, no trappings indicating grief, none but a few cut flowers, none but immediate members of the family to go to the cemetery, no expenditure of money by clubs or societies, the use of material for the coffin which will decay quickly, early interment, disuse of family vaults, removal of body to a mortuary instead of retaining it in rooms occupied by the living,...the substitution of a simple garb of muslin or linen in dressing the dead,...use of churches for funeral services instead of homes, and burial where a grave can be had for $4."[48]

Finally, Reform Jews weighed in for simplicity and economy. At a paper read before the Central Conference of American Rabbis, Rabbi Joseph Stolz of Chicago decried "the needless expensiveness, the indecent display, the bootless waste at our modern funerals." After tracing the modern critique of funeral excesses to Biblical times, he suggested forgoing the cemetery committal service. Even the funeral service at the home or synagogue should be quick, simple, and rational. A funeral sermon of more than fifteen or twenty minutes was, in his words, "a torture and a cruelty." Extravagant floral decorations were in "bad taste."[49]

As this passage indicates, ritual arguments against the Victorian funeral often segued into economic and social analysis. More money was spent each year in the United States on funerals, it was argued, than on public education. Moreover, those who could afford the costly trappings typically did not indulge in them. The poor felt most acutely the social pressures to buy garish paraphernalia, and they suffered disproportionately as a result. It was not uncommon for poor families who had just lost their breadwinners to spend the family fortune and go into debt in order to pay for a "proper" funeral. The typical Victorian funeral benefited no one except the undertaker and the liveryman, critics claimed. For economic and social as well as ritualistic reasons it was time to do away with all the "costly paraphernalia of woe."[50]

But not everyone was ready to give up on the Victorian funeral, and not all funeral reformers became cremationists. In a front-page article and an accompanying editorial (each called "Facts about Funerals") the Pilot, a Boston-based Catholic paper, applauded the optimistic turn in death rites but denounced funeral extravagances, especially among the poor. Its editors suggested, however, that "it may be that handsome hearses, coffins, and other such things dissipate in part the gloom associated with death." The front-page article listed the wholesale and retail charges of undertakers. After conceding that undertakers made "large profits," the paper concluded that those profits were justified.[51]

Dueling Metaphors

The struggle between cremation and burial, like the Gilded Age war between science and religion, was largely a battle of metaphors. It was as if both sides knew that logical arguments alone would not carry the day, that the matter of the disposition of the dead was too important to be decided on the basis of reason or utility alone. Admittedly, both sides debated doctrines such as the bodily resurrection, but opinions turned not so much on doctrine as on what comparative religionist Bruce Lincoln has called "sentiments of affinity." Cremationists frequently derided their opponents as sentimentalists, but both sides tugged at the heartstrings of the American public. The successes and failures of the cremationist cause, in other words, turned less on doctrines than on metaphors.[52]

Enemies and allies evaluated key terms in the debate (fire, earth, body, soul, self, heaven, hell, God) differently. When traditionalists thought of the crematory they thought of hellfire: the retort was the devil's furnace. The cemetery, by contrast, was "God's acre," a beautiful place of rest. But cremationists, citing a source no less authoritative than Shakespeare ("graveyards yawn, and hell itself breathes out contagion on the world"), depicted the cemetery as a site of incessant and gruesome decay—the "Devil's Acre," not God's. Cremation they associated not with hell but with heaven. Fire, some believed, liberated the soul.[53]

Perhaps because most Americans stood with the traditionalists on the association of fire with hell, cremationists insisted repeatedly that fire never actually touched the body. But they also attempted to spread among the public more positive images of fire as "the purest of mundane things." When you think of fire, they were saying, think not of punishment but of purification, not of the pits of hell but of "the fire of the immortals." Citing the story of Moses and the burning bush, cremationists said that fire was a "symbol...of the divine presence." And citing the Book of Revelation, they argued that "the world is saved, not lost, by fire." While opponents associated cremation with the valiant efforts of Phileas Fogg to rescue a beautiful girl from suttee in *Around the World in Eighty Days* or with the tragic fire that leveled the Brooklyn Theater on the day of the De Palm cremation in 1876, supporters linked the crematory flames with the romance of the Fourth of July:

> FIZZ-BANG! The rockets whizzed aloft,
>   And on they sped with ease.

"I love," she whispered low to Jack,
  "Such fiery works as these."

Oh, see that stick in swift descent,
  It's fallen on the lawn.
"I dote on pyre-otechnics, love;
  Cremate me when I gone."[54]

Cremationists and their opponents also viewed the living body, the corpse, and the self very differently. The notion that the self is both material and spiritual is, of course, a long-standing Hebrew and Christian assumption. In the early Christian period some gnostics had challenged this view with the Platonic and Hellenistic claim (informed by a fundamental mistrust of matter) that the essential self is spiritual and immaterial, but they failed to gain control of the Church, and their claims became heretical. By the nineteenth century the Judeo-Christian idea that the self was a psychosomatic unity of body and soul had become for most Americans an obvious truth. From this popular perspective the body possessed both "a divine tincture" and "an infinite dignity." It was "sacred flesh" not only in life but also in death. Because a corpse was thought to be dead only for a time (sown in the earth, it would be harvested at the end of times as a new and glorious resurrection body), it made no sense to discriminate sharply between living and dead bodies. ("Human reason refuses to see in the corpse," one Catholic wrote, "an abnormal condition of the body.") In life, death, and the afterlife the body was a temple deserving special care. The self, fragmented by death into spirit and matter, would at the end of time be miraculously reconstituted once again as a body-soul unity. The problem of the body's decay would be resolved supernaturally through a miraculous bodily resurrection. To burn a corpse in the face of these facts was, quite literally, a desecration.[55]

When pondering the living body, the corpse, and the self, cremationists worked with very different metaphors. Some, citing Plato, called the body a tomb that during life holds the pure soul captive in polluted matter. Others termed it "a cage in which the bird of Paradise is imprisoned" or "a tangle of wire fence that held the person a prisoner." Either way, the body was more burden than glory, and according to at least one cremationist it had "no significance in eternity." Most cremationists were content to adopt the ancient Christian metaphor of the corpse as seed. But they insisted that if sown in the earth, that seed would bring forth fruit long before Gabriel blew his trumpet. They also insisted that the fruit would be toxic not tonic: contagion, illness, and death. There was therefore nothing sacred about a corpse. The body, wrote *Modern Cremation,* was merely "the house we live in...essential while here, to be wisely looked after, but to monopolize neither our thought nor our endeavor, and surely to be put off when we come to the noble gateway that gives entrance to the World of Spirits." Others, citing Job—"Thou hast clothed me with skin and flesh, and hast fenced me with bones and sinews" (Job 10:11)—dubbed the corpse the "cast-off clothing of [the] soul." In either case, it was to be stoically set aside at death. Once emptied of its immortal inhabitant, the corpse was "a mere habitation of worms."[56]

If cremationists had a low view of the living body and the corpse, they had a lofty view of the human person. Most cremationists seem to have viewed the self as soul-only. The real person was a spiritual entity trapped during life in a body. The real resurrection occurred, therefore, not at the apocalypse but at the moment of death, when "the bird of Paradise" winged its way to the heavens. The corpse would be made incorruptible not by God but by technology, and not in the by and by but in the here and now. With a little technological intervention, "nature's purifier" could carry out the designs of Mother Nature more quickly and efficiently than she could herself.[57]

Ultimately, all these metaphors and associations supported very different views of cremation itself. Was cremation a desecration or a purification and spiritualization of the body? Was it crisping and crackling or sweetness and light? Was it like charring a pig on a spit? Or was it "like snow [disappearing] in the genial warmth of the sunshine" or, better yet, "like laying your friend robed in white upon a bed of roses"? Was earth the great purifier? Or was fire? It all depended, of course, on who had your ear.[58]

Purity and Pollution

The Gilded Age, America's age of debate, was also an era beset with binary oppositions. Capital pitted itself against labor, and science wrestled with religion. Whites passed anti-Asian legislation in the West and Jim Crow legislation in the South. Boxing, not baseball, was the national pastime. According to one social historian, at the end of the nineteenth century there was an obsession with social and racial hierarchies and with ranking individuals and groups on a continuum from dirty to clean. There was also "a popular fixation on the dirt associated with the bodily functions of human beings: their excrement, urine, blood, pus, and other secretions." This historian does not mention in his work the popular fixation on the oozings of the dead body itself—perhaps the most polluting of those "other secretions." But there is no reason to exempt those fluids from his analysis. Both sanitary reformers in general and cremationists in particular divided American society into high and low, "washed" and "unwashed," pure and polluted. The movement for sanitary reform was obsessed with these categories, and the debate over the disposal of the dead was littered with references to them. Partisans of burial appealed on occasion to the rage of the age for purity (for example, when they insisted that cremation would pollute the atmosphere with "the reeking stench of burning bodies"). But denunciations of pollution were largely the coin of the cremationists, for whom "pure air, pure water, pure soil" was a mantra.[59]

To the cremationists burial was polluting on both sanitary and ritual grounds. In fact, so intertwined were the movement's appeals to sanitary and ritual cleanliness that it is impossible to disentangle them. Consider the many ways in which, from the cremationists' perspective, the old-fashioned urban graveyard mixed up what should not be mingled. It caused the living to interact with the dead. It also brought the dead into contact with one another, as flesh and bones shifted and sank, and as the fluids of one corpse drained into the fluids of a neighbor. In another instance of bringing together what should be left separate, the burial of the Union dead in what were to become Southern cotton fields brought Yankee bones into unseemly contact with the heirs of the Confederacy. Burial was even said to mix up the races and sexes in ways that were unimaginable among the living, since in at least one exhumation the bones of an African-American man were found to be nuzzling up against the remains of a white woman in what had become a shared grave. Cremation would, of course, solve all of these problems and more—as long as crematory operators were scrupulous about incinerating only one body at a time and used magnets to separate out unwanted iron flakes from the pure, white ashes of the dead. Placing those ashes in individual urns would eliminate the possibility of untoward mixing of races or genders in the world of the dead.

According to Catherine Bell, the ritualization process does far more than create rites; it also fabricates worldviews. Bell sees three key dynamics at work in ritualization. First is the construction of a series of binary oppositions. Second is the ordering of those dyads into a hierarchy where some are seen as superior (+) and others as inferior (−). Third is the arrangement of the binary oppositions into a loose scheme in which each element is related to every other. All these dynamics were at work in the Gilded Age cremation movement, which developed not only an alternative means of disposal of the dead but also a new way of viewing the world.[60]

There were two key binary oppositions in the cremationist worldview: burial and cremation, and pollution and purity. The cremationists evaluated pollution negatively and purity positively, and they associated burial with the former and cremation with the latter. Hence the most basic scheme in their worldview was:

Burial (−)   Cremation (+)
Pollution (−)   Purity (+)

To this basic scheme cremationists added a series of elaborations, which appear in table 1. The webs of meaning spun by the cremationists run down the columns (for associations) and across the rows (for contrasts). So, for example, cremation was associated with purity, which was associated with cleanliness and science, but contrasted with burial, which was associated with pollution, uncleanliness, and superstition. In the world the cremationists made, the soul was pitted against the body and seen as superior to it. The body was viewed as tomb, not temple. And belief in the immortality of the soul was said to be spiritually superior to the doctrine of the resurrection of the body. Modernity and medievalism, science and superstition, cosmopolitanism and parochialism, Eastern religion and Western religion were also arrayed in hierarchically arranged pairs. In this world, women were associated with matter and the body, and men with spirit and the soul. Blacks and immigrants were associated with burial and, through it, with sentiment, parochialism, and the past.

Cremationists believed their reform would appeal to all Americans, but as this taxonomy makes plain, it was really designed by and for genteel elites. Those who knew themselves to be white, male, liberal Protestant, and refined no doubt felt welcomed in that world. But for Blacks, immigrants, women, and Roman Catholics, such a world must have seemed unappealing and perhaps dangerous. In the social order of the cremationists' making, genteel elites worked hard to uplift the "unwashed" to a higher level of culture and civilization. But they also felt free to sneer at those who stubbornly resisted their largesse.

If, as many scholars have argued, attitudes toward the body ("the individual body") mirror attitudes toward society ("the social body"),

TABLE 1

The World According to
Genteel Cremationists

Burial	Cremation
pollution	purity
dirt	cleanliness
body	soul
materialistic	spiritual
medieval	modern
stasis	progress
tradition	innovation
past	future
barbarous	civilized
West	East
superstition	science
sentiment	reason
vulgarity	refinement
parochial	cosmopolitan
uneducated	educated
conservative Catholic	liberal Protestant
Christianity and Judaism	Asian religions
"unwashed"	"washed"
"dangerous classes"	"advanced thinkers"
immigrants	U.S.-born
women	men
feminine	masculine
black	white
darkness	light
low	high
below	above
wet	dry
slow	fast
earth	fire
cold	warm
low tech	high tech
corpse preserved indefinitely	corpse destroyed quickly
extravagance	simplicity
expensive	economical
body as temple	body as tomb
self is body and soul	self is soul only
resurrection of the body	immortality of the soul

then the cremation movement can be seen as an effort to free the soul of American society from ties that held it captive to the past. In this sense Gilded Age cremationism was a quintessential Enlightenment project—a cleansing of the waste of medieval superstition by the fires of modernity. The movement might also be seen, however, as a working out of sorts of the Northern myth of the Civil War: America would have to go through a great fire in order to be free. But there is another, more ominous reading of what the cremationists had in store for the American "social body." Subtly encoded in the logic of cremation was a desire to purify that social body, not merely by separating it from the pollutants of the past but by banishing pollutants in the present. If Mary Douglas is right that in addition to everything else it is, ritual is also "an attempt to create and maintain a particular culture," then cremation in the Gilded Age was an attempt to create and maintain the culture of gentility.[61]

Sanitary Spirituality

The culture of gentility aimed to rid the United States of many pollutants. But religion per se was not one of them. And neither was ritual. It is an ancient strategy to dismiss religious innovators as secularizers—to see in their new theologies not new religious impulses but no religious impulses at all. Denouncing ritual innovators as unceremonious is also old sport, dating back to the Protestant Reformers and the Hebrew prophets. And cremation's opponents (and in some cases the cremationists themselves) were clearly engaged in that strategy and that sport. True, U.S. cremationists rejected the Victorian way of burial, along with its emphases on formalism, tradition, and repetition. They typically denied the doctrine of the bodily resurrection, the popular conception of the self as a psychosomatic (body-soul) unity, and the view of the body as a temple of the Holy Spirit. They commonly refused to submit themselves to the authority of the Christian tradition, whether that authority was perched in the Vatican or in a venerable American Protestant pulpit. And they repeatedly stated that the cremation versus burial question should be decided on the basis of sanitation not scripture, science not spirituality. But those denials were almost always accompanied by a series of vehement affirmations. In short, while the cremationists said no to traditional religious beliefs and rites, they said yes to religious and ritual alternatives. Like the cremation of Baron De Palm—neither a secular nor an unceremonious affair—cremation's early history was unorthodox but by no means irreligious or antiritualistic. "Cremation is just as solemn and religious" as burial, one nineteenth-century cremationist rightly affirmed. He and his colleagues, from Olcott and Le-Moyne on, contributed not to the secularization but to the diversification of American religion.[62]

It is now commonplace to describe American religious history as a march from Protestantism to pluralism. Historians differ on when that march began, but most now see religious diversity as one of its key characteristics. Gilded Age cremationists made important contributions to that diversity. Although most cremationists would have called themselves Christians, they typically refused to deride practitioners of Asian religions as heathens. Moreover, they took seriously the alternative spiritual worlds of Theosophists, Spiritualists, Hindus, and Buddhists. Cremationists also contributed to the diversification of American ritual life by championing alternatives to the Victorian ritual regime. The cremation rites they fashioned were more idiosyncratic, more personalized, and more likely to be led by laity than the burial rites of their contemporaries. Their efforts to displace the remains of the dead from coffins to urns and from cemeteries to backyard rose gardens represented not a giving up of religion but a resituating of it (in many cases from the public to the private sphere). And while many cremationists did want to put an end to the practice of visiting dead bones in cemeteries, they hoped to popularize the practice of communing with the spirits of loved ones at home. Such communion, they believed, would be informed not by thoughts of sin, redemption, and resurrection, but by memories of a life well lived, images of the cycles of the seasons, and a certain hope in the immortality of the soul.

Gilded Age cremationists paved the way, therefore, not only for the powerful emergence in the 1960s of alternative spiritualities but also for the revolution in ritualization that came to the United States as the counterculture went mainstream. Finally, Gilded Age cremationists contributed to the diversification of American popular theology—the metaphors, narratives, symbols and beliefs that make up the theology of everyday life. Observers of American religious thought now agree that popular thinking about the self, the body, death, and the afterlife changed significantly over the course of the Gilded Age. When compared with their early-nineteenth-century compatriots, early-twenty-first-century Americans were far less likely to believe in hell or the bodily resurrection and far more likely to affirm reincarnation or to view themselves as essentially spiritual. The cremation movement participated in the development of a new, modern American self, liberated not only from the constraints of the irksome body but also from the constraints of traditions and customs—free to seek new experiences in both life and death. Exactly how or when these transformations in popular theologizing occurred is not clear. What is clear is that the Gilded Age cremation movement contributed to this revolution too.

In "Cremation in Boston," an unpublished manuscript written in 1895 as the period of cremation's birth was drawing to a close, J. Wetherbee linked the rise of the cremation movement with the emergence of new rituals and new theologies. "A change has gradually come in the method and form of funeral services," wrote Wetherbee. "We rarely hear the officiating clergyman speak of the corpse in the casket as being in that sleep that knows no waking, or waiting for the resurrection trumpet when all shall rise from the dead. He says oftener today that the body in the coffin is not the man, that he has left it." In fact, it was by 1895 an "almost universal" conviction, according to Wetherbee, that the "dead human body vacated by the soul is not the real man, only a vacated tenement"—that the "real man" is the "thinking soul" and "does not die and is not buried." Wetherbee, who favored cremation, embraced these changes as glorious advances and saw them as "very fitting for the successful introduction of the new idea of cremation." He was exaggerating when he said that almost everyone in America had embraced these new beliefs and new practices, but he was right to link such innovations with the growing acceptance of cremation, which as the twentieth century dawned had secured a place in America's repertoire of religious rites.[63]

PART TWO

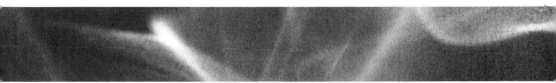

Bricks and Mortar
1896–1963

4

The Business of Cremation

SHORTLY AFTER THE DE PALM INCINERATION the *New York Times* ran an article called "The End of Cremation." The practice was laboring under such "heavy disadvantages," wrote the *Times*, "that it will be surprising if it does not give way under them and disappear." Another source reported around the same time that "the public are as much, if not more inclined to old-fashioned burial than ever." It looked at first as if the public would stay that way. After an initial flurry of activity in 1874, the cremation movement mimicked a depressed economy by going into what even supporters admitted was "a profound sleep." The New York Cremation Society languished, newspapers ignored the topic, and for a period of nearly three years advocates could not arrange a single cremation. One stumbling block was an underdeveloped infrastructure. When Dr. LeMoyne opened his crematory in 1876, it was the only one in the country, and it retained that distinction for nearly a decade. His facility, moreover, was never fully public. LeMoyne reportedly turned down more than thirty requests for every one he granted. In one case, a father was not allowed to cremate his dead son because the father had separated from his wife (and so was considered unfit for the honor). The facility was used only forty-two times before closing in 1901. Cremationists who tried to raise money to build crematories were routinely frustrated. The New England Cremation Society, during the three years following its incorporation in 1885, sold only 750 of the 2,500 ten-dollar shares it expected would be necessary to build a public crematory. The society refunded the money and resigned its charter.[1]

In the mid-1880s and early 1890s, however, the movement picked up steam. The 1884 cremation of Dr. Samuel Gross, a one-time AMA president and, according to the *Philadelphia Record*, "one of the most distinguished surgeons that this country has produced," provided a much-needed boost. Publications on cremation boomed in the mid-1880s, and the cholera epidemic of 1892 kept the matter of the disposal of the dead in public view through the early 1890s. Massachusetts passed a groundbreaking law permitting cremations, and at least two efforts to outlaw the practice (one in Pennsylvania and another in New York) were handily defeated. Three previously mentioned pro-cremation monthlies—*Modern Crematist* of Lancaster, Pennsylvania; New York's *The Urn*; and Philadelphia's *The Columbarium*—began publication. Shortly before the turn of the century *Chambers's Encyclopedia* reported that over 3,000 works on cremation had been published. More significantly, two forms of cremation organizations sprang up in major metropolitan centers in New England, the Middle Atlantic states, the Midwest, and the Far West: reform societies devoted to preaching cremation to the American public and nonprofit organizations intent on raising capital to build crematories. The number of American crematories grew slowly at first. Not until 1884 did the country's second (and first fully public) crematory open in Lancaster, Pennsylvania. By the end of the 1880s, however, cremations were also being performed in New York City, Buffalo, St. Louis, Philadelphia, Cincinnati, Los Angeles, Detroit, Pittsburgh, and Baltimore. By 1899, twenty-four crematories were operating in fifteen states. During the nineteenth century, the families of over 10,000 Americans chose cremation over burial as the best way to dispose of their dead. Americans, the *Boston Transcript* quipped, were finally "dying to be cremated."[2]

Still, there continued to be setbacks. A crematory in San Antonio, Texas, was torched by a traditionalist with a mean streak and a keen sense of irony. And one crematory in the making collapsed during a wind storm. Various efforts to build a national cremation organization—the "American Cremation League," "The American Crematorium and Funeral Reform Association," the "National Cremation Association," and the "Benevolent Society of the United States for the Propagation of Cremation"—failed for lack of support. But by the turn of the century prophesies of "the end of cremation" were few and far between. In 1895 a minister remarked that it was "no longer considered an altogether pagan and mad thing to be burned rather than buried." Four years later the *New York Tribune* determined that "modern cremation is not a fad; it has come to stay. With common-sense as godfather and sanitary science as nurse, its success is assured." Just after the turn of the century editors at the *New York Times* observed that cremation "no longer shocks the public sense" and that "a preference for it over burial does not now class the one expressing it as a 'crank' and a moral outlaw." A steady increase in cremations, said the *Times,* was "to be expected." The cremationists' fin de siècle assessments were less cautious. One likened the movement to "a snow-ball rolling down a snow clad hill [which] grows as it progresses," while *The Urn,* noting that cremation was being eagerly discussed "from Maine to California," boldly prophesied that "in the very near future, [cremation] is to be the most common, if not the only mode of disposal of the dead."[3]

The numbers, at least in the Gilded Age, did not justify such optimism. At no point in the nineteenth century did the ratio of cremations to deaths approach 1 percent. Burial remained the preference of the overwhelming majority of Americans. *The Urn* consoled the faithful with the truism "that any new idea or reform, no matter how important, can make only very slow and unsatisfactory progress," and the *Lancaster Examiner* reminded its readers that "the law of gravitation was not accepted, but was denounced as infidel for seventy-three years after the death of Newton." *Modern Cremationist,* before itself succumbing to indifference, likened the cremation campaign to the vaccination movement, which eventually triumphed over vigorous opposition.[4]

The movement's progress may have disappointed the faithful, but it was not so terribly slow. Between 1884 and the end of the century cremation grew in popularity. The number of U.S. cremations rose during that period at a compound annual growth rate of 38 percent per year, and by the start of the twentieth century the United States was the leading Western country for cremations. Neither Italy, where the movement began, nor Great Britain, where Sir Henry Thompson gave cremation its strongest boost, could match it. In the United States, total cremations jumped from 16 in 1884 to 1,996 in 1899. (See figure 1.) In Italy during the same period the practice stagnated. More Italians than Americans were cremated in 1884 (113) but far fewer (only 265) in 1899. In Great Britain the number of cremations advanced from zero to a mere 301 in the century's last year. During the nineteenth century Italy built more crematories than did the United States, but Americans cremated nearly three times as many corpses as did the Italians and more than five times

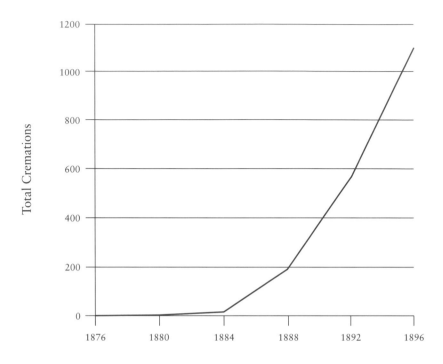

FIGURE 1. Cremations in the Gilded Age, 1876–1896

as many as the British. In fact, there were more cremations in those years in New York State alone than in either Italy or Great Britain.[5]

In light of these comparisons, America's nineteenth-century cremation movement must be judged at least a modest success. The cremation of Baron De Palm in 1876 was a national scandal reported in virtually all U.S. newspapers. Individual cremations were infrequent and notorious enough to make news into the mid-1880s. By the mid-1890s, however, cremation was old news. During that decade, a Lancaster, Pennsylvania, reporter noted that "cremation does not now attract any more attention in this city than an ordinary funeral." And in Chicago cremation had become "so common it [was] ceasing to cause comment." During the mid-1890s polemical works on both sides of the cremation question declined sharply. By 1896 the great cholera scares had passed and all three major cremationist journals had ceased publication. What the *World* had described as "this curious controversy between the sextons and the stokers" was over and a new era in the history of American cremation had begun.[6]

In the years between 1874, when the cremation debate began, and 1896, when the demise of the pro-cremation publications brought this period of controversy to an end, advocates had transformed cremation from a stigmatized practice into an acceptable alternative to burial. In 1885, only months after the cremation of Dr. Gross had nudged the cremation cause a bit closer to respectability, the *New York Times* reported that cremationists were "no longer regarded as demented or even eccentric." By the turn of the century antagonism toward cremation had cooled even more. In 1900 an article in the *Journal of American Medicine* reported that religious objections to cremation "are no longer heard." In 1909 the Massachusetts Cremation Society proudly proclaimed that the cause had "outgrown the period of argument." Such boasts were not, strictly speaking, true. But cremation had outgrown the period of widespread revulsion. "Cremation," the *Scientific American* editorialized in 1916, "is indeed a method no longer on trial." And that was no inconsiderable achievement.[7]

Following the period of intense public controversy from 1874 to 1896, cremationists turned to new challenges, which would preoccupy them into the 1960s. In this middle period in cremation's American history cremationists continued to make their case in print and to publish the names of notable recruits (among them, settlement house pioneer Jane Addams, temperance advocate Frances E. Willard, socialist Eugene Debs, sculptor Daniel Chester French, Congregationalist preacher and best-selling author Charles M. Sheldon, the Reverend Harry Emerson Fosdick of New York City's First Presbyterian Church, and Rabbi Stephen S. Wise of the Free Synagogue of New York). But the emphasis was clearly shifting from arguments to action, from preaching to practice, from creeds to deeds.

Back in the early 1880s, while the cremation movement was still in its infancy, the *New York Tribune* had accused the New York Cremation Society of doing little more than meeting and gabbing. "A single cheap crematory," its editors had written, "would do more to convert the public to the faith and practice of cremation than all the interminable arguments." Some time later, in the pages of the *San Francisco Examiner,* Ambrose Bierce (the satirist who once opined that "death is not the end; there remains the litigation over the estate") challenged cremation reformers to "Put up or shut up." "A man ought to support his convictions," Bierce wrote. "Why don't they build the crematory?" America's cremation societies were dogged from the start by such critics, who urged them to stop talking about cremation and to do something about it instead. But those complaints evaporated as the twentieth century dawned and the cremation movement moved into its bricks and mortar stage.[8]

As the century turned, nonprofit cremation societies yielded to for-profit businesses, and making the case for cremation took a back seat to building and operating crematories. In short, the old preoccupation with purity yielded to practicality. While John Storer Cobb was researching *A Quartercentury of Cremation in North America* (1901), he uncovered only one example of a crematory run in "a business-like spirit." At no other facility, he wrote, did he find "any indication of a disposition to balance personal interest with the general welfare." A long-time member of the New England Cremation Society, Cobb was relieved by this finding, since it was his wish that "in this matter, the pursuit of private material gain, as the cardinal motive for advancing what is conceived to be a public good, may be confined to its present narrow limits." But Cobb's wish would not be granted. As he was writing his book, cremation was becoming less a social reform and more a pragmatic enterprise. Among U.S. cremationists, power was shifting from idealists to managers. As the Gilded Age yielded to the Progressive Era, the business of cremation was becoming business.[9]

Dr. Hugo Erichsen and the CAA

The Cremation Association of America epitomized this shift. Loosely modeled after the National Funeral Directors Association, the CAA (today the Cremation Association of North America, or CANA) was founded in Detroit in 1913. Some early CAA members operated crematories inside cemeteries. Some were funeral directors with on-site crematories. A few were independents. Virtually all, however, worried less about public attitudes toward cremation than about the cremation industry's bottom line. In 1919 the CAA included roughly seventy U.S. crematories, nearly all of them run as businesses. This organization was, therefore, one of the chief engines driving American cremation away from the ideological posturing of nineteenth-century social reform toward the pragmatic spirit of compromise characteristic of twentieth-century businesses.

The CAA was the brainchild of Dr. Hugo Erichsen, whose life embodies the changes and tensions the cremation movement experienced as it entered a new century. Born in Detroit in 1860 to German-speaking parents, Erichsen was educated at the German-American Seminary in

Detroit, the Realschule in Kiel, Germany, and Detroit Medical College. He later received his medical degree from the University of Vermont. Though his father was an atheist, Erichsen became a Unitarian in his youth and attended a Unitarian church for the rest of his life. He first pondered cremation after reading, at the age of sixteen, a newspaper report on the 1876 De Palm incineration, and his long career in the movement continued until his death in 1942. Erichsen's pro-cremation work thus bridged the reforming zeal of the cremation reformers of the nineteenth century and the pragmatism of the cremating businessmen of the Progressive Era and beyond.

Erichsen's *The Cremation of the Dead Considered from an Aesthetic, Sanitary, Religious, Historical, Medico-Legal, and Economical Standpoint* (1887) was the first great pro-cremation work written by an American. Like Sir Henry Thompson, his British counterpart, Erichsen was a surgeon. And like Thompson, his early agitation for cremation was highly partisan. Erichsen responded to the Vatican's 1886 cremation ban, for example, by lambasting the Pope as the "ancient personage with the threefold crown and the herdman's stick." Over time, however, Erichsen devoted less energy to anti-Catholic fulminating and more to building and administering effective cremation organizations. He assisted at the foundation of the International Cremation Congress in 1886 and served as the CAA's first president.[10]

Under Erichsen's guidance the U.S. cremation movement entered its bricks and mortar stage, which began in 1896 when the Gilded Age debate drew to a close and ended in 1963 when the contemporary cremation boom began. As the debate between burial and cremation concluded in the mid-1890s without a clear winner, "How to cremate?" replaced "Why cremate?" as the cremationists' most pressing concern. After the CAA came into being in 1913, practical matters such as designing, building, and operating a nationwide cremation infrastructure quickly rose to the top of the cremationist agenda. Crematory operators began to experiment with the architecture, technology, and rites of cremation. What should a crematory look like? Should its furnace (or furnaces) be fired by coal, oil, electricity, or gas? What was the ideal columbarium? During this bricks and mortar period, cremationists occupied themselves with these practical questions. No longer obsessed with purification, cremationists turned in this middle period in cremation's U.S. history to ways and means—to the everyday challenges of improving crematory technologies, constructing crematories and columbaria, and administering a burgeoning infrastructure.

A Model Crematory and a Futuristic Columbarium

At the turn of the century the American crematory was still an ongoing experiment. Some crematories were rustic and some classical in design. Some boasted beautiful grounds with roads, walkways, trees, flowers, and shrubbery. Others consisted of little more than the crematory itself. Most crematories operated inside cemeteries, but in San Francisco a fraternal order ran one. An Episcopal church built a crematory in Milwaukee, Wisconsin. An undertaker operated one in the basement of his funeral home in Pittsburgh. The Swinburne Crematory outside New York City was government-run. Equally experimental was the technology of cremation. While some furnace designers preferred coal-fired units, others championed oil, and a few experimented with electricity. In these fluid circumstances, cremationists mused not so much about novel arguments for cremation as about building the perfect crematory and the perfect columbarium.

At the beginning of this bricks and mortar period one forward-looking New Yorker fantasized about a rich donor bequeathing one million dollars for "the model crematory of the world." If money were no object, what sort of crematory would he design? This writer's story invites readers to visualize themselves arriving in an electric car at a modern, scientific crematory in the heart of an American metropolis. Visitors pass through heavy bronze doors, entering a gracious sanctuary that rivals the finest European cathedrals. Worlds apart from the shabby and ill-appointed reception room of America's first crematory in "Little Washington," this "imposing" structure is constructed out of marble in the Gothic style. Elegant urns sit in niches along the walls, which are themselves adorned with "memorial windows and inlaid onyx decoration."[11]

A funeral service is in progress, so all respectfully lower their voices. Officiating is the Episcopal priest of St. George's Cathedral, and he is assisted by two additional ministers. The casket set in front of the altar is draped in purple velvet embroidered in gold with a large cross. Clearly, this is no pagan practice and the deceased no freethinker. In fact, the sexton whispers to the visitors that the deceased was an Episcopal bishop. As a professional choir breaks into song, accompanied by the pipes of the chapel's stately organ, the traditional Episcopal burial liturgy is read with only minor alterations. ("Ashes to ashes, dust to dust" becomes "Dust to dust, ashes to ashes.") Then the casket is lowered, smoothly and silently, on a hidden elevator to the furnace room below. The service, however, is not yet over. As heat speeds the transformation of the corpse from an empty shell of the soul into pure, white ashes, the priest holds the congregation "spellbound" with a homily that focuses not on death but on life, not on hell's horrors but on the hope of the resurrection. In less than thirty minutes the service reaches its climax, as the "pure remains," which have ascended in a "handsome bronze urn" from the fiery depths, are given over to the family.

Following the service visitors are taken on a grand tour. One is amazed by the efficiency of the furnace room, which is equipped with ten state-of-the-art furnaces (five at the front of the chapel for paying customers and five to the rear for the poor). Upstairs, the tour courses through reception rooms, a ministers' room, and, in a nod to Gilded Age pamphleteering, a cremation library. Outside, the crematory grounds anticipate the sort of landscape that will emerge in the teens as the memorial park. The land is "laid out in plots...[and] dotted all over with little white, engraved marble plates, level with the lawn, each covering a tiny grave of ashes." The grounds are both beautiful to behold and easy to mow.

Not long after this futurist wrote his story, another forward-looking cremationist imagined the ideal columbarium. No fan of either scattering or burying cremains, he was convinced that people only strewed or buried ashes because they had not yet figured out how to display them tastefully and securely. Solve that problem with an elegant columbarium and perpetual care, he reasoned, and Americans would happily give up scattering and burying. The first step on the road to this "Columbarium of the Future," he wrote, would be small family columbaria. Placed in cemeteries, these memorials would look like the family monuments popularized in the rural cemetery movement, but their foundations would incorporate receptacles for ashes. The next step would be large community columbaria suitable for "fraternal orders as well as religious denominations" and, eventually, for counties and even states. As these larger structures became popular, the smaller family columbaria and memorials—"a necessary evil"—would yield to fewer yet finer specimens. In the process, America's landscapes of death would become greener and more parklike. Gradually, the cemetery would be remade in the image of the memorial park, put into practice most famously at Forest Lawn (established in 1917) in Glendale, California.[12]

The final step would be a massive "national columbarium." This memorial would require a spectacular natural backdrop, perhaps "a mountain top among the clouds, with an environment of Nature that would lift [it] above and away from the cares of life and place it in a realm of its own." Outfitted with "corridors and colonnades grand beyond description," it would boast "bronze and marble memorial urns, tablets and sculpture of infinite design," and a library "similar to the inner temple of an Egyptian temple" (for biographical works on the resident deceased). The grandeur would rival the glories of the pyramids of ancient Egypt, and put Americans alongside pharaohs in the ranks of the world's greatest memorializers.[13]

From Homeliness to Elegance

Like this model crematory and this futuristic columbarium, America's actual crematories were designed with criticisms of the LeMoyne crematory in mind. The Gilded Age cremation movement was hurt by the homeliness of the America's first crematory, and advocates went to great lengths to insulate later facilities against accusations of inelegance. In 1882 *American Architect and Building News* had noted that, despite advances in cremation, U.S. crematory design remained "in an early stage of development." That was no longer true by the mid-1890s, when nearly two dozen crematories dotted the land and architects were busy designing dozens more.[14]

The crematories and columbaria built in the United States around the turn of the century did not quite actualize the fantasies of the fin de siècle futurists, but they were a far cry from the plainness of the LeMoyne crematory and its makeshift bookcase columbarium. The first truly public facility, in Lancaster, Pennsylvania, was a modest brick building constructed in the Gothic style just off the grounds of a local cemetery. Four rooms crowded its single story: an auditorium, a waiting room, a preparation room, and a furnace room. The floor, even in the auditorium, was unadorned Portland cement. There was no altar or stage and no columbarium. Architecturally, Lancaster distinguished itself from "Little Washington" largely through its designer's efforts to mask its use. While LeMoyne's crematory had three chimneys, Lancaster's had only one, and it was concealed behind a small rooftop observatory (the building's only effort at ornamentation). Also designed in this simple style were the crematories built in the 1890s in Boston; Chicago; Davenport, Iowa; and Waterville, New York.

The simplicity of those buildings, however, ran against the architectural grain of the times, which edged inexorably toward elegance. As cremationists gained respectability, they articulated their newfound

status in more ornate architecture. One step in this direction was the
Baltimore crematory, constructed on cemetery land in 1889 by the Cremation Cemetery Company of Baltimore. Like many of the simpler crematories, it was rustic, built on one floor out of craggy stone with an occasional granite accent. The auditorium, which looked like a chapel,
complete with oak pulpit and pews, was ornamented with stained glass.
Two urns stood like sentries posted on either side of the front door, and
above that door was a prominent marble tablet proudly marking the
place "Crematorium."

The Baltimore crematory was in many respects a compromise between the simplicity of the Lancaster crematory and the grandeur of
later examples at St. Louis, Philadelphia, San Francisco, Buffalo, and
(above all) Troy, New York. The later type articulated in space the argument that cremation was a modern revival of an ancient rite. Most of
these crematories were built in the Grecian style and on a grand scale.
And in keeping with the emerging fashion in deathways—ushered in at
the Reverend Beecher's "flower funeral" of 1887 and stretched to its
logical conclusion in the mawkishly cheery Forest Lawn Memorial
Park—they emphasized life over death, light over darkness, gaiety over
gloom. Most had at least two floors. The first was given over to what
was now clearly a chapel, complete with high ceilings, pews, a pulpit,
an organ, hardwood or tile floors, frescoed walls and ceilings, carved
oak doors, and stained glass. The basement floor comprised a body
preparation room, a furnace room, and, in some cases, a living room for
the janitor. The most elegant early example of this type was the crematory in Troy, built by a father as a memorial to a deceased son. The most
expensive crematory constructed in Gilded Age America, it included an
elaborate mosaic floor, an onyx altar, carved bronze doors, and five Tiffany stained glass windows.

These modern crematories cum chapels, already elegant at the turn
of the century, became only more extravagant over time. The "new
model chapel and crematory," constructed just before World War I at
the Forest Lawn Cemetery in Omaha, Nebraska, was built in the classical style, underscoring once again the conception of American cremation as a modern revival. Marble, stained glass, and mosaics created a
warm but cheery chapel that "eliminated everything in any way sugges-
tive of the somber atmosphere of mortuary structures." The symbolism
inside was said to suggest both the Tree of Life and "the four ideas of
Faith, Hope, Love and Memory." (Charity lost out in the translation.)[15]

Columbaria Light and Dark

In the early stages of American crematory design columbaria were strangely neglected. Although some fantasized about ideal columbaria, few built them, and those who did were often careless in their design. The Mount Auburn crematory, highly praised for its design at its opening in 1900, initially included no columbarium. When columbaria began to appear in New England and the Midwest, they were clearly afterthoughts. The chapel and crematory at Lakewood Cemetery in Minneapolis was lauded by *Park and Cemetery* as "one of the most notable architectural creations of its generation," but its architects relegated the columbarium to a dark, wet basement. The Detroit crematory built a columbarium, but its architect made its niches the size of post office boxes, so few standard urns fit inside. Cremationists stumbled when it came to columbaria because for roughly the first quarter of the century they saw themselves as cremation providers rather than memorializers. If the business of cremation was business, that business was cremating corpses, not selling urns or columbarium niches or committal services. Most crematory operators did little more post-cremation marketing than keeping a few dusty urns in a back room. Families who chose cremation for their deceased relatives typically buried or scattered the ashes.[16]

At the 1925 convention of the CAA, Herb Hargrave, an independent crematory operator from Fresno, California, reported on an unsettling tour he had taken of East Coast crematories. Some of those crematories offered no columbarium niches at all, and the columbaria he saw were typically in dark and uninviting basements. Such retrograde facilities were, in his view, a major barrier to the advance of cremation. His recommendation was to build new columbaria and spruce up the old ones. "I firmly believe that more cremations result by way of the beauties of a Columbarium," Hargrave said. "The act of cremation should be considered as a means to the beauties of the Columbarium." Then, in a key development, he suggested selling prospective cremation families not on the retort but on the niche. This strategy would work, he said, only if every crematory had a properly designed columbarium. New columbaria should be built above ground and bathed in light. Such facilities, he concluded, would stimulate both post-cremation sales and cremation itself.[17]

Like much in cremation's U.S. history, the columbarium first gained popularity on the West Coast and largely among independent crematory operators like Hargrave, who saw niches as a way to compete more effectively with cemetery-based crematories. Paving the way for this West Coast revolution in the American way of cremation was the San Francisco crematory and columbarium of the International Order of the Odd Fellows, an all-male fraternal organization. Within a decade of its opening in 1895, this facility, which *The American Architect* praised as "the most magnificent" crematory in the country, became the most popular site in the country for cremation. In the first five years of the twentieth century, the Odd Fellows crematory did 3,415 out of the 14,040 cremations performed in the United States, or 24 percent of the total.[18]

Initially, crematory operators in New England and the Midwest resisted the columbarium. Most crematories in those regions had sprung up in cemeteries, which by the turn of the century were often generations old. Cremation customers, therefore, typically had parents and grandparents buried in cemeteries, and while they were willing to be cremated, they wanted their urns to be buried in family plots. Pro-cremation families that rejected urn burial, moreover, typically requested scattering. For many years, the Forest Hills crematory outside Boston had scattered ashes in a pine grove in its cemetery, and family members of its crematory customers had strewn many more ashes hither and yon. As early as the teens, however, it became clear to crematory operators nationwide that the West Coast crematories were onto something in emphasizing the columbarium over the crematory. While during this decade the ratio of cremations to deaths remained well below 1 percent in New England, that ratio topped 10 percent in California, Oregon, and Washington. In the twenties, seven of the ten leading crematories in the country were located in California. And in the thirties, roughly one third of all the nation's crematories were in that one state.[19]

There is a saying in recent U.S. presidential politics: "As California goes, so goes the nation."[20] That may or may not be true, but in cremation's American history it certainly was the case. As news of West Coast successes traveled eastward, crematory operators across the country came to see the virtues of the columbarium, and the West Coast way of cremation began to migrate too. The columbarium came into its own in the Midwest at Chicago's Bohemian National Cemetery. Founded by Americans of Czech descent in 1877, this cemetery built a crematory with a chapel in 1913. It added elaborate columbarium niches in 1931 and soon came to be known as the Midwest's equivalent of the Odd Fellows crematory and columbarium. In Chicago as in San Francisco, columbaria were seen not merely as spots to deposit ashes but also as places to visit the dead. Moreover, in a nod to the customization of culture that would take hold in late-twentieth-century America, families were encouraged to personalize niches with photographs and decorate them with flowers. Mount Auburn did not allow its customers such free rein, but it too made niches available in the 1930s. In 1934 Mount Auburn retrofitted the first floor of its crematory chapel for columbarium niches, and demand was so great that it constructed additional niches on the chapel's second floor in 1936. By the 1930s the columbarium was taking hold across the country. In that decade Hugo Erichsen told an audience of cemeterians that no crematory was complete without a columbarium. Still, the practice of inurning in a columbarium remained uncommon (except on the West Coast) well into the twentieth century.

The Cemetery Site

One of the most surprising facts about the first hundred years of U.S. cremation is how frequently cremated remains were buried. To anyone who participated in the Gilded Age burial versus cremation debate, that fact would come as a surprise. Early cremationists championed their method as an alternative to burial, not a precursor to it, so scattering, not burial, was their preferred post-cremation rite. This cremate-and-scatter approach made sense as long as crematories were independent operations ill-equipped to handle inurnment in niches or burial in cemetery plots. But as the business of cremation expanded in the early twentieth century, cremationists entered into a curious alliance—first, with officials at rural cemeteries and lawn-park cemeteries and later (following World War I), with entrepreneurs at memorial parks. This coming together of private crematories and private cemeteries was, according to one historian of the American cemetery, "a unique American pattern." In Europe the emerging crematory regime was controlled by a coalition of cremation societies, which built many of the early crematories, and municipal governments, which emerged in the twentieth century as the leading crematory builders and operators.[21]

Back in the 1870s Dr. LeMoyne had tried to construct his crematory on the grounds of a nearby cemetery, but the local cemetery operator had turned him away, so he built it instead on his own land. The Lancaster, Pennsylvania crematory was placed next to a cemetery, but it too was independently run (by the Lancaster Cremation and Funeral Reform Society). In fact, the first five U.S. crematories were all independents. Independent crematories dominated into the 1890s, when battles

over the relative merits of cremation and burial made compromise between cremationists and cemeteries unimaginable. And even into the
early bricks and mortar period, most U.S. crematories were financed,
built, and run not by cemetery managers but by cremation reform societies. In 1912, on the eve of the foundation of the Cremation Association of America, Hugo Erichsen worked tirelessly to win over the undertaker but considered the cemeterian to be a lost cause. "Our
competition," Erichsen wrote, "was with the cemeteries."[22]

As the era of debate gave way to the era of crematory construction,
however, competition yielded to cooperation, and the cemetery crematory emerged as the dominant American model. While funeral directors
continued to ignore or impugn cremation into the late twentieth century, cemetery superintendents decided that it made more sense to profit
from cremation—through urn burials and sales of columbarium niches
or burial plots—than to perpetually thumb their noses at it. Moreover,
some cemeterians were prescient enough to see that their land would be
eaten up far less quickly by urn burials than by whole-body burials and
that interring urns could be a far more efficient (and profitable) use of
space than interring caskets. Cremationists, meanwhile, made peace
with the cemetery by, among other things, embracing the concept of memorialization. Some crematories, particularly on the West Coast, continued to be run by independent cremationists or undertakers, but the
cemetery site became the national norm.

Modern Cemetery, the official organ of the Association of American
Cemetery Superintendents (or AACS, established in 1887), gave a boost
to the cemetery crematory by endorsing cremation repeatedly during its
five-year publication run in the 1890s. "The proper place for a crematory," it editorialized in 1892, "is in the cemetery." In 1900 Mount Auburn Cemetery, the doyen of the rural cemetery movement, converted a
chapel on its grounds into a crematory. But not all crematories located in
cemeteries were cemetery-managed. Of the twenty-four open for business in the United States at the turn of the century, fifteen were located in
cemeteries, but just over half of those were cemetery-run. As the century
progressed, however, the cemetery crematory became the norm. When
the CAA was founded in 1913, its rolls included many cemetery managers but only one Gilded Age–style reform association (the Massachusetts Cremation Society). Relations between cremationists and cemetery
superintendents eventually got so cozy, however, that the CAA and the
AACS held joint meetings and even considered merging. By 1917 a cemetery superintendent could claim with some justification that "the day is

not far distant, in fact, may be said to be already here, when no cemetery of any importance will be considered fully prepared to accommodate its patrons if not equipped with a crematory." In the 1920s in a speech before the AACS, a cemetery superintendent argued that a crematory in the cemetery was both "good business policy" and "a profitable investment." "A crematory," he added, "may now be considered an essential part of the equipment of the up-to-date cemetery." In the 1930s, Glendale's Forest Lawn gave a stamp of approval to the cemetery crematory when it found room in the midst of its 200 acres of kitsch to construct a crematory. By 1939 roughly 60 percent of the crematories in North America were run by cemeteries. The rest were run by independent operators, funeral directors, nonprofit organizations, or local, state, or federal governments.[23]

Two examples, one from each coast, illustrate this shift from the nineteenth-century model of society-run independents to the twentieth-century model of privately managed cemetery crematories. These two facilities, one outside Boston and one in San Francisco, were originally built by cremation reformers. The crematory and columbarium at Cypress Lawn opened in 1893 thanks to the efforts of the San Francisco Cremation Company, which despite its name was actually a society for cremation reform. The crematory of the Massachusetts Cremation Society, the first in Massachusetts, opened one year later across the street from the Forest Hills Cemetery in Jamaica Plain. Both were eventually taken over, however, by less ideological and more pragmatic concerns. In 1897 Cypress Lawn took out a lease on the San Francisco Cremation Company's land, and by 1913 the company had folded and the cemetery was running both the crematory and the columbarium. The Massachusetts Cremation Society held out longer. It turned its crematory over to Forest Hills Cemetery in 1925.

The decision to hitch the future of cremation to the cemetery site was a mixed blessing for cremationists. The alliance with cemeteries lent the cremation cause legitimacy and expanded its infrastructure. A few leading cemeteries promoted cremation aggressively and successfully. (During the thirties, Mount Auburn did more cremations than it did wholebody burials.) But many cemetery-based facilities promoted cremation halfheartedly or not at all. Some even opposed it. In 1920 the president of a San Francisco–area cemetery with a crematory operation argued in a letter to the editor of *Park and Cemetery* that cemetery men should avoid speaking out for cremation, which was in his view "merely another name for burning."[24]

Ritualization

As this bricks and mortar stage progressed and cremationists settled on
the cemetery site, they also routinized the rites of cremation. Whereas in
the 1990s most cremations in the United States proceeded without
family members present, crematory attendance was the norm until the
early twentieth century. At the De Palm cremation in 1876 witnesses
had watched the proceedings through a peephole in the side of the furnace. Over roughly the next half century, attendance and ritualization
at the crematory remained the norm. Peepholes were a standard feature
in early crematory furnaces. The Cincinnati crematory even instituted a
rule in the late nineteenth century mandating that "each incineration
must be attended by one or more members of the family of the deceased." And as late as 1932 the Forest Home Chapel and Crematory in
Milwaukee was encouraging family members to witness the placing of
the corpse in the cremation furnace.[25]

Rites practiced at America's crematories were modeled on the traditional graveside committal service. In fact, for decades crematory services were virtually identical to committals except for a few changes in
liturgical language. Instead of saying, "We therefore commit his body to
the ground, earth to earth, ashes to ashes, dust to dust," officiants might
say, "We therefore commit his body to the flames, ashes to ashes, dust
to dust." Frank Bates Flanner, an undertaker and cremationist from Indianapolis, Indiana, said he conducted his early-twentieth-century cremation services just as he conducted burials. He washed, embalmed,
dressed, and shaved the body. He put it in a casket, and had it carried
by pallbearers into the crematory. At the crematory a rabbi or minister
would conduct a committal service.

Most early American crematories had only one floor. The room devoted to ritualization lay next door to the room devoted to the technology of cremation. At the height of the ritual the casket would be ma-
neuvered from one room to the next, usually through a door or a hole
in the wall designed for that purpose. Beginning in the late nineteenth
century, however, and continuing into the early twentieth century, architects began to place the working elements of crematories in the basement. These designs allowed for more elegant chapels on the first floor
and provided a more dramatic exit for the corpse. While at Washington
and Lancaster officiants had carried or slid the dead body from the
meeting room to the furnace room next door, at these newer crematories officials lowered the corpse, as in a burial, to the furnace room
below. Following this emotional moment, and away from wet-eyed

mourners, the basement furnace would do its work of purifying the body, releasing the soul.

Like the decision to place the furnace directly beneath the chapel's altar in order to transform the crematory rite into a committal service, the prominence of the chapels in these modern facilities provides evidence refuting the thesis that cremation promoted secularization. While Dr. LeMoyne's crematory emphasized the technological, these modern crematories emphasized the spiritual. They did so, however, in a distinctive way. The chapels in many of these facilities were grand—larger and more ornate than the secular space below. Crematory rites, however, were simple. "As cremation comes more and more into general favor, one effect is noticeable," the *Boston Transcript* reported in 1908. "That is the simplification of funerals. The whole tendency of cremation customs is toward the elimination of superfluous display." So while crematory rites were the norm, those rites were more low than high church. Simplicity was their spiritual style.[26]

During the teens and twenties the tide began to turn against certain forms of cremation ritualization. This trend, too, seems to have begun on the West Coast. In 1912 the California Crematorium in Oakland covered up the peepholes in the front of its cremation furnaces. A pamphlet from the Los Angeles Crematory (undated but likely from the 1920s) describes another strategy for distancing ritualization from cremation itself. According to that pamphlet "no part of the actual cremation" was "witnessed by those attending." The closest family members could get to the actual crematory was a distant balcony. Over time, U.S. cremations would proceed at an even greater remove from relatives. An undated typescript found in the archives of the Forest Hills Cemetery outside Boston provides evidence of changes in cremation ritualization that seem to have begun to take hold in the 1920s. This typescript underscores the importance of cremation services, but notes that at the end of the services "the flower embowered casket is left in its position and is not removed until after family and friends have taken their departure."[27]

This distancing of family and friends from the act of cremation itself privatized what in the De Palm case had been eminently public. But in no way did it put an end to ritualization. The covering up of peepholes and the banishing of friends and family from furnace rooms merely relocated the key cremation rite, which moved first from the furnace room to the cremation chapel and later from the chapel to the columbarium. As columbarium services became more popular, priests, ministers, and rabbis accommodated themselves to inurnment in niches. In *The Funeral: A Source Book for Ministers* (1942), Andrew W. Blackwood of Princeton Theological Seminary included a lengthy explanation of the columbarium, pointing out that the word literally means "a resting place for doves." He instructed the Protestant ministers reading his book to keep an open mind about cremation rites. "God is as near to sorrowing people in a columbarium," Blackwood wrote, "as at a cemetery." According to Blackwood, the columbarium rites should proceed much like whole-body burials, again with just minor alterations. For example, instead of saying, "We therefore commit *his* body to be dissolved" (the language in the Scottish *Book of Common Order*) the minister should say, "We therefore commit *his* ashes to this resting place." ("In no case," Blackwood added, "should there be any use of the word 'flame,' or 'fire.'")[28]

Cremation Technology

While crematory operators were experimenting with architecture and ritualization, they were also experimenting with cremation technology. Inventors devised and patented a variety of Rube Goldberg contraptions in an effort to profit from cremation's advance. There were efforts to make cremation portable—to bring the crematory to the body rather than the body to the crematory. A "Hygienic Wagon and Portable Furnace" patented in 1907 ran on rails "in the manner of a road-locomotive." An earlier mobile crematory designed for cemeteries used a series of pipes to pump fiery gases underground, burning already-buried bodies. In 1910 there was talk of placing a small crematory on every ocean liner "so as to obviate the burial at sea of persons who die in the course of a voyage." Engineers experimented with different fuels and various types of tile, brick, and cement for furnaces. Urn designers innovated too. One patented a model shaped like a bust, complete with a hole in the back of the head to receive the ashes. Another invented a crystal Masonic urn with a slot for a photograph of the deceased. During the first few decades of the twentieth century, however, cremation technology was rapidly routinized. An American way of cremation was beginning to emerge.[29]

During the early bricks and mortar era, crematory engineers experimented with furnace designs, fuels, and burners. Virtually all the options had problems. Many early furnaces followed the patented coke-and-coal design used at the Lancaster crematory. Later engineers experimented with wood. All these strategies, however, produced lots of smoke and noise. Some furnaces had to be preheated for as long as twenty-four hours. And because corpses were introduced into a white hot retort, cremations typically began in a frightful blaze. In retorts fired by wood, coke, or coal, moreover, the corpse mixed with fuel, making it impossible to extract pure ashes. Oil-burning furnaces eventually replaced these early models, first at San Francisco's Cypress Lawn and later in locations across the West Coast. Oil retorts were economical. They did not need to be preheated, so the corpse could be introduced to a cold furnace. But oil-burning technology only added to the noise and smoke, and corpses continued to be consumed directly by fire. Some witnesses reported seeing partially burned clothing drifting down from the smokestacks. "One had to be a 100% cremationist in those days," one crematory operator later said, "to face all of these horrors."[30]

That crematory operator was Lawrence Moore of the California Crematorium in Oakland, and he based his judgment of cremation's early "horrors" on a nationwide tour of U.S. crematories he took in 1912. What he found disgusted him: "All of the crematories had high smokestacks and all of them had black smoke coming out of them, with the roar of the machinery and the shoveling of coke or coal. They stripped the casket of its handles and metal, then chopped or hammered up the handles and ornaments. There were a lot of ornaments on caskets in those days. They heated up the furnace quite hot to receive the caskets, and one of the accompaniments of such procedure was the screams of the mourners who saw their loved ones put in these red hot furnaces."[31]

One cremationist who struggled to resolve these problems was Frank Gibson, who got his start in cremation when he attended the De Palm incineration in 1876. In 1883 he went to work as the crematory operator at Cypress Lawn in San Francisco. The Odd Fellows crematory in San Francisco later lured him away, and still later he built and ran crematories in Denver and Portland. Early in Gibson's career it was standard practice to remove the corpse from the casket before the cremation. But "it was a disagreeable experience not only to the family but to those that had the handling of the body," Gibson said. "We had to handle the body, wrap it in a winding sheet and place [it] in the furnace, and at the same time we had the grief of the family standing around seeing the body go into the furnace." So Gibson cremated a casketed corpse at the Odd Fellows crematory in 1897. That decision cost him his job, but the undertaker in charge of the funeral warmed to the innovation, vowing he would refuse in the future to take bodies out of caskets. "That," Gibson recalled, "was the beginning of that practice."[32]

Gibson was also responsible for another important innovation. During the first decade of the twentieth century a group of Masons came to his Denver crematory to conduct an elaborate cremation rite. Unfortunately, Gibson had not been told they were coming. He improvised a plan: to place the corpse in a cold retort, remove it after the mourners had left, then preheat the retort and reintroduce the body. The Masons, however, insisted on seeing their brother cremated. So all Gibson could do was insert the corpse, fire up a cold furnace, and proceed. To his surprise, both casket and corpse were consumed with minimal smoke, and from that day forward Gibson never preheated a furnace.

In 1940 Lawrence Moore was able to report that most of cremation's technological problems had been solved. After a brief flirtation with electricity (abandoned as uneconomical), crematory engineers had adopted oil as the fuel of choice. The oil furnaces were now fired indirectly rather than directly, however, so the corpse was not consumed by direct flames. These new furnaces also consumed the corpse without smell or smoke. Moreover, they did not have to be preheated; corpses could be placed into a cold retort. And new methods of directing air into the furnace rendered the high smokestack obsolete. Thus, after much experimentation, cremationists adopted technologies that allowed cremations to proceed with "no vibration, no noise, no smoke, no odor." According to Moore, U.S. cremations now included:

> Lovely and gracious buildings, in which the services are held; understanding, intelligent and gentle personnel; the actual process under ideal conditions—invisible and inaudible to the "passer-by"; ... the ministry of music skillfully played on a fine organ, representing the religious beliefs of the family now being served; the entire absence of death symbols, of black; a hallowed atmosphere of calm; the placing of cremated remains in an urn in a memorial niche in a columbarium of cheer and light; of lovely flowers; of the singing of birds; or the interment of a bronze urn in a plot, marked with a memorial inscription; the financial endowment of the perpetual care of all memorial premises.[33]

Gradually, but perceptibly, an American way of cremation was emerging out of all this experimentation. By World War II, cremationists had forgotten about ocean-going crematories or burning the buried. They no longer suggested stirring cremains into glue and casting the mixture into statues. Even urn design had become more formulaic. Both a flame motif and the classical style predominated on the American urn.

And columbarium designers adapted themselves to standard-size urns. The time it took to cremate a body had fallen from three hours to roughly one. Oil had been "almost universally adopted" as the fuel of choice. In most major American cities, cremations were readily available for between $25 and $50 (less for children). Crematory operators had come to see themselves not as purveyors of cremation but as sellers of urns, cemetery plots, and columbarium niches. The cemetery had emerged as the most popular crematory site, and cremation rites had become more private, though no less spiritually charged. Finally, the nonprofit cremation societies of the nineteenth century had given way to the crematory businesses of the twentieth, and crusaders after purity had yielded to pursuers of the Almighty Dollar.

But even as this new way of cremation was emerging and the infrastructure to support it was being built, the time-honored rationale underlying cremation was eroding. With the discovery of germ theory in the late nineteenth century, the tight connection between cremation and sanitary reform had begun to unravel. Cremation had lost its primary justification.[34]

5

The Memorial Idea

DURING ITS BRICKS AND MORTAR PHASE from 1896 to 1963, the U.S. cremation movement grew modestly and expanded its geographic reach. In 1900 there were twenty five crematories operating in the United States—four in California and the remainder in the Northeast and Midwest. In 1919 there were roughly seventy, including eighteen in California. There were still none in the South, however, and none in Kansas, Oklahoma, Texas, New Mexico, Utah, or Arizona. Over the next two decades, new crematories were built at a rate of roughly six per year, and the option to cremate came to the South, Southwest, and Pacific Northwest. At the outbreak of World War II there were approximately 200 crematories in the United States. By 1966, there were 267.[1]

Accompanying this geographic expansion was a demographic diffusion. In the nineteenth century cremation was practiced largely by "advanced thinkers" for whom it was a novelty. During this era, cremation got a boost from immigrant groups for whom it was a tradition. In the first few decades of the twentieth century, immigrant Sikhs—adherents of a religious tradition born in the Punjab in the eighteenth century that creatively combines elements of Hinduism and Islam—came from India to the West Coast. Hardly any Sikh women immigrated, so many Sikh men married Mexican-American Catholics and adapted themselves to Catholic beliefs and practices. But when they died, their families saw to it that they were properly cremated, typically in Sacramento. There, in a creolization of the ancient Sikh way of death, the closest relative would press the retort button to commence the cremation. The ashes would be scattered into a body of water—either the Pacific or in a river or ocean back in India. At least until 1924, when the Asian Exclusion Act severely restricted immigration from Asia, Buddhists from Japan and Hindus from India came to America too, and they brought their cremation traditions with them.[2]

The cremation rate also increased during the bricks and mortar phase, though the rate of growth was far more modest in the first half of the twentieth century than it had been in the last quarter of the nineteenth century. In the early 1920s the ratio of cremations to deaths topped 1 percent for the first time. It hit 2 percent in the early 1930s and exceeded 3 percent in the 1940s. In comparison with the progress of cremation in Great Britain, the American turn to cremation was sharp in the nineteenth century but was far more gradual in the twentieth. Americans cremated at least five times as many corpses as Great Britain in virtually every year through 1930. But that gap narrowed quickly in the forties, and by the fifties Great Britain had passed the United States, in large measure because of British policies favoring cremation, including the construction of dozens of municipal crematories. By 1967, when cremation overtook burial in Great Britain as the preferred mode of disposition of the dead, the American cremation rate was just over 4 percent.[3]

These statistics present at least two interpretive tasks. The first is to explain why cremation progressed as rapidly as it did. The second is to explain why the vast majority of Americans blithely ignored it. Why, on the one hand, did cremation refuse to die at the turn of the century as some had predicted it would? Why, on the other hand, did the cremation rate not rise to even 5 percent? Why did the practice fail to become, as optimists had predicted it would, America's leading method for disposal of the dead?

Inhibitors

Many factors inhibited cremation's growth. One was inertia. Cultural practices are extraordinarily resistant to change. Of all these practices, the most stubborn are religious rites, and of all religious rites, the most entrenched are the rites of death. Historians will continue to debate the correctness of the claim of French historian Fernand Braudel that change proceeds exceedingly slowly over the *longue durée* (long duration), but death rites typically fit that bill. During the French Revolu-

tion—a moment of rapid historical change if ever there was one—revolutionaries repeatedly tried to supplant the traditional rites of Roman
Catholicism with new rites of "the religion of humanity." Among those
attempts at dechristianization was an effort to institute cremation. But
the French people resisted these so-called advances. Voltaire may or
may not have returned to the comforts of Christianity on his deathbed,
but the myth that he did communicates an important truth: When faced
with death, even the most forward-looking people tend to look back to
traditional comforts. "Mere ritual" is an oxymoron, at least at the end
of life. Rituals matter, especially the rites of death; and burial is nothing
to be trifled with. A version of the Voltaire deathbed conversion myth
seems to have plagued the U.S. cremation movement. As the first generation of cremationists began to die, many eschewed cremation for the
comforts of burial. Notables the movement had counted as stalwart
converts repeatedly proved to be lukewarm sympathizers—examples of
the "Hyde and Jekyll character who preaches cremation and practices
earth burial." "The greatest embarrassment that the cremationists have
to encounter," one observer wrote around the turn of the century, "is
the fact that when their most eminent disciples depart this life they are
generally buried."[4]

Cremation was also hurt by high capital expenses. Although it cost
little to fuel a single incineration, the investment required to build a crematory was considerable. Because the crematories that opened for business in the movement's first few decades remained idle most of the time,
cremation's economic benefits remained largely theoretical well into the
twentieth century. Cremationists were also frustrated by the fact that
the important philanthropists who had made pro-cremation declara-
tions—among them, Andrew Carnegie, Courtlandt Palmer, and William
Waldorf Astor—did not put their money where their convictions were.
The U.S. cremation rate could not rise much until crematories were
built, but crematories could not be built until capital was raised, and
raising that capital was always a struggle. *The Urn* repeatedly chided its
readers for not giving enough to the cause, urging wealthy advocates to
contribute at least as much to cremation as they gave, say, to Christian
missions. But few philanthropists came through, and the movement
struggled financially.

Successful innovations in American cemeteries—first the popularization of the lawn-park cemetery and later the emergence of the memorial
park—also inhibited cremation's growth. Each of these innovations in-
sulated cemeteries from the criticisms of overcrowding, unsanitariness,

and ugliness leveled against the old urban graveyards. The cremation movement was hurt as well by the inauguration of the mausoleum, which like the crematory was promoted as a sanitary alternative to burial. In his history of American cemeteries David Charles Sloane has referred to the period between 1880 and 1920 as "the golden age of the private mausoleum." And early-twentieth-century cremationists did see mausoleums of all sorts as a competitive danger. CAA president C.J. Buchanan, at his organization's 1925 convention, referred to the community mausoleum as "the greatest enemy to cremation." That statement was hyperbole, but the popularity of mausoleums in the early part of the century no doubt slowed cremation's growth.[5]

Yet another inhibitor of cremation's advance was the failure of its leaders to win the imprimatur of the state. Whereas in Japan and many European countries governments passed laws that made burial difficult, in the United States government officials remained aloof from the questions of the disposal of the dead. A key factor in the success of cremation in Great Britain, for example, was the transfer of authority over death from the Church of England to local governments, who by the end of the twentieth century were running over 150 crematories as a public service. Cremationists occasionally argued for laws mandating the cremation of the indigent or victims of contagious diseases, and they supported efforts to build municipal crematories. But in the twentieth-century United States, cremation remained almost entirely in the hands of private entrepreneurs and nonprofit corporations. The federal government did build a crematory in the Panama Canal Zone in 1914. And a few more government entities (most notably, municipal hospitals) eventually followed the example of New York State, which built the first government-run crematory on Swinburne Island in 1889. But local, state, and national governments for the most part steered clear of the business of cremation. A 1935 tally of U.S. crematories found 116 commercial establishments and only eight run by local or state governments. At least in the United States, the burial versus cremation debate, like the contemporaneous contest between Methodists and Baptists, was to be settled by the free competition of ideas, not by state intervention.[6]

Vulgar Utilitarianism

The cremation movement was also hit hard by lingering memories of its early radicalism. Newspaper coverage of the De Palm incineration seared into public consciousness associations of cremation not only with paganism, Freemasonry, and Asian religions but also with callousness and indiscretion. The perception that cremationists looked upon the corpse as something utterly profane—a perception that would not be totally erased even in the early twenty-first century—was reinforced by the brazenly utilitarian arguments of a few pioneering cremationists. Some had been content merely to paraphrase English philosopher Jeremy Bentham (who offered up his corpse to the dissecting table) in portraying cremation as "one of the ways by which the greatest amount of good can be done for the greatest number of people." But others had performed a more detailed calculus.[7]

Sir Henry Thompson, for example, misstepped when he argued for cremation on the grounds that cremating the 80,000-plus people who died in London each year would yield over 200,000 pounds of high-grade "bone-earth" worth approximately 50,000 pounds sterling. He also miscalculated when he described cremated remains in utterly materialistic terms—as nothing more than a profane mix of "carbonic acid, water, and ammonia, and the mineral elements." Picking up on Thompson's suggestion, a number of American sources argued for scattering ashes on the theory that placing them in urns away from the reach of trees and plants amounted to thievery. One American doctor who wanted to see cremains used as fertilizer added, apparently in all seriousness, that the dead could make themselves even more useful to the living by having their "skins tanned into leather" before incinerating what remained into fertilizer. This crude utilitarianism reached its apogee in a text published around 1880 entitled "After the End of Life: A Positive Dissertation." Among the "positive" uses of the corpse discussed in this dissertation were burning it as "candle-coal...for gas-lighting." Given the 250 deaths per day in New York City and a corpse's average weight of 180 pounds, the author calculated that "not less than thirty thousand and six hundred pounds of fat substances could be had; therefore, every evening in the boilers of the gasometers, there would be ready about 190,000 cubic feet of bright illuminating gas." Moved by this logic, one civic-minded New Yorker published a codicil to his will indicating a desire to have his remains taken to the Manhattan Gas Works, where they might "add their share to the duty of illuminating the city."[8]

That the public was not moved by this cold-hearted calculus is clear from the fact that of the 800 letters Sir Thompson reportedly received (many of them from U.S. citizens) in the six months after his article appeared, about 600 were hostile. Even the *New York World*, America's most unabashedly pro-cremation newspaper, blanched at the "suggestion that we should use our fathers' ashes as turnip-dressing." If we were to follow the distinguished surgeon's analysis, the *World* wrote, "there would soon be something to be said for the cannibals, who treat a defunct man as a 'long pig.'" The vulgar utilitarianism of Thompson and others no doubt hurt the movement most in its infancy, but the effects lingered long into the twentieth century.[9]

Women, Undertakers, and the Church

Yet another factor inhibiting cremation was the diffidence of women. As pro-cremation texts frequently noted, the cause was supported by a number of prominent women's rights activists, and at least a few important American women chose cremation. Lucy Stone Blackwell, for example, was the first person cremated at Boston's Forest Hills Crematory, and sharpshooter Annie Oakley was cremated following her death in 1926. As a rule, however, women were indifferent, in part because pioneering cremationists did little to cultivate their support and in part because the logic of cremation aligned femininity with sentimentality and sentimentality with burial. Cremation writers did, however, lament women's lack of interest in their cause, and statistics seem to bear the lamentation out. Only 10 of the 42 people (24%) cremated at the Le-Moyne crematory were women, and of the first 1,101 cremations at Fresh Pond, 325 (30%) were of females. Only at the Forest Hills Crematory in Boston (where Lucy Stone Blackwell set a prominent example) is there evidence of a rate approaching 50 percent. Some early cremationists argued that women were in the vanguard of the movement—that they were "by far the best, the most enthusiastic and the most energetic apostles of cremation." Others claimed "a majority of the converts to the reform are of the gentler sex." But both statements were wishful thinking. Many a male cremationist complained that, try as he might, he just could not win over his wife.[10]

Admitting that women exhibited "a sentimental conservatism... which has retarded, hitherto, the movement," more realistic cremationists published lists of "women from the better class" who had joined cremation societies or otherwise signed on to the cause. They also made excuses for women who refused to see the light. Drawing on Victorian stereotypes, they said that females were "less accessible...to logical argument than to impression" and that "the average woman's sense of fairness and justice is not developed to its full capacity of impartial discernment." Some responded to this recalcitrance by working to educate women, much as they had tried to uplift immigrants, by cajoling them to attend to reason rather than sentiment. Those less certain about a woman's ability to change what many thought to be her true nature tried to entice her by emphasizing cremation's tender mercies. A far less useful approach was to vent about those who either refused cremation for themselves or ignored the pro-cremation wishes of their husbands (or both). ("Aunt Prejudice, on a visit from Customville," one writer labeled this type.) By most accounts, none of these approaches to "the woman problem" was particularly successful. Astronomer Maria Mitchell may have joined the chorus of "the college-bred women of the nation" humming the hymns of cremation, but few American women were singing along.[11]

Also refusing to praise cremation were the tradesmen who made a living off burial: cemetery operators, coffin makers, undertakers, and even grave robbers. Of all these foes, the most outspoken were the undertakers. Before the Civil War virtually all burial preparations had been done by relatives and close friends of the deceased, notably, wives, mothers, sisters, and daughters. During the war, however, authority over the dead began to shift from women to men, from kin to strangers, and from home to funeral parlor as a new cadre of death experts emerged. Capitalizing on the rise of consumer culture, these death experts sold caskets, rented hearses, embalmed bodies, and "undertook" funerals all for a tidy profit. Although embalming had been around in some form since the time of the pharaohs, it was popularized during the Civil War as families sought ways to preserve fallen loved ones for transport from battlefield to home. Like cremationists, "embalming undertakers" seized on the growing interest in sanitary science by arguing that embalming could sanitize even the bodies of victims of epidemics. They too had their journals (for example, *Casket* and *Western Undertaker*) and their voluntary associations (the National Funeral Directors Association). Given the tendency of cremationists to describe their practice as an economical alternative to burial, undertakers were understandably wary. Convinced that economic arguments for cremation were direct attacks on their financial well-being, they fought back, attacking cremation and defending the emerging embalm-and-bury regime in organs such as *Casket*. At least in the beginning, cremationists responded by branding the undertakers "our natural enemies." "If there be one obstacle greater than any other," one cremationist wrote, "it is to be found in that immense and powerful body, the undertakers."[12]

A third anti-cremation group comprised Catholics and other traditional Christians. While women merely passively resisted cremation and undertakers lacked the social power, cultural authority, and organizational expertise to severely restrain it, conservative Christians actively and effectively opposed the movement, meeting the cremationist onslaught with effective propaganda of their own. The Holy Office of the Roman Catholic Church took cremation seriously enough to issue three separate decrees against it in the 1880s and 1890s. In accordance with these mandates, Archbishop Ryan of Pennsylvania refused to allow funerals to be held in his cathedral over the bodies of parishioners slated for cremation. By portraying cremationists as sacrilegious secularists in league with "heathenism," and by insisting that cremation threatened to undermine long-standing Christian beliefs and practices (most notably the resurrection of the body), Catholics and other Christian traditionalists (many of them immigrants) served as the leading stumbling block to cremation's acceptance.[13]

What motivated individual Catholics, undertakers, and women to oppose cremation is difficult to determine. What is clear is that the cremation movement threatened to undercut the social power and cultural authority of all three groups. Before the rise of cremation and the funeral industry in the last quarter of the nineteenth century, death rites had been the domain of women and the church. Women prepared the body for burial, while ministers and priests officiated at last rites. In the end, the corpse was entrusted to the church, often in a churchyard plot (which women were typically charged with tending). Cremation threatened to upset both this American way of death and the emerging paradigm of the embalming undertaker. Early cremationists thought little of either the corpse or bodily preparations and they disdained much of the Victorian funeral as overly ritualized mumbo-jumbo. Funeral rites were important, cremation reformers believed, but they should be kept simple and they could be performed by lay people just as efficaciously as by clerics. Undertakers, by abrogating to themselves many of the duties associated with the corpse and its disposition, were also poised to undermine the authority of the women and church. But those undertakers were threatened, in turn, by the cremationists, who by resisting embalming and burial challenged not only their aspirations to professional status but also their livelihood itself. About this power struggle, Catholic critics were the most explicit. Some of them worried that state legislatures would pass laws mandating cremation and then enforce that fiat on unwilling Catholics. Others, noting how the municipal cemetery had grown at the expense of the churchyard, insisted that authority over both corpse and cemetery rested by natural and divine law with the Mother Church, not with an overbearing state. "It is eminently right and proper," one wrote, "that the mother should have full control of the dormitory where her children sleep."[14]

African Americans and the Poor

While undertakers, women, and traditional Christians opposed cremation, Blacks and poor whites (many of them immigrants) ignored it. During the nineteenth century cremationists argued repeatedly that cremation represented a boon to the impoverished—that the burying regime hurt the poor far more than the rich because funeral expenses were for them more of a burden. The cemetery, moreover, was said to discriminate scandalously between the "haves" and the "have-nots." One supporter estimated that the average cost for cremation was one-quarter that for burial. Dr. LeMoyne argued that the widespread adoption of cremation would save billions of dollars. He pointed out that burial practices drew a great divide between the wealthy, who could afford extravagances, and the destitute, who could not: "Thus the custom of inhumation separates the rich and the poor in their final homes as effectually as false religious customs separate the pariah from the higher castes in India." Cremation, of course, would obviate this difficulty, since one of its aims was "to bring rich and poor to a level in their last homes, that the common brotherhood of man may be practically demonstrated." "Cremation treats the body of a prince as it does that of the peasant; the body of the king as that of the commoner; the patrician as the plebeian; the President of the United States as the obscurest citizen."[15]

Other believers in the brotherhood of humanity cited similar social benefits. At the first cremation in New York State a friend of the deceased applauded the fact that the funeral occurred at a crematory, where "all are alike," instead of a cemetery, "where distinction is made between rich and poor with costly monuments and little wooden crosses." Others said cremation would make it more economical for people of all social ranks to ship home the remains of loved ones who died away from home. Dean George Hodges of the Episcopal Divinity School translated this socio-economic argument into an ethical imperative. "It is immoral," Hodges stated flatly, "so to spend money which might buy bread for the people."[16]

These arguments may have been designed to win the poor to cremation, or they may have been aimed instead at stroking the social con-
sciences of well-to-do cremationists. What is clear is that cremationists
did a poor job of persuading working-class Americans to reject burial.
In the nineteenth century cremation advocates had made their pitch almost exclusively to genteel elites (and to others with aspirations to gentility). In the process, they had alienated immigrants and the poor. In the
bricks and mortar period, cremationists only rarely described their
postmortem practice as an avenue to either godliness or cleanliness, but
the damage had already been done. Poorer Americans no doubt re-
sented how the logic of cremation associated them with pollution, and
they avoided the practice as if it were polluted itself.

Condescension tipped toward contempt when it came to attitudes toward African Americans. There is very little discussion about race in
pro-cremation sources, but a debate held on the floor of the 1943 CAA
convention is instructive. When asked whether they cremated "colored
people," only twelve members raised their hands. One said he took
"colored" cremations after hours, but would not allow an urn holding
African-American ashes to be placed in his Jim Crow columbarium.
CAA President Currie said the rules at his crematory allowed only Caucasian cremations; he did not take African Americans. Clearly there was
no groundswell of interest in cremation among African Americans in
early-twentieth-century America. One reason for this indifference is no
doubt the influence of the Black church, which opposed cremation for
many of the reasons other traditional Christians did. But the insistence of
many crematory operators on cremating only whites—and the insistence
of a few that cremation was an "Aryan" activity—also kept African-
American cremation rates down. And the logic of cremation, which
aligned Blacks with dirt, the body, and superstition, did little to win African Americans to the cause.[17]

The Educated and Enlightened Classes

Still, cremation had its supporters. One of the stock boasts of cremationists was that their reform attracted the "brightest citizens," and cremation does seem to have enjoyed success among physicians, sanitarians, clergymen, lawyers, scholars, journalists, writers, and artists—the
white, middle-class professionals whom *The Urn* dubbed "the educated
and enlightened classes." In the bricks and mortar period, notables such
as singer Fanny Brice, scientist Albert Einstein, painter Winslow Homer,
psychologist William James, musician Fats Waller, actors W. C. Fields

and Humphrey Bogart, and authors Horatio Alger, Sinclair Lewis, Zane Grey, Jack London, and Henry James were all cremated.[18]

From its inception in 1874 the cremation movement had commended itself not only to atheists and freethinkers but also to Spiritualists and Theosophists, Unitarians and Universalists. And though initially cremationists were unable to recruit many mainline Protestants, that changed markedly as the bricks and mortar period approached and mainline lay people and ministers, along with a few renegade Catholics, signed on. An early-twentieth-century pamphlet on "Religion and Cremation" claimed support among Episcopalians, Presbyterians, Unitarians, Methodists, Congregationalists, and Baptists. Support came earliest from Episcopalians. In the 1870s Episcopalian bishop William Stevens had pronounced cremation "the freak of a disordered brain" and burial a "Divine ordinance," but by the 1890s a number of leading Episcopal clergymen, including the Reverends George Hodges and William Lawrence of Massachusetts and the Reverend William Ford Nichols of California, had endorsed the torch over the spade.[19]

Although most American Jews opposed cremation, some Reform Jews supported the cause. Reform Judaism became the dominant form of American Judaism during the last quarter of the nineteenth century, and during that same period some Reform rabbis embraced cremation as an alternative to burial. In 1891 Rabbi Schlesinger of Albany, New York, concluded in a paper on cremation read before the Central Conference of American Rabbis (CCAR) that cremation was not only rational but Jewish—the original Hebrew method of disposing of the dead. Two years later, the CCAR, the leading body of Reform Jewish rabbis in America, passed a cremation-friendly resolution that allowed rabbis to officiate at cremations. At the CAA convention of 1940 Rabbi Louis Wolsey of Philadelphia admitted that Orthodox Jews were opposed to cremation on the theory that it amounted to an unlawful mutilation of the body, but he argued nonetheless for the practice's propriety. In 1941 *The Universal Jewish Encyclopedia* reported that among Reform Jews in Europe and the United States, cremation was "being practised instead of burial with increasing frequency," in part because these Jews had given up the doctrine of the bodily resurrection for a belief in the immortality of the soul. As soon as the world learned about the atrocities wrought by the Nazis at World War II death-camp crematoria, however, Reform Jews in the United States joined their Conservative and Orthodox colleagues in denouncing cremation. Not until late in the twentieth century would cremation start to make headway in Reform congregations, and even then acceptance would be limited largely to the West Coast.[20]

German Americans also gave cremation an early boost. Although there is little good demographic data on cremation in Gilded Age America, it is clear that German Americans led the way. Both the body of Baron De Palm and the first body cremated in New York State came into the world in Bavaria. At a funeral held at the Fresh Pond crematory on Long Island the deceased was eulogized in German and a choir sang "Abendlied" ("Evening Song"). "A Cremation Catechism," published by *The Urn* in 1893, concluded that the "nationality" that showed "the most preference for cremation" in America was "the Germans," who "outrank all others four to one." Available cremation data seems to back the predilection, if not the ratio. Of the first 1,062 bodies cremated at the Fresh Pond crematory in New York, for example, 539 (51 percent) were German-born.[21]

German Americans were also active in cremation societies. The Michigan Cremation Society, in which Erichsen actively participated, was described by one observer as "almost purely German." In fact, it was so dominated by German Americans that at first it advertised only in German-language papers. *Neue Flamme,* a Berlin-based monthly, advertised regularly in *Modern Crematist.* And both *Modern Crematist* and *The Urn* published numerous articles—including front-page stories—in German. Two cremation organizations, the "German Working-men's Cremation Association" of Buffalo and the "Allgemeine Feuer-bestattungs Verein" of New York, seem to have catered exclusively to German Americans. Why Americans of German descent were so attracted to cremation is difficult to determine. Some sources, hinting at the tradition of "fire-burial" in old Germany and references to it in German fairy tales, explained the propensity as a return to ancient customs. But cremation did not do nearly as well in Germany in this period as it did in the United States. Perhaps the German-American propensity for cremation can be traced to the strength of free thought in Germany. It may also reflect an aspiration by German immigrants and their German-American descendants to achieve genteel status in their adopted homeland.[22]

Accommodation

Despite the support of German Americans, physicians, Reform Jews, and liberal Protestants, cremation did not exactly thrive in the United States in the first half of the twentieth century. It did survive, however—largely because of a strategy of accommodation. Many historians have noted the tendency of U.S. social reform movements to foster resistance, then compromise, then co-optation. The cremation movement was no exception to this rule. As the Gilded Age gave way to the Progressive Era and early pro-cremation ideologues to a new generation of practical businessmen, the movement remade itself. Chastising female opponents as "Aunt Prejudice" or describing their hometown as "Customville" was out. Sentimental appeals, intended to win over the "gentler sex," were in. Also in fashion were efforts to demonstrate that the cremation movement was "in accordance with true religion"—a friend rather than an enemy of authentic spirituality. Calculations of how many pounds of fertilizer or how many kilowatt-hours of light could be generated by incinerating a year's supply of a city's dead disappeared from the cremationist literature. And most advocates came to see that Sir Henry Thompson had erred in appealing to "grossly utilitarian considerations."[23]

As the funeral industry gathered steam, cremationists also tried to work with rather than against undertakers. Bashing undertakers as unscrupulous con men concerned only with the Almighty Dollar had been around as long as the undertaking trade. Such denunciations were not quite as popular among early cremationists as they would become among consumer rights advocates in the 1960s and 1970s, but when cremationists talked of cutting funeral costs by 75–80 percent, they knew who would take the hit. Back in 1886 a pro-cremation poet had conceded that cremation "Contemplates obliteration/Of the sexton's occupation" and was "A sure annihilator/Of the faithful undertaker." That same year members of the Lancaster Crematorium and Funeral Reform Society had published advertisements urging readers to do an end run around undertakers by shipping corpses directly to its crematory. "All that is necessary," their copy read, " ...is to enclose the corpse in a cheap casket...and have the casket checked as baggage."[24]

Cooperation supplanted confrontation, however, as the cremation movement matured and shed its radicalism. In articles published in the 1890s under patently sycophantic headlines (e.g., "Our Friends the Undertakers"), *The Urn* urged its readers to look at undertakers not as competitors but as partners and to distance themselves from funeral reform. Extravagance, *The Urn* argued in an article called "Mind Your Own Business," was in the eye (and pocketbook) of the beholder. "It is to us and should be to every incinerating company a matter of serene indifference, whether a body reaches the crematory followed by one or twenty coaches as long as it is brought there at all," *The Urn* wrote. "It

is a serious blunder for advocates of cremation to eliminate the undertaker....By the utterance of words naturally tending to rouse in undertakers a spirit of antagonism, cremationists are doing their cause a
grievous harm." After all, a body scheduled for cremation still had to be
cleaned and dressed. It might need to be iced or embalmed. Some sort
of coffin would have to be procured. In the vast majority of cases there
would be funeral services to attend to. Rather than instructing readers
to toss the corpse in the baggage car of the closest train, *The Urn*
printed a list of undertakers who "have attended to cremations before,
know about all the special arrangements, and can be recommended as
thoroughly reliable." "Just tell your undertaker you want a body cremated," *The Urn* suggested, "he does the rest." Hugo Erichsen, who
early in his career was convinced that cremation would (and should) cut
into the undertaker's bottom line, also learned the art of compromise. In
a 1912 article in *Sunnyside,* an undertaker's trade journal, he insisted
that cremationists felt "no call to enter the province of the undertaker."
Nowhere was this effort to placate funeral directors more plain than on
the floor of CAA conventions. There crematory operators repeatedly
apologized for their radical forebears who, by pitching cremation as an
inexpensive alternative to burial, turned funeral directors into antag-
onists. Many a speech listed "getting the co-operation of funeral directors" as one of the organization's top priorities.[25]

Well aware that undertakers made most of their money on caskets,
crematory operators focused their efforts at reconciliation on the casket
sale. One crematory operator urged his customers to purchase "the kind
of casket which will best represent your social and financial standing as
well as your sentimental regard for the deceased." Another, noting that
"a funeral is a memory," insisted that the quality of that memory was
determined by the quality of the casket. "If a casket is beautiful in its
furnishings, in fabric, in construction and design, it is a beautiful memory," he argued. "If common, or tawdry, it is a poor memory." The same
rule applied, he said, to the quality of the embalming. The most brazen
advocate of this new approach was Frank Flanner, an undertaker/
crematory operator from Indianapolis, Indiana. "The undertaker is the
man we must win to our side if we would have cremation grow," he
wrote in 1915. And the best way to win over the undertaker was to jet-
tison the "bugaboo" of the cheap casket and the "fallacy" that cremation is cheaper than burial. "To those who say, 'Why burn the casket?'
I say, 'Why bury it?'" Flanner wrote. "There is as much reason in one
case as in the other."[26]

In the twenties and thirties some cremationists began to speak of creating an integrated "memorializing movement" that would "unite in one craft" not only the crematory operator and the funeral director but also the cemetery superintendent, the casket maker, the funeral florist, and the mausoleum operator. Of all these professionals, however, crematory operators coveted most the goodwill of undertakers, who in many cases had the power to make or break their businesses. Some paid a 10 percent commission for undertakers' referrals. Others threw parties or handed out cigars. One crematory operator who worked hard to spread the good news that "cremation in no way affects the funeral" was Frank Gibson. After he opened his crematory in Portland, Oregon, in the first decade of the twentieth century, he made a point of visiting every undertaker in the city and promising not to "talk against caskets." After all, he reasoned, "If you place the casket in the ground, it rots and you never see it again. The same is true when you place the body in a retort." Gibson further promised the undertakers that he would not mix himself up in their affairs. "I am not going to interfere with your business," he told each of them, "and I don't want you to interfere with mine."[27]

The only problem with this non-interference pact was that it was horribly one-sided. Crematory operators seem to have been angling for a gentleman's agreement that would have split up postmortem responsibilities into separate spheres. Crematories would sell urns, columbarium niches, and (in the case of cemetery-based crematories) cemetery plots. Funeral homes would sell caskets and funeral services. And neither would stand in the way of the other.

But while most undertakers were happy to have the casket market to themselves (or to take a 10 percent commission on crematory sales), some insisted on selling urns as well. Few vowed not to talk against cremation, and plenty continued to "hold up their hands in horror" at the mere mention of that practice. Although in the 1890s both *Casket* and *Western Undertaker* extended an olive branch to the cremationists, in fact few undertakers were ready to make peace. The Great Depression that followed the stock market crash of 1929 strained profit margins at funeral homes and therefore relations between undertakers and crematory operators. Relations were further strained in 1933, when Forest Lawn was licensed to add a mortuary to its cremation and cemetery facilities. In 1935 *Mortuary Management* lamented the advance of cremation in Oregon, Washington, and California, complaining that the tendency to purchase inexpensive caskets for cremations had cut into revenues. In that same decade, a crematory operator conducted an informal survey concerning relations between crematories and funeral homes. When asked whether "the undertakers in your territory knock cremations," nearly three-quarters (71%) said yes.[28]

Cremationists also suffered the slings and arrows of mausoleum operators. One mausoleum company from Seattle found multiple reasons to oppose cremation, not all of them pecuniary. Its 1916 pamphlet promoting "the endowed community mausoleum" spilled nearly as much ink decrying "the terrors of the torch" as promoting its own "temples of peace." The pamphlet's author had witnessed a number of cremations and was sickened by them all. Modern and ancient cremation were indistinguishable, he argued, since both amounted to "roasting." The body mutilation did not cease when the fire went out either, since the bones still had to be brutally crushed, mortar-and-pestle style, into fragments sufficiently small to fit into an urn. All in all, what greeted the corpse when it was shoved into the retort was not "beautiful rosy light" but a "miniature hell."[29]

Christianization

In addition to working to befriend undertakers, cremationists reached out to traditional Christians. Embarrassed by early associations with Asian religions and frustrated by the insistence of the Catholic Church that cremation was in cahoots with Freemasonry, cremationists bent over backwards to make their movement look and feel Christian-friendly. People like Frederic Harrison, an advocate of "the Religion of Humanity" who agitated in a 1908 book for a post-Christian way of cremation, were not entirely flushed from the movement, but they were no longer running it either. Convinced as the turn of the century approached that "cremation would prosper more ... if the cranks would not champion it so much," cremationists insisted that their method was in perfect harmony with Christian practices and principles.[30]

Perhaps the clearest indication of this Christianization trend, which took hold as the bricks and mortar period began, is that cremationists spoke of their beloved practice in explicitly theological terms. Cremation was "a last baptism by incandescent heat," and the pure flame ascending to heaven was "the symbol of the Holy Spirit." Their cause was "the gospel of incineration" and its promotion "missionary work." In a clear nod to the abiding public power of American Christianity (and a clear rebuke of his atheistic father), Hugo Erichsen wrote: "Every cremationist must be a missionary for the cause and embrace every suitable occasion to spread its gospel, the glad tidings of a more sanitary and more aesthetic method of disposing of our beloved dead."[31]

But more than the rhetoric had changed. Influenced by the free-thought critique of ritualizing as so much priestly superstition as well as by the more moderate (and widespread) Protestant tendency to emphasize scripture at the expense of practice, the cremation movement in its infancy had been hostile to traditional Christian deathways. Beginning in the 1890s, however, cremationists began to argue that their practice was as decorous as it was Christian. In a typical cremation at Fresh Pond in that decade, the corpse was conveyed to the crematory in a funeral procession that according to an eyewitness "looked like any other respectable, well appointed funeral." At the crematory a superintendent (nattily dressed in a "handsome black" broadcloth uniform ornamented with red velvet) received the body as mourners stood "in solemn silence and with heads uncovered." "The manner of handling the dead," he said, "was eminently dignified and reverential." Following the cremation, loose particles that had fallen from the iron crib on which the body had been placed were removed by a magnet. Then the ashes were sealed inside a simple yet attractive black tin canister. Most Fresh Pond cremations were preceded by clergy-officiated funerals in the home, but religious services would also be held at the crematory's Urn Hall, which gave "the impression of a chapel." That impression was strengthened by the presence of an organ, whose strains accompanied the short service that was provided free of charge with every incineration. This service regularly featured a rendition of Handel's *Messiah,* and was "particularly satisfactory to the ladies," whose eyes were (at least according to cremationists) also delighted by the handsome iron gate, the immaculate lawn, the extensive flower beds, the pure white marble columbarium, the glistening ribbon-wrapped niches, and the elegant stained glass (one depicting a woman holding a torch).[32]

Some Christian cremationists looked forward to the possibility of bringing the now-harmless dead back into cities and churches. "What sentimental value cathedrals, chapels, and church-yards would take on if their niches, crypts and mounds were filled with the cenotaphs and vases that ensafe the snowy ashes of the dear departed!" wrote the Reverend Howard Henderson, an Episcopal minister. "Every great city would have its Westminster, every capital its Escurial." The Reverend Hodges, another Episcopalian, also saw great artistic and didactic possibilities for a "house of the departed...set in the midst of the city." "Such a building," he said, "would offer large opportunities to art and artists. It would be a building that would uplift the thoughts of all who enter, made splendid perhaps with paintings, teaching the great truths of the present and the future...[on] memorial windows, through whose pictured panes the sun would tell the story of the cross as the symbol of redemption, and of the altar as the symbol of the life to come."[33]

Scattering

One of the most important concessions cremationists made to conservative Christianity concerned the disposition of the ashes. Like the problem of the disposition of the corpse, the problem of what to do with ashes admits of multiple solutions. Ashes can be scattered or placed in an urn. If scattered, they can be strewn on land, at sea, or (today) from the air. If inurned, they can be deposited in a columbarium, placed on the living room mantle, nestled into a church wall, or squirreled away in a safe deposit box. They can also be buried. Ashes can even be commingled. Husband and wife can lie together after death in a common urn, making good this cremationist prayer:

> Let not their dust be parted
> For their two hearts in life were single-hearted.

Conversely, ashes can be divided and disposed of in different ways at different places. The ashes of Helena Blavatsky, cofounder (along with Henry Olcott) of the Theosophical Society, were reputedly divided into three parts and inurned in Theosophical shrines in India, London, and New York.[34]

Ashes also had more fanciful uses. While visiting Japan during the Gilded Age, Buddhist sympathizer Lafcadio Hearn learned from a geisha of the practice of drinking a combination of sake and ashes. In the United States a physician reportedly mixed the ashes of a "tramp" with glue and then cast them as a small statue. (The result was said to be "charming.") A would-be poet suggested yet another use in this "Ode to Sir Henry Thompson":

> I think the apartment is pleasant,
>   The ornaments, too, are on suite;
> That hour-glass you see was a present
>   From Bolus of Requiem Street.
> It holds what remains of Aunt Lizzy—
>   The notion, I think, is sublime;

Humanity's ashes are busy
  In place of the sands of Old Time.[35]

Many of America's first generation of cremationists echoed Sir Henry Thompson in favoring scattering. Colonel Olcott followed the Hindu example when he spread De Palm's ashes over water, and Mr. Benjamin Pitman, influenced more by a love of nature than by Hinduism's Vedas, reportedly placed the incinerated remains of his beloved wife at the roots of a rose bush. At a ceremony billed as the first Buddhist cremation in America, the ashes were "scattered to the four winds, so that no man should know whence they had gone."[36]

In many respects, early cremationist logic demanded scattering. As one observer noted:

> The more ardent adherent of cremation not only regards earth burial as pernicious but he usually looks upon the cemetery as an unwarranted waste of land.... [H]e reminds us that Nature is economical and most exacting in demanding obedience to her laws, which are immutable and decree that nothing shall be wasted or misapplied, and as Nature has supplied all the elements constituting the human body, they must be returned to their original sources sooner or later. Therefore, says this zealous cremationist, the ashes must be consigned to the earth as soon after death and as directly as possible; but since the cemetery is condemned by him and must be abandoned, there is but one disposition to make of the ashes, and that is, to use a popular phrase, "Scatter them to the four winds."[37]

During the nineteenth century and into the early twentieth, most cremationists saw cremation as final disposition (not a preparation for burial or some other disposition). For Gilded Age cremation reformers the climax in the postmortem drama was the moment of cremation, and scattering a fitting denouement. Whatever death rites were to be celebrated were typically observed at the crematory. The functional equivalent of burial, cremation minimized the ritualization of death. Scattering was merely the quickest way to return what remained of the physical body back to earth.

If cremated remains were scattered sufficiently widely (for example, on the ocean), the dead person was quite literally displaced. This displacement of the dead satisfied early cremationists both theologically and practically. From a practical perspective, the dematerialization of the dead, who via scattering disappeared with nary a trace into nature, made postmortem memorialization difficult if not impossible. At least in cases of widespread scattering, there simply was no place to go to mourn obsessively, and there certainly was no body left to "listen" to

your prayers or "see" your tears. Scattering was also economical, insofar as it obviated the needs for an urn, a columbarium niche, and perpetual care. Scattering was equally efficacious from a theological perspective. More than any other method of disposal of the ashes, it was in
keeping with the view that personal identity resided in spirit. Cremationists regularly complained that the emerging embalm-and-bury regime, by lavishing undue attention on the material husk of the deceased,
amounted to "spiritual materialism." Scattering ashes to the wind, on
the other hand, wonderfully exemplified the belief that the real person
had already passed into immortality. He or she was to be remembered
spiritually, not attended to materially.

Cremationist logic may have initially demanded scattering, but even
the early cremationists were not always entirely logical. Though it may
seem odd for a lot so passionately opposed to burial, many saw to it that
their ashes were buried in cemeteries, and over time that practice became
commonplace. At the crematory at Chicago's Graceland Cemetery at the
close of the nineteenth century ashes were usually buried. In fact, Graceland officials could think of only two cases of scattering. Early in the
twentieth century the Massachusetts Cremation Society estimated that
out of the first 2,500 cremations in its Forest Hills crematory, ashes had
been scattered in a nearby pine grove in only 200 cases. (In "many in-
stances" they were buried in a cemetery.) At the close of World War I the
crematory at Forest Home Cemetery in Milwaukee was burying approximately half of its ashes. Burying ashes was also the norm around
the same time at the Detroit Crematorium. In the early 1930s W. B. Currie of Chicago's Oak Woods Cemetery conducted a study of thirty cemeteries in the Midwest. Most of Currie's respondents did not keep rec-
ords of the disposition of their facilities' cremated remains, but those
that did reported that 11 percent of cremated remains were scattered, 11
percent were placed in a columbarium, and 8.5 percent remained with
the undertaker. A significant portion (29%) were kept at home, but the
most popular option (31%) was burial. Cremation was "not intended to
do away with any of the sacred ceremonies attendant upon burial," advocates of urn burial pointed out. Apparently, among the "sacred ceremonies" slotted to endure was burial itself.[38]

The trend away from scattering and toward some other form of memorialization must have pleased the nation's undertakers and cemetery
managers, who vehemently opposed scattering. The emphasis on memorialization at a sacred site therefore simultaneously accommodated
not only traditional Christians, for whom scattering was a scandal, but

also death professionals, for whom it was an economic threat. It also helped to commend cremation to women, who were historically in charge of tending to the graves of kin and who may also have been slower than men to give up the traditional psychosomatic conception of the person for the utterly spiritualized self. Whereas the first generation of cremationists saw incineration itself as a method of *disposing* of the dead, the second generation was coming to view cremation (much as others saw embalming) merely as a method of *preparing* the corpse for its final disposition. No longer a substitute for burial, cremation was becoming a prologue to it.

The Memorial Idea

As the American cremation movement shifted from the social reform agenda of the nineteenth century to the business agenda of the twentieth, a great silence fell over the cremation question. By the mid-1890s most newspaper editors had decided that ordinary cremations were no longer newsworthy. All three leading cremationist publications had ceased to be, and many of the pioneering cremation societies were defunct. The cremation movement was now in the hands of practical businessmen. For the first two decades of the twentieth century, those businessmen had focused on building and operating crematories, not spreading the good news of cremation. Moreover, the CAA had assiduously followed a no-propaganda policy. Because many members were also cemetery operators, the CAA was intent on promoting cremation without disparaging burial. Initially that meant swearing off advocacy. But as the Great Depression gripped the country, straining businesses of all sorts, cremationists began to do something about their invisibility. In the 1930s they embarked on their first marketing campaign. Initially, that campaign focused on the rhetoric of cremation. Crematory operators vowed to speak not of retorts but of cremation vaults, not of incineration but of cremation. A few even called for an end to the word "cremation" itself. But above all, cremationists focused on sales. "Too much attention is being paid by crematories to the mechanics of installation and the operation of plants," Forest Lawn's Leslie Hoagland complained in 1934, "and too little attention is being paid to selling." After decades of quiet, cremationists decided it was time to pitch their products and services—to get their message out.[39]

What exactly was that message? That cremation was not an end but a means to an end. And what was that end? Memorialization. While the movement's pioneers had promoted cremation as final disposition, these profit-minded crematory operators promoted cremation as a preparation for either inurnment in a columbarium or interment in a cemetery. No cremation was complete, they told their customers, without an urn, a final resting place, and a rite of committal.

It is difficult to determine precisely when this strategy emerged. Apparently it was articulated first sometime in the 1920s and became ubiquitous in cremationist circles in the early 1930s. In 1927 and 1928, in speeches delivered to both crematory and cemetery operators, Walter B. Londelius, the superintendent at Glendale's Forest Lawn, argued for "the memorial idea," which he termed "a sacred obligation which [families] have no right to disregard." After tracing that idea back to the pyramids of Egypt, the Taj Mahal, and Westminster Abbey, Londelius argued that it applied to cremation as surely as it did to burial. After a cremation the postmortem process was only one-third complete; that was because "urn interment" included three "inseparable" features: "cremation, niche and urn." "Cremation alone is a losing proposition," he argued. "There is no money in that." But cremation followed by the purchase of an urn and a columbarium niche—that was a winning proposition, particularly if other crematory operators followed Forest Lawn's practice of quoting one comprehensive price (a minimum of $100) for the package.[40]

In a 1929 address to the CAA, Henry Adams of the Boston-area Forest Hills Cemetery put an East Coast spin on Londelius's West Coast strategy, calling cremation "a preparation of the body for the ground." Cremation was not an alternative to burial, he contended, but a supplement to it. During the 1930s CAA secretary Lawrence Moore tried to mediate between the East Coast bias toward urn burial and the West Coast preference for niches. "The important thing to all of us," Moore said, "is to *encourage the memorializing of the dead,* in one way or the other." Soon cremationists across America were promoting what they collectively referred to as the memorial idea and "cremation as a preparation for memorialization" had become the mantra of their marketing, public relations, and advertising efforts. Some followed the lead of Forest Lawn, offering package deals that included not only cremation but also an urn, a columbarium niche, and a crematory or columbarium service. But virtually all agreed to stop talking about cremation as an inexpensive alternative to burial.[41]

The memorial idea was actually a cluster of ideas and ideals, or to be more precise, a rhetoric that supported a variety of practices. Those practices included: some sort of rite before cremation; inurnment of the cremated remains in an appropriate urn; the placement of that urn in a cemetery plot, columbarium niche, or mausoleum; a rite of committal at the place of memorialization; and a suitable marker at that site. What those practices decidedly did not include was scattering, which was, according to Hubert Eaton of Forest Lawn, "a menace to the memorial idea." Roy Hatten of the American Cemetery Owners' Association termed scattering "irreverent and a desecration to human remains," and Hugo Erichsen called scattering "an abomination." Harold Wright, a cremation-friendly funeral director from San Francisco, put the matter succinctly: "Some don't want an expensive type of funeral, that starts it; then they don't want to go to the crematory. They go down and get the ashes and "scatter" them. There is no sentiment, no urn, no memorial for the person departed." "Do away with the memorial idea," he concluded, "and we are all through."[42]

In an effort to put an end to scattering, one crematory operator argued for national legislation against disposing of cremated remains "anywhere except within the bounds of a permanently endowed cemetery, columbarium or mausoleum." Others called for a national advertising campaign. But for the most part crematory operators took the matter into their own hands. One West Coast operator explained his art of persuasion like this:

> If the family wishes the ashes scattered we inform them that we do not scatter ashes under any circumstances and insist that they come to our office and get the ashes and scatter them themselves. Upon the arrival of the person who is to take the ashes away, we show them the ashes (which by the way we do not crush) and we endeavor to have them realize the advantage of a niche memorial. If they are still insistent upon scattering the ashes we deliver same to them, taking a proper receipt for the delivery. We insist that some permanent disposition must be made of every case coming to our crematory.[43]

As this passage shows, some cremationists attempted to discourage scattering by refusing to crush cremated remains. In the late nineteenth century, as in the late twentieth, cremated remains emerged from the retort not as fluffy ashes but as clanking bone fragments. Crematory operators typically processed those remains, through either grinding or pounding, in order to fit them into urns and make them look more like ashes. As crematory operators embraced the memorial idea, however, some began to argue that such processing was sacrilegious. They were also aware, of course, that relatives were far less likely to scatter unprocessed bone fragments than to scatter crushed remains. In fact, many ridiculed the romantic notion of gently scattering ashes to the four winds as a physical impossibility.

Initially the anti-processing initiative was largely confined to the West Coast, but like so much else in cremation's U.S. history, it eventually moved eastward. In a 1931 survey of forty-five crematories in the United States and Canada, Herbert Hargrave of California's Fresno Crematory found a sharp discrepancy between California crematories and facilities elsewhere in the United States. "Almost the entire State of California leave the remains in fragments," he reported, "while other sections of the country generally grind them." Ten years later CAA spread the anti-pulverization message nationwide when it reprinted a catechism of sorts initially published by the Interment Association of California. In this *Manual of Standard Crematory-Columbarium Practices,* the CAA came out against both the scattering and the processing of cremated remains. In big, bold type the CAA urged its members:

NEVER CRUSH OR GRIND CREMATED REMAINS.

The text went on:

This is very important. We have no right to crush, grind or pulverize human bone fragments. They should be placed in the temporary container or urn, just as they were removed from the cremation vault (after the foreign matter has been removed). To do otherwise encourages desecration, gives an impression of valueless ash, and will eventually destroy the memorial idea.

On the following page, the manual insisted (again in large, heavy type):

NEVER SCATTER CREMATED REMAINS.[44]

Twentieth-century crematory operators promoted the memorial idea for a number of reasons. Financial considerations carried weight. Cremation by itself was not a profitable proposition. But if every cremation came with the sale of an urn and a cemetery plot or columbarium niche, cremation would be economically viable. Crematory operators also promoted memorialization in an effort to improve relations with undertakers. While cremation with scattering represented a serious threat to American funeral directors, "cremation as a preparation for memorialization" did not. The memorial idea was as compatible with a pricey casket as it was with a top-of-the-line urn. Finally, many cremationists promoted the memorial idea because they truly believed that anything less was irreverent and irreligious. As the high priests of this new funerary rite, many cremationists felt obliged to make cremation spiritual. And at least in the first half of the twentieth century, no one could convince them that scattering was anything other than wholly secular.

By all accounts, efforts to promote the memorial idea were at least moderately successful. Although the funeral industry did not pull together into "one craft" as some cremationists had hoped, cremationists and crematory operators achieved a level of cooperation that would have been unthinkable in the nineteenth century, when cremation reformers were blasting the cemetery as the Devil's Acre. Cooperation between funeral directors and cremationists was rare, but in some cities those groups did follow something like a nonaggression pact. Cremationists were successful, moreover, in opposing scattering and promoting memorialization. In 1940 one West Coast crematory operator reported that he placed over two-thirds (68%) of his facility's cremated remains in columbarium niches. And over time, many operators in New England and the Midwest discontinued what in many cases had been a decades-long practice of scattering ashes on site.[45]

Memorial Societies

Although crematory operators worked hard to win support for the memorial idea, not all cremationists fell in line. Perhaps the most conspicuous dissenters were members of American memorial societies, reformers who carried the ideals of the pioneering cremation societies of the Gilded Age into the beginning of the twenty-first century.

The memorial society movement can be traced to the burial cooperatives of the American frontier, the mutual cremation societies of the Gilded Age, the burial clubs of medieval Europe, and even to the burial assistance compacts of the Israelites in captivity in Babylon, but its more recent roots go back to Seattle, Washington, in 1937, when the Reverend Fred Shorter and other members of his nondenominational Congregational Church of the People began to meet to discuss alternatives to the embalm-and-bury regime. As advocates of inexpensive yet dignified death rites, Shorter and his congregants were attracted to cremation. They were also attracted to memorialization. But their way of cremation diverged significantly from the so-called memorial idea.[46]

The founding members preferred direct cremation: quick and inexpensive incineration performed without embalming, viewing, expensive coffin, or funeral. Initially, they considered starting and running their own crematory, but they decided instead to establish a nonprofit funeral cooperative aimed at helping members obtain low-cost death care. On January 12, 1939, the People's Memorial Association (PMA) was organized as the first memorial society in the United States. Shortly thereafter, the PMA signed a contract with Seattle's Bleitz Funeral Home, which agreed to pick up members' corpses, cremate them, and return the cremated remains for a flat fee of $50.

Both the PMA and the memorial society movement grew slowly at first, but in the late 1950s, as newspapers and magazines hammered away at the high cost of dying, both expanded rapidly. PMA membership grew from 650 in 1952 to over 7,000 in 1960. Buoyed by the publication of the first edition of Ernest Morgan's memorial society primer, *A Manual of Simple Burial* (1962), PMA membership swelled to 30,000 later in the 1960s. The success of the PMA spawned a variety of imitators, which came together in 1962 to form the Continental Association of Funeral and Memorial Societies (now Funeral and Memorial Societies of America).

Like Gilded Age cremation societies, some of these memorial societies limited themselves to educating the public about simple and inexpensive alternatives to what one sympathizer characterized as the "barbaric funeral ceremony complete with gussied-up bodies, expensive caskets, parades, and regalia." But most, like the PMA, went further, contracting with local funeral directors to provide members with simple, inexpensive death care at a fraction of the going rate. Some offered cremation only. Others added to their list of options simple burial and body donation. But all were forceful advocates for the dignity, propriety, and economy of cremation. All championed spiritual over material values, criticizing the traditional funeral as materialistic and praising cremation as spiritual. Most were staffed entirely by volunteers, and many were led by Unitarians, Quakers, and other liberal Protestants. Members suggested charitable donations in lieu of flowers, scattering in lieu of urns, and the memorial service (whose defining feature is the absence of a corpse and casket) in lieu of the funeral director's funeral. "Honor the memory," their slogan went, "not the remains!" Because of their shared commitment to cremation, these societies functioned as an important adjunct to the crematory infrastructure that had been constructed largely in the first half of the twentieth century. While they did not typically put bricks and mortar together to make crematories, their vast network of grass-roots organizations spread the gospel of the dignity, simplicity, and economy of cremation.[47]

Though memorial societies did not typically put it in these terms, what they were after was an alternative to the cremate-and-memorialize strategy of the new pragmatic businesses: a return to the cremate-and-scatter approach of the reform-minded pioneers. Now that the memorial idea had taken hold, cremation was increasingly preceded by the purchase of a lavish casket and followed by burial in an equally lavish urn. Memorial society members wanted to cut down on the costs associated with this extravagant way of cremation. They also yearned, however, for a simpler aesthetic. Moreover, they wanted to take control over cremation ritualization away from crematory operators and funeral directors and put it back in the hands of lay people like themselves. The success of the memorial society movement demonstrates that Americans in this bricks and mortar period were crafting not one way of cremation but many. From the late 1930s when they got started through the early 1960s when they came together to form a national organization, memorial societies were responsible for a small minority of the nation's cremations. But by providing an alternative to the new memorial idea regime, they opened up a host of possibilities for post-1960s reform.

Light, Like the Sun

As germ theory replaced miasma theory in the 1880s and 1890s cremationists adjusted to the new paradigm in public health and bacteriology by casting fire as a "germ destroyer." Initially this strategy worked. The sanitary argument continued to be the strongest argument for cremation until the end of the century. But as scientific research regarding the nature of infectious diseases advanced, as outbreaks of infectious diseases subsided, and as undertakers spread the word that embalming sanitized dead bodies as effectively as cremation, the claim that buried bodies represented a major threat to public health evaporated. As early as 1895 an article in the *Journal of the American Medical Association* noted "a growing feeling that the dangers apprehended from cemeteries have been considerably overestimated." As the article explained: "Before much was known about bacterial agencies of disease, many evils which could only be conjectured were charged to cemeteries. As the science of bacteriology was gradually unfolded, an explanation of how cemeteries may produce disease was afforded by supposing that the germs of infectious diseases, buried with their victims, infected the air and water in their vicinity. Outbreaks of contagious disease near burial grounds were often attributed to this cause without seeking for positive proof."

New studies, however, had brought the connection between ceme-teries and disease into question. Although the 1895 article did go on to endorse cremation as "a safe and cleanly method of disposing of the dead," it added that earth burial, when properly regulated, was "also a safe and satisfactory method for disposal of the dead." By World War I this had become the new consensus. *Park and Cemetery* claimed in 1917 that it could show "conclusively, that there is no reason to appre-hend danger of contamination of the water or air by the modern ceme-tery." In a 1922 study published in the *American Journal of Public Health,* only three of twenty health officers and sanitarians surveyed be-lieved buried bodies could spread contagious diseases. Eight said it was possible but not probable, while nine said buried bodies were perfectly benign. In 1929 even ardent cremationists had to admit that the argu-ments from sanitation had been "almost wholly abandoned."[48]

Stripped of its prime justification in sanitary science, cremation after World War I became a rebellion in search of a cause. It found one in the arena of aesthetics. In the twenties and thirties, around the same time undertakers were promoting the memorial idea, cremationists stopped championing their practice as a sanitary alternative to burial and began promoting it for its beauty. Cremationists continued to contrast their fa-vored practice with burial, but now the claim was that cremation was beautiful and burial ugly. In order to make good on this claim, crema-tory operators scurried to make their facilities more attractive. They fes-tooned their chapels with flowers, plants, elegant rugs, and modern fur-niture. They brought their columbaria up from basements and opened them out to sun-drenched gardens. Some even employed song birds. In short, they did all they could to suggest sweetness and light. Scuttling the outmoded emphasis on cremation's purity, they emphasized in their promotional literature the beauty of the chapel and columbarium. One West Coast crematory operator, who referred to his vocation as a "min-istry of beauty," described his ideal crematory and columbarium in en-tirely aesthetic terms:

> In outward appearance—of charming dignity, and preferably, church-like buildings (with no stack nor exterior evidence of cremation, either of sound or odor visible) in which one would love to enter, the chapel bright with the cheer of not only its form, but also its color, the song of birds, the music of beautiful organs. A Memorial columbarium should have no dark corners in it. Indoor gardens will lift it from the common place; the niches themselves should be very substantial, the urns well selected as to form and inscription, the walls adorned with messages of cheer from the Scriptures and poets; sun-

shine should enter, fountains add their note, and where possible, gardens should open to the outdoors.[49]

In keeping with this new focus on the beauty of cremation, advocates promoted cremation as a "way of nature." "The rocks, the trees, the rivers, the air around you, are of the same composition as is your body," argued a 1916 pamphlet from the Missouri Crematory Association. "Nature has loaned to your soul, for its time upon earth, the use of the materials of which your body is made—to serve as an earthly home—a dwelling.... And in return, what is your debt to nature?" How will it be paid? Before you answer, the pamphlet advised, "you must realize that not your material body, but *your soul*—your intellectual being—is *you!* Your loved ones, your friends, are likewise their own *souls,* not their material bodies." Your responsibility, the pamphlet concluded, is to return your body—the inessential you—to Nature, to "give it all back to the forests, the earth, the water, the air." This new ecological argument for cremation recalled Sir Henry Thompson's claim that burial amounted to thievery, but it differed from Thompson's manifesto in one important respect: it was driven by environmentalism rather than utilitarianism. Why return your body to nature? Not because it would yield this much lime and that much phosphorus, but because it is proper to restore to nature what is rightfully hers. Cremation was praiseworthy not because it was useful but because it was natural—because it participated in the cycle of life, death, and rebirth. "I Restore to Nature" was the cremationist's new boast.[50]

The core text for this new view of cremation was an essay called "Light, Like the Sun." Written by Mrs. Frances Newton, this short piece first appeared in *The Forum* in 1937. Before the year was out, Newton had won a $1,000 *Reader's Digest* prize and her story had been published as a book. Over the ensuing decades, "Light, Like the Sun" was reprinted repeatedly in *Reader's Digest* and other venues. In cremation's bricks and mortar period, it was the nation's most influential pro-cremation document.[51]

"Light, Like the Sun" is autobiographical. It is set in winter. The death of Mrs. Newton's father is fast approaching, and doctors have told Newton to begin to make "arrangements." Initially the author refuses to consider cremation. "It was bad enough to die," she writes, "without becoming a bonfire." Besides, she likes the idea of burial—"of returning to the earth again, of enriching the soil and becoming part of nature." But the rural churchyards are full and even the best city cemetery is undesirable. The day is cold and wet, and the cemetery is crowded, expensive, and squalid—cluttered with "unending rows of graceless, ugly blobs of stone, each a memorial to some loved one, in mass a monstrous blight upon the land."

Newton's story turns on an unlikely premise. While she is visiting the city cemetery, the young man charged with selling her a plot (for $1,700) has pity on her and decides to come clean. "If I had to do what you're doing today," he confides, "I'd choose cremation." "Never," she instinctively replies. But he is persistent and suggests that she visit the cemetery's crematory. She finally agrees, and after a ride through the "ghoulish artificiality" of the cemetery she arrives at the crematory chapel. "Tell me everything," she says.

As the attendant complies, readers look on and listen in. We see a "friendly and unpretentious" Gothic chapel. There are flowers on the altar. "Warm colours" cascade through a stained-glass window, playing off lily-white walls. "The casket is brought in," the attendant explains, "and the usual Committal service for the dead is read. At the words 'earth to earth, ashes to ashes, dust to dust' the casket is sprinkled with ashes and with dust. I press this electric button, and the casket sinks a foot below the floor, leaving only the flowers showing. The priest gives the benediction and the service is over." The casket is then whisked away to the retort where, under the watchful eyes of a friend of the family, the body is reduced to ashes. The ashes, in turn, are placed in a lovely urn "to be placed either in a niche in the chapel or given to relatives to dispose of as they wish."

Mrs. Newton is coming around, but she still can't abide the thought of flames consuming her beloved father. "Does it burn?" she asks, "like a bonfire?" No, she is told, the body is consumed not by flames but by heat and light—"light, like the sun." With that explanation, Mrs. Newton is born again:

> Light, like the sun.
> A sense of triumph came over me. Sunlight over Father working in his garden. Sunlight on his white head as he sat on the terrace reading. The warmth of sunlight bringing life to growing things, falling benignly on the aging.
> When Father's time comes, I told my aching heart, I shall bring him here.

And she does. After her father's death and the celebration of a simple Episcopal funeral service at a local chapel, she drives his body past the cemetery "with its soot-stained stones and snow, its uncovered ugly clay" to the crematory chapel where the casket is bathed in "warmth and colour, light and beauty." She then uses the money she had saved to establish a scholarship at her father's university. "To me, he has not died," Newton concludes. "To these unknown students he is bringing 'Light, Like the Sun.'"

A funeral director's nightmare, Newton's narrative translated the pro-cremation argument into an idiom one historian has termed "nature religion." As the fear of premature burial faded and advances in bacteriology and embalming stripped cremation's sanitary arguments of their force, Newton and other cremationists found aesthetic and environmental reasons to prefer cremation over burial. Back in the 1880s *Modern Cremation* had informed its readers that "God writes the gospel, not in the Bible alone, but on trees, flowers, clouds and stars." That nod to nature's beauty was at the time a minor chord in the pro-cremation repertoire. Between World War I and World War II, however, it became a standard refrain: Cremation was both more natural and more beautiful than burial—as natural and beautiful as the sun. The practice restored to nature elements that, before death, constituted a living human body and, after death, nourished plants and animals. It was, moreover, a sensible use of land.[52]

Still an Abomination

While the new aesthetic and environmental approach seems to have resonated with women, who as the century wore on began to choose cremation about as frequently as did men, it did not sit well with Roman Catholic leaders, who continued to view cremation as unchristian. In 1908 *The Catholic Encyclopedia* noted that the Roman Catholic Church still believed it "unseemly that the human body, once the living temple of God, the instrument of heavenly virtue, sanctified so often by the sacraments, should finally be subjected to a treatment that filial piety, conjugal and fraternal love, or even mere friendship seems to revolt against as inhuman." A 1923 article on "The Ethics and History of Cremation" traced cremation's history back to murder by suttee, its ethics to pagan atrocities, and its rationale to "pseudo-science and blatant infidelity." In 1928 the *Catholic Medical Guardian* insisted that cremation amounted in most cases to "a public profession of irreligion and materialism." In 1937 and again in 1946 the Catholic periodical *Sign* quoted an anti-Catholic Freemason—"Our task is not confined to the mere burning of the dead," he had written, "but extends to burning and destroying superstition as well"—to make the same point. *Catholic Mind*, in 1941, worried that cremation would do away with relics of the saints and of the practice of pilgrimage to the grave.[53]

Nowhere is the continuing Catholic disdain for cremation more plain than in the reaction of the American Catholic hierarchy to Mrs. Newton's "Light, Like the Sun." In the late thirties and early forties, *Ave Maria, The Catholic Digest, The Catholic Mind, Sign,* and *America* all denounced the piece as yet another pagan assault on the revered rite of burial. They called Newton's book "propaganda" and reminded readers that, as Father De Leo had said in the Tennessee Williams play *The Rose Tattoo* (1950), cremation was "an abomination in the sight of God." The most pointed critique, however, came from James P. O'Hara, whose article "Cremation" appeared in *Tablet, Catholic Digest,* and *Catholic Mind.* According to O'Hara, cremation was no sweet science. It was, on the contrary, "immediate destruction by fire for the sake of efficiency, in the same manner as is used in the destruction of refuse." Cremated remains were not pure ashes but bone fragments mixed up with "soot from the oil flame,... wood from the casket, cloth from the clothing, and particles of brick-dust from the fire-brick." And they had to be beaten to a pulp after the cremation in order to fit into an urn. All this might not be so bad if the cremationists' motives were pure. But the cremation businessman was in it for the "financial kill." And after the cremation came the deluge: urns to buy and columbarium niches and cemetery plots to consider. So there was "no lowering of cost."[54]

Sign, which noted that "nearly everything in the great outdoors looks ugly at times during winter, even crematories," tried to beat the cremationists at their own game by insisting that burial was more natural than cremation. "Not many will be convinced by the article 'Light, Like the Sun,'" it wrote. "Rather, Christians would say 'Risen Like the Saviour, Who died and was buried,' and Who, by the way, is the Creator of the Sun." *Catholic Digest* poked fun at the new obsession with land use in a satire about a salesman going door-to-door peddling cremation. "It is ill-bred," says the salesman (who is fond of playing with matches), "on so small a planet to take up more room than you need." "Mrs. Everyman" replies, "I'm sure I only want to do what is right. Do you want to cremate me now?"[55]

Happily, the salesman's answer was no. In the thirties, forties, fifties, and sixties, however, there were plenty of cremation buyers. Cremation had not overtaken burial, as some overly optimistic supporters had predicted, but nineteenth-century reformers had carved out a place for cremation as a legitimate postmortem alternative. And twentieth century crematory operators, by constructing a nationwide network of crematories, had gradually brought that alternative to more and more Americans. After a period of experimentation with crematory and columbarium design and with the technology, rites, and vocabulary of cremation, advocates had come to at least a tentative agreement on what the American way of cremation should look like. Each of these achievements was possible only because, as the first generation of cremationists yielded to the second, a spirit of rebellion gave way to a spirit of accommodation. While ideologues and nonprofit cremation societies had to a great extent ruled the movement in the Gilded Age, pragmatic businessmen took over as the movement matured in the Progressive Era and beyond. Here, as in other aspects of American life, purity had given way to practicality.

The story of cremation in America from 1896 to 1963 is, therefore, a story of moderate success through accommodation. That accommodation, however, did not go unchallenged. Just as the cremate-and-memorialize strategy of the cremation businessmen was taking hold, memorial society advocates blasted the memorial idea as a co-optation of true funeral reform. And as they organized themselves into a nationwide association to be reckoned with they began to craft an alternative way of cremation—a way that drew more on the purity concerns of the Gilded Age than on the practicality of the bricks and mortar period. In this way, they helped to set the stage for the cremation boom to come.

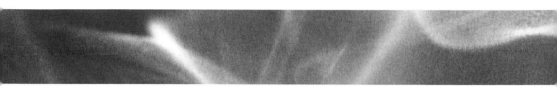

PART THREE

Boom
1963–Present

6

Consumers' Last Rites

JUST AS 1874 MARKED THE BIRTH of the American cremation movement, 1963 ushered in the cremation boom. The year did not start auspiciously. When Paul Bryan, the immediate past president of the Cremation Association of America, stepped to the rostrum at the Congress of the International Cremation Federation in Berlin in June 1963, the CAA was commemorating its golden anniversary. But there was little cause for celebration. Cremation was suffering, Bryan noted, from "declining acceptance" in the United States. "There is still a strong and emphatic feeling," he said, "that cremation is a pagan practice, that those devoted to their religion and the Christian way of life both abhor and decry." He then launched into a jeremiad, mourning the lost enthusiasm of the nineteenth-century cremation crusaders. Bryan's speech, like other lamentations for lost Edens, dug deep into hyperbole. But Bryan exaggerated little about cremation's dire straits.[1]

After surging in the nineteenth century and growing slowly during the first half of the twentieth century, American cremation stagnated following World War II. (See figure 2.) The national cremation rate was 3.7 percent when the war ended in 1945, and nearly two decades later it stood at 3.7 percent again. When Bryan delivered his speech, moreover, that figure seemed more likely to fall than to rise. The booming postwar economy had produced an affluent society. Garish and expensive were in; simplicity and economy were out. In the age-old battle between purity and pollution, pollution was winning. Automobiles, those

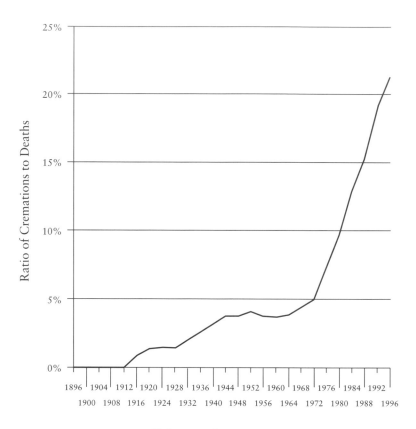

FIGURE 2. U.S. cremation rate, 1896–1996

great definers of design (and belchers of impurity), recalled not the
spare aesthetic of the Shakers but the extravagance of the Baroque. For
undertakers, cemeterians, and florists the 1950s represented a wonder-
ful opportunity for gaudy excess. Just as the Civil War had ushered in
the golden age of the embalmer, World War II brought on a period of
prosperity for undertakers. At least until 1963, the funeral industry
served up to its customers the funerary equivalent of the sinuous
chrome bumper, the erotic headlamp, and the oversized tail fin. In this
industry, too, conspicuous consumption was the order of the day. It was
not, to say the least, a moment friendly to the growth of cremation, a
practice that for roughly a century had allied itself with values such as
naturalness, simplicity, economy, and purity. In the summer of 1963,
however, Pope Paul VI and the British satirist Jessica Mitford entered
the picture. In November so did assassin Lee Harvey Oswald. Together

Mitford, Paul VI, and Oswald—the sixties' unlikeliest bedfellows—unwittingly conspired to rescue a dying rite.

Aggiornamento and the American Way of Death

Between 1962 and 1965 the Roman Catholic Church inaugurated a new era of *aggiornamento* (updating) when it convened the Second Vatican Council. Among the elements slated for updating was the liturgy. After Vatican II—notably, after the publication of *Constitution on the Sacred Liturgy* (1963)—lay people came to play a far more prominent role in the mass, and the ruling ritual style in the Roman Catholic Church became far less formal. On May 8, 1963, in the midst of Vatican II, the Supreme Congregation of the Holy Office (now the Sacred Congregation for the Doctrine of the Faith) endorsed an "Instruction with regard to the Cremation of Bodies." On July 5 of that year Pope Paul VI endorsed the measure, which relaxed the 1886 ban against cremation codified in Canon 1203 of the *Corpus Juris Canonici* ("The bodies of the faithful must be buried; their cremation is forbidden"). But this was no ringing endorsement. The Pope and the Holy Office urged Roman Catholics to continue to practice burial, and they outlawed cremation in cases where it was chosen as a deliberate affront to resurrection doctrine. Church officials also banished cremated remains from the funeral mass and forbade priests from accompanying corpses to crematories or conducting services there. Nonetheless, after the summer of 1963 Catholic cremationists were no longer branded publicans unworthy of last rites. The Church still strongly urged burial, but cremation was no longer a sin. In a crucial decision that effectively put an end to a century of religious condemnation of cremation, Vatican disapproval had grudgingly given way to toleration.[2]

In the summer of 1963, just months after Pope Paul VI relaxed the cremation ban, Jessica Mitford's *The American Way of Death* hit the bookstores. The book was a searing exposé of the contemporary funeral industry, but it turned on a historical premise. According to Mitford, the "traditional American funeral" marketed by postwar funeral directors was actually a recent invention, conjured up not to meet the needs of bereaved families but to fatten the wallets of dismal traders. Not until Victorian times, Mitford wrote, did the simple deathways of the Puritans begin to give way to the "baroque wonderland" of the modern American funeral home—"the full treatment display of the embalmed and beautified corpse reposing on an innerspring or foam-rubber mattress in an elegant 'casket', 'visitation' of the deceased in the mortuary 'slumber room', an open-casket ceremony at which the mourners parade around for a last look at a burial vault that allegedly affords 'eternal protection', elaborate 'floral tributes' from family and friends, a 'final resting place' in a 'memorial park' or mausoleum." Smart consumers, she concluded, would trade in that American way of death for cheaper and simpler death rites (like cremation).[3]

Mitford thought her rant might stir polite cocktail party conversation among "Unitarians, earnest consumer advocates, university eggheads, and the like." Instead it shot to number one on the *New York Times* bestseller list, transforming the British-born writer into an American celebrity, the Ralph Nader of the death care set. Piggybacking on Mitford's popularity, CBS aired a documentary, "The Great American Funeral"; MGM called in Mitford to consult on "The Loved One," a film (based on the eponymous 1948 novel by Evelyn Waugh) starring Liberace, the doyen of 1950s excess, as a sleazy casket salesman; and NBC wrote an ambulance-chasing funeral director into an episode of its Dr. Kildare soap opera called "The Exploiters." Prompted by the press, which coronated Mitford "Queen of the Muckrakers," the public received *The American Way of Death* as a revelation. But Mitford was no pioneer.[4]

The first family in a long line of American Mitfords were the Puritans. At least among their first New World generation, their funerals were simple, short, and to the point. And the point was this: Since death comes to everyone, all should live each day in preparation for it. Staunch critics of what they saw as the hyper-ritualization of both Catholicism and Anglicanism, early Puritans shaved death rites to the bone—no scripture, no sermons, no prayers for the dead. Death was to be accepted as part of life, and there wasn't anything to be gained by making a fuss over it.

Of course, for undertakers, who emerged as professionals after the Civil War, there was something to be gained. Working hard to keep those gains to a minimum, however, were Gilded Age funeral reformers, who regularly upbraided undertakers for fleecing the bereaved. Gilded Age cremationists, meanwhile, hammered home the point that cremation was less expensive than burial. That it was "cheaper to live than to die" was a major theme of the *New York World* cremation series of 1874. And lampooning undertaking as "the dead-surest business in Christendom" was a duty Mark Twain took up with glee in *Life on the Mississippi* (1883). "As for me," Twain concluded there, "I hope to be cremated."[5]

Critics of the high cost of dying were also prevalent in the twentieth century. In *Funeral Management and Costs* (1921), Quincy L. Dowd wrote that "it is impossible to state the problem of burial burdens in all its horrible details." A 1928 study conducted by John Gebhart on behalf of the Metropolitan Life Insurance Company documented the high cost of dying. So did *Burial Reform and Funeral Costs* (1938) by Arnold Wilson and Hermann Levy. In 1944, in the midst of World War II, the Federal Council of Churches conducted its own survey of funeral costs. "Are funerals being commercialized?" they asked. The answer, again, was "Yes."[6]

Caveat Emptor: Cremation for Consumers

There is an important distinction, however, between Mitford and earlier critics of the high cost of dying. Before World War II, cremationists and funeral reformers offered little advice on how to shop for a coffin or weigh the costs and benefits of embalming. Their concerns were more aesthetic than economic. After World War II, however, complaints about vulgarity gave way to complaints about cost.

The consumer revolution that contributed to the contemporary cremation boom took its cue from the critique of "conspicuous consumption" presented in *The Theory of the Leisure Class* (1899) by American economist critic Thorstein Veblen (who was himself cremated following his death in 1929). That revolution was aided by the foundation of the Consumers' Union and the inauguration of *Consumer Reports,* both in 1936. It did not really take hold, however, until the focus of the U.S. economy shifted from production to consumption after World War II. As Americans learned how to shop smart for automobiles, toasters, and washing machines, the centuries-old lament of funeral extravagance was reborn as a consumer critique. In the late 1940s articles with titles such as "The Vicious Scandal of Funeral Fees" and "It's Cheaper to Live" appeared regularly in popular magazines. A play about an unscrupulous undertaker, "The Biggest Thief in Town," hit Broadway. In 1959, only two years after the publication of *The Hidden Persuaders,* Vance Packard's landmark critique of Madison Avenue's contributions to conspicuous consumption, sociologist Leroy Bowman's *The American Funeral: A Study in Guilt, Extravagance, and Sublimity* appeared. The *Saturday Evening Post* ran an article in 1961 asking, "Can You Afford to Die?" In 1963, Ruth Harmer wrote *The High Cost of Dying.*[7]

Mitford's tome, therefore, was not a book with a revolution in it. It was far too derivative for that. But it was witty and wicked and was reviewed (favorably) in all the right places. What delighted the critics most was Mitford's biting satire of funeralese—the morphing of dying into "passing away," corpses into "loved ones," undertakers into "morticians," embalming schools into "colleges of mortuary science," ashes into "cremains," the "Snodgrass Funeral Home" into "Little Chapel of the Flowers." What finally sold the book to American readers, however, was Mitford's ability to distill a widespread yet vague sense of dissatisfaction with funerals into two clear complaints. The first was economic: Funeral directors were sleazy salesmen fattening their wallets by ripping off the unsuspecting relatives of the corpse. The second was aesthetic: The fare those hucksters were selling was as tasteless and fake as their chapels. Happily, Mitford had a simple solution to both problems: inexpensive yet dignified funerals. The best way to avoid getting swindled into buying a monument to bad taste, Mitford advised, was to forego the Cadillac funeral for the postmortem equivalent of the VW Bug. In order to do that, however, you would have to take your business to a low-cost cremation provider or a not-for-profit memorial society.[8]

Funeral directors who read Mitford's book as an extended advertisement for memorial societies and cremation were not entirely mistaken. Mitford dedicated the book to her husband, Robert Treuhaft, an Oakland lawyer and a major player in the Bay Area Funeral Society, who first suggested she investigate the death industry. The last two chapters of *The American Way of Death* are given over to the memorial society movement, and the book concludes with one appendix listing memorial societies in the U.S. and Canada and another on "How to Organize a Memorial Society." The book clearly gave a boost to the memorial society movement, which gained in strength in the 1960s and 1970s and appears to have peaked in the early 1980s. That movement, in turn, aided cremation. In the late 1990s, the pioneering People's Memorial Association of Seattle claimed 87,000 members, and although the organization had come to offer low-cost burial as well as cremation services, roughly 90 percent of PMA members had chosen to be cremated.[9]

The FTC and the NFDA

As public opinion turned against the death merchants Mitford so savagely satirized, state and national legislators began convening hearings on the costs of dying, and Protestant, Catholic, and Jewish clergy began to speak out against funeral fraud. In 1964 the attorney general of New York State recommended a law requiring undertakers to provide an itemized list of funeral costs, the Anti-Trust Subcommittee of the U.S. Senate held hearings on funeral industry collusion, and Minnesota's Father Alfred Longley, in an endorsement of memorial societies printed in *Ave Maria*, reminded U.S. Catholics that "the Cross had no inner-spring mattress." In January 1966, Moses I. Feuerstein, the president of the Union of Orthodox Jewish Congregations of America, called the public ogling of embalmed corpses and the "lavish floral displays and unholy musical extravaganzas" of American funerals a "desecration." Later that same year, the Reverend John J. Krol, Philadelphia's Roman Catholic Archbishop, told the National Catholic Cemetery conference that funeral directors were conning "emotionally charged and grieving relatives" into wasting money. Their industry, he said, was ruled not by spirituality but by "extravagance, escapism and commercialism."[10]

The seventies debate was dominated, however, by the Federal Trade Commission (FTC), which began to investigate the funeral industry in 1972. For nearly a century America's funeral directors had counted on the licensing authority and the good graces of state legislators to protect their profits. Now the machinery of the state seemed to turn against them. In 1972 California required its funeral directors to provide consumers with an itemized price list of its products and services. Then came the FTC. After an exhaustive inquiry, it issued in August 1975 what *Business Week* characterized as a "blistering report." These were the proposed regulations:

Prices must be itemized.

Permission of next of kin must be obtained before embalming.

Prices must be quoted over the telephone if requested.

The most inexpensive casket must be displayed along with the others.

This FTC funeral rule also would have outlawed both false claims (for example, that certain caskets could provide everlasting protection from the elements or that embalming was legally required) and efforts by undertakers to blackball cut-rate funeral homes and cremation providers.[11]

In the summer of 1978, after more hearings, the FTC released a 526-page final report on what had become a $6 billion industry. The *New*

York Times summarized the litany of funeral industry abuses uncovered by the FTC:

> removing bodies from hospitals without authorization and refusing to release them to their families; embalming without permission; misrepresenting the legal requirements, hygienic value and preservative properties of caskets and vaults; persuading survivors that an expensive casket is needed to transport a body to be cremated; overcharging for such things as flowers and clergy; failing to itemize clearly the prices of the elements in the funeral ritual; harassing undertakers who try to sell low-cost funerals.[12]

This report proposed more lenient rules than those floated in the 1975 FTC report, but added new proposals, including a regulation that would have outlawed "misrepresenting the need of a casket for cremation, particularly when cremation is not preceded by a ceremony or a viewing." The FTC also strongly suggested the use of rental caskets for cremations, but stopped short of requiring them on the mandated price list. Taking a page out of Mitford, who had stated repeatedly that her criticisms were directed at the vast majority of U.S. funeral directors, the report concluded that "the practices addressed by the rules are not isolated occurrences confined to an unethical few. In fact, the most significant funeral problems which consumers face are practices which are widely used and even condoned by a large percentage of the nation's 20,000-plus funeral homes."[13]

In the face of muckraking by someone of Mitford's talents, the grassroots organizing muscle of the likes of the Continental Association of Funeral and Memorial Societies, and findings by an agency as powerful as the FTC, industries charged with high crimes against consumers have a few options. One is to offer up a mea culpa accompanied by an argument against outside interference: Mistakes were made, there might be an unscrupulous operator here and there, but the industry is basically sound and its problems can be easily resolved internally (or, if necessary, through a legislative or regulatory compromise). When the media turned on the funeral industry, casting it as Goliath versus Mitford's David, the National Funeral Directors Association (NFDA) and the American Cemetery Association (now the International Cemetery and Funeral Association) would have been well-advised to admit to an error or two and make a show of internal reform. But they reformed little and admitted less. Convinced Mitford had drawn first blood in a bout for their good name, they fought back instead, defending their livelihoods and the American way of life against atheists, "burial beatniks," and other cheapskates. But their public relations blitz did little more than fatten Mitford's royalty checks and pump up public sympathy for what NFDA executive secretary Howard Raether disparaged as the "disposal movement." In many respects, the funeral industry was its own worst enemy.[14]

In the early 1950s *American Cemetery,* irate that America's journalists had described "cemetery profiteers" as "on a par with the body-snatching morticians," had responded to a spate of negative publicity with a show of astonishing tactlessness. Rather than responding to specific charges, it smeared the smearers as "anti-American." According to *American Cemetery,* the author of a widely read cost-of-dying piece had connections "with various organizations generally regarded as communistic" and his article was "slanted along the lines of communistic thinking." A cartoon in another issue of *American Cemetery* likened the author of another exposé to Stalin. "Attacks on American standards of burial," the caption read, "are in line with the Communist program to break down confidence in the American way of life." James B. Utt, a Republican congressman from California, brought the red-baiting into the 1960s when he branded Mitford (who earlier in her life *had* been a member of the Communist Party) "pro-Communist, anti-American" and blasted her book for striking "another blow at the Christian religion." Rabbi Julius J. Nodel of St. Louis denounced Mitford's advocacy of "'assembly-line' burials" as propaganda for her "socialistic philosophy." *American Funeral Director* judged her politics merely "slightly pink in hue" before settling on the epithet of "liberal." In the world according to *American Cemetery* and *American Funeral Director,* Mitford didn't just want to bring down the costs of funerals, she wanted to bring down church and state.[15]

As the FTC kept the spotlight on the death industry in the 1970s, there was no retreat among funeral directors or cemetery superintendents from confrontation and ad hominem arguments. Red-baiting had gone out of fashion, but rhetorical excess had not. Funeral directors, rather than cooperating with the FTC on regulations they could stomach, dug in their heels, dispatching lobbyists to Washington and angry letters to the editor protesting the socialization and secularization of funerals. Once again the attack was handled with all the nuance of a bare-knuckles brawl. *American Funeral Director* denounced the FTC's hearings as "an expensive and hypocritical charade." *Mortuary Management* complained that the agency was foisting its "agnostic, atheistic ways on the God-fearing, traditional family-oriented American." The NFDA called the FTC's 1978 report "shrill, unfair and lopsided." In addition to denouncing its critics as unpatriotic and treasonous, funeral industry representatives defended the "traditional American funeral" as integral to old-time religion and the American way of life. The Reverend Paul Irion had spoken for the funeral directors when he argued in *The Funeral: Vestige or Value?* (1966) that what Mitford and the memorial societies really wanted was "to do away with the funeral altogether." Roger L. Waltrip, chairman of Service Corporation International, read FTC investigating attorney Arthur R. Angel the same way. "Angel just doesn't like funerals, period," he said.[16]

In an effort to shore up what they saw as America's eroding commitment to the funeral, Waltrip and Irion insisted that the funeral was no passing fad. While Mitford viewed the funeral as (in Irion's words) "a vestige of past eras, an anachronism, a wasteful, unneeded, empty ceremony that outlived its usefulness long ago," they recognized its social, psychological, and religious value. To go over to the Mitford side was, from this perspective, tantamount to denying death and rejecting religion. While the traditional funeral fostered acceptance of death by forcing would-be deniers to gaze at the embalmed and coffined corpse, pray over the departed soul, and watch the casket disappear into the ground, cremation and the memorial service fostered denial by banishing the body from last rites. This denial bred both individual neurosis and social chaos. "Disposal funerals," moreover, bordered on heresy, since according to Irion they were rooted in an erroneous Greek understanding of the self (as spirit only) rather than the proper Judeo-Christian understanding of the self as both spiritual and material.[17]

In an effort to rescue Americans from this pathological (and heretical) denial of death, the NFDA published a series of pro-funeral, anti-memorial society brochures, including "What about Funeral Costs?" and "Why Do We Have Funerals Anyway?" *The Director,* the in-house NFDA organ, invoked the authority of anthropologists, psychologists, theologians, and sociologists in an effort to prove that "where there is a death there should be a funeral... where there is a funeral there should be a body," and where there is a body there should be a casket. Any and all alternatives to the embalm-and-bury regime were "maladaptive and neurotic responses."[18]

Convinced that "the funeral is a rite for the dead and a RIGHT of the living," the NFDA urged Congress to block the FTC from implementing any reforms. Because of the power of the death care lobby and its friends in high places, the FTC's 1978 regulations amounted to little more than simple disclosure requirements. "Undertakers would still be allowed to peddle those solid brass coffins guaranteed to withstand a direct hit by a nuclear warhead," wrote the *New York Times,* "but they would also be required to show grieving relatives the plain pine box." Nonetheless, funeral directors fought even those watered-down rules. Federal regulations would not merely gut the American way of life, their argument went, they would raise costs and reduce choices. Better to leave the regulating to state boards stacked with funeral directors.[19]

Besides, the funeral directors claimed, funerals weren't unreasonably priced. Following a strategy pioneered in 1876 by the Catholic-run and Boston-based *Pilot,* the NFDA commissioned its own studies on the cost of dying, which it found to be a bargain. Findings issued shortly after the 1978 FTC report fixed the average adult funeral bill for 1977 at only $1,412, up a paltry 5 percent over the previous year's average. Moreover, this $1,412 figure (which did not include costs for vaults, cemetery services, monuments, clergy honoraria, flowers, burial clothing, or obituary notices) was not all profit, since funeral directors incurred at least sixty different types of expenses, including furniture depreciation, automobile repairs, stationery costs, and owners' "total salaries, and bonuses and/or other compensation." Add that all up and the pre-tax profit was only $90 per funeral.[20]

The war between the funeral industry on the one hand and Mitford, the memorial societies, and the FTC on the other produced no clear winners. While the FTC investigated and the NFDA stonewalled, little changed. In 1974 a New York Public Interest Research Group study of funeral practices found that two-thirds of undertakers did not cooperate in providing price information over the phone. In 1978 a three-part investigative series by the *New York Times* uncovered evidence of "body-snatching (one undertaker claiming a body before a competitor), price gouging, misrepresentations of the need for embalming and, on occasion, assaults on the cultural and religious beliefs of people trying to cope with the death of a loved one." In a May 1981 series called "The Death Merchants," the Chicago *Sun-Times* concurred. "Deception, fraud, scare tactics, outright lies," it editorialized, "almost nothing is beneath these vultures as they seek to peck the last dime of profit from a bereaved relative."[21]

The FTC did more investigating than acting. Not until July 1982, nearly two decades after the publication of Mitford's book, did the FTC finally adopt a modified trade rule, but it postponed enforcing that rule until 1984. In 1994, the commission amended the rule, opening the way for funeral directors to bundle a variety of services together under one undeclinable fee. Moreover, enforcement even of the existing rules was unenthusiastic at best. The FTC brought few formal enforcement cases, and in 1996 the NFDA and FTC announced a new agreement allowing funeral homes to enter into a Funeral Rule Offenders Program rather than pay fines. Meanwhile, the average undertaker's bill rose, according to the NFDA's own estimates, from roughly $1,000 in 1963 to nearly $6,000 (cemetery expenses excluded) in 1999.[22]

Bake and Shake

The hue and cry that followed the publication of *The American Way of Death* did little to modify the behavior of undertakers or cut funeral costs, but it did a lot to promote cremation. Mitford, who devoted a full chapter of her book to the subject, was an outspoken champion of cremation as an inexpensive alternative to burial. Her advocacy of memorial societies, moreover, accelerated cremation's growth, since the vast majority of memorial society members endorsed cremation. In the two decades that followed the appearance of *The American Way of Death*, funeral directors and cemetery managers concerned themselves largely with attacking the FTC and defending the old-time funeral. There was an occasional article on cremation in *Casket and Sunnyside* and *American Funeral Director* in the 1960s and 1970s, but for the most part the funeral industry ignored the subject. Its fixation on the evil triumvirate of Mitford, the memorial societies, and the FTC, however, created an opening for a new brand of cremation entrepreneurs who viewed the average cost of funerals as opportunity rather than scourge. In an effort to capitalize on the popularity of nonprofit funeral and memorial societies, many of these profit-making cremation businesses masqueraded as cooperatives. Two of the most successful, the Telophase Society and the Neptune Society, even called themselves societies and charged membership fees. Following the example of the earliest American crematories, these new cremation businesses operated as independents. By offering no-frills cremations sans funeral, plot, marker, and bouquets, they threatened not only funeral directors but also cemeterians, monument makers, and florists. They also solidified the century-old association between cremation and eccentricity.

The Telophase Society was the brainchild of biochemist Thomas B. Weber, who got into the cremation business in 1971 in San Diego, California, after running into roadblocks while trying to cremate his dead father. His oddly-named business—"telophase" refers to the final stage in cell division—pioneered direct cremation for profit. Operating out of a modest storefront, the Telophase Society charged members (who initially paid a $10 initiation fee) $250, or roughly the equivalent of the Social Security death benefit. Weber, who did not run his own crematory until 1974, would pick up the corpse, bring it to a crematory, and scatter the cremains, typically at sea. The Telophase Society offered one-stop shopping but only one product. Like most cremation businessmen at the turn of the century, Weber focused on selling cremation itself, rather than products and services. If you wanted cremation preceded by a funeral or followed by burial, Weber would turn you away. And any memorial service you might want was strictly up to you.

In 1977 the San Francisco–based Neptune Society entered the direct cremation business. Its CEO was Dr. Charles Denning, a goateed chiropractor who was dubbed the Colonel Sanders of the death industry until someone came up with an even better moniker: "Colonel Cinders." A pioneer in both direct cremation and the fun funeral, Denning distinguished himself from Weber by offering a complete cremation menu rather than just one cut-rate course. A popular extra (for an additional fee) was a lavish scattering bash aboard a hundred-foot teak-paneled yacht. Denning, attired in a blue blazer and a captain's hat, would skipper the ship himself. His dapper outfits—a far cry from the staid dark suits of the typical funeral director—were West Coast casual. His demeanor, a stark contrast to the grim Midwestern solemnity of his competitors, was California cheery. By the end of the decade Denning's laid-back approach had trounced not only the funeral directors in his area but also Weber's austere minimalism. In 1980 he attended to more dead than any other business in California except Glendale's massive Forest Lawn.[23]

Funeral directors and other death care providers reacted to the success of direct cremation by disparaging firms like Telophase and Neptune as "bake and shake" and "burn and scatter" outfits that treated deceased loved ones, literally, like trash. It's "just a disposal service," complained one funeral director, "a completely pagan method of disposing of remains." But funeral directors did more than call Weber and Denning names. They tried to legislate them out of business. Shortly after the Telophase Society opened, the California Funeral Directors Association found a sympathetic legislator to sponsor a bill that, by classifying "cremation clubs" as funeral homes, would have subjected them to the regulations of the undertaker-controlled state Board of Funeral Directors and Embalmers. Consumer groups cried foul. "It's like having the railroads regulate the airlines," said Weber. The Telophase Society eventually lost the battle, but after getting his funeral director's license Weber was back in business. Still the opposition did not stop. The state Board of Funeral Directors and Embalmers sued him, as did the Cemetery Board, which tried to classify his business as a cemetery. In roughly thirty lawsuits, however, he eventually prevailed.[24]

Critics of direct cremation also took a page out of the books of Gilded Age cremationists by attacking this new way of cremation as ghoulishly insensitive. In the nineteenth century cremationists had repeatedly spun tales of the horrors awaiting the buried corpse. Now funeral directors, armed with stories about the postmortem misadventures of cremains, waged their own war by anecdote. In a debate with Mitford in *Good Housekeeping* in 1968, freelance writer Kate Holliday complained that the urn of a friend of hers "clunked and rattled" and looked like "a can of tar." In 1976 *American Funeral Director* gleefully reported that the U.S. Postal Service had lost an urn in shipping. Three years later the same publication devoted a series of articles and editorials to a cremation scandal in St. Petersburg, Florida. Cremated remains had been found spilling out of large trash bags near the garage of a man who worked part-time scattering ashes in the Gulf of Mexico. It was, the magazine concluded, a "callous desecration." Christian critics weighed in too. In *Cremation: Is It Christian?* James W. Fraser answered the question posed in his title with an emphatic no. According to Fraser, cremation was "of heathen origin, an aid to crime, a barbarous act, also anti-Biblical." "To a person of refined Christian culture," he wrote, "it must be most repulsive to think of the body of a friend being treated like a beef roast in an oven, with all its running fats and sizzling tissues."[25]

What is striking about the funeral industry's response to Mitford, the FTC, and the new cremation entrepreneurs is how closely it mirrored the critics' responses to cremation in the Gilded Age. Like those critics, funeral directors denounced cremation as secularization and its supporters as secularists. Mitford was a godless communist who "just [didn't] believe in ceremony." The FTC's ways were agnostic and atheistic. And the services of Weber and Denning were pagan. But in the 1960s and 1970s, as in the 1880s and 1890s, the critics were wrong. Neither Mitford nor the FTC nor the new cremation entrepreneurs were preaching an end to religion or ritual. What they were preaching were alternatives to the embalm-and-bury regime. In the sixties and seventies, as in the Gilded Age, the cremation movement fostered not secularization but the diversification of religion and ritualization.[26]

Efforts by traditionalists to associate cremation with godless communism and other forms of secularity no doubt dissuaded some from choosing cremation. But cremation grew rapidly nonetheless in the sixties and the seventies. In a 1970 report on the growing threat of cremation, NFDA executive secretary Howard Raether argued that "it's clear that most of the American public does not want cremation. There have been cremation societies for more than 100 years, and there is certainly no strong move in that direction." Raether was incorrect, at least about the trend. After the appearance of Mitford's book in 1963 the cremation rate turned gently upward, hitting 4.5 percent in 1969. But cremation grew faster in the 1970s. Spurred by the success of the Neptune and Telophase societies and their imitators, the cremation rate reached 6.5 percent in 1975 and 9.4 percent in 1979. (See figure 2.) The number of crematories expanded too, nearly doubling from 238 in 1963 to 506 in 1978. In the late seventies, membership in the Telophase Society topped 20,000. So did membership in a similar direct cremation firm, the St. Petersburg–based National Cremation Society. In the early eighties, an estimated 170 memorial societies claimed 750,000 members, the overwhelming majority of them pro-cremation. Thanks to the Pope, Mitford, and the direct cremation entrepreneurs, American cremation had become a growth industry.[27]

A New Puritanism

Both long-term and short-term factors played a role in the post-1963 cremation boom. The undeniable influence of Mitford, the FTC, and the memorial society movement would seem to suggest that cremation benefited in this period primarily from economic considerations—that cremation won its popularity by riding the wave of consumerism just as it won its legitimacy a century earlier by riding the wave of sanitary reform. There is some truth to this claim. After 1963 consumer calculations dominated the public debate. Changes in the treatment of the dead continued to be proposed on behalf of the living, but now their financial rather than physical well-being was said to be at stake. In 1977 the editors at *Consumer Reports* published a book called *Funerals: Consumers' Last Rights*. Once *Consumer Reports* was training death rites buyers to act like consumers, it was only natural for some to select the cheapest way to go. Moreover, after the FTC required funeral directors to include a cremation option on a mandated price list and direct cremation outfits were up and running, making that selection became much easier. "You can get yourself cremated for about $250," someone told a Northwestern University researcher in a study on death attitudes published in 1981. "Why pay $3500?"

Another accelerator of the cremation rate was the rise of environmentalism, which earned nationwide recognition when the United States first celebrated Earth Day on April 22, 1970. Since the late nineteenth century cremationists had criticized burial as land-hungry and praised cremation for consuming far less land. And in the 1930s, in "Light, Like the Sun," Frances Newton had found ecological reasons to prefer cremation over burial. But environmental considerations remained a minor chord throughout the movement's first century. In the 1970s, by contrast, environmental considerations became important to many Americans choosing cremation, and "Save the Land for the Living" emerged as a leading pro-cremation slogan.[28]

While both consumer and environmental considerations clearly played a part in cremation's rapid growth, each of these factors can be overplayed. Although, as a 1970 *New York Times* article on the rise of cremation noted, finances were a "principal reason" for cremation's growing popularity, they were not the principal reason. The most important cause of the cremation boom was a matter not of money but of style. Cremation gained at the expense of burial not because it was cheaper but because it was simpler and more authentic. Or, as a woman interviewed for the *Times* article testified, "It just seemed a lot purer."[29]

The American Way of Death has been hailed as a consumer classic on par with Ralph Nader's *Unsafe at Any Speed*. But it was really akin to "Light, Like the Sun." Like Newton's classic, Mitford's book was fundamentally an aesthetic critique. As an Englishwoman and a former communist, Mitford did believe funerals should be performed at low or no cost to the consumer, preferably (as was increasingly the case in Great Britain) as a public service. But this was not a view shared by many Americans. When activist Herb Klein sent out a call in 1975 for a "cremation crusade," demanding legislation mandating "free cremation for all who choose it," few Americans answered the call. U.S. citizens did not believe their government should foot the bill for their death rites, and they did not expect funeral homes to be run as charities. Where Mitford and her American readers came to a meeting of the minds was in their shared sense that the American funeral had become a tacky parade of the fake. Americans had been ambivalent about greed since the wealth of the robber barons and the depredations of the slums arose simultaneously in the Gilded Age. But they were not ambivalent about bad taste, and as

Mitford repeatedly demonstrated, the American way of death had become by the early 1960s a boulevard to bad taste. The vice of Mitford's villains—the funeral directors, cemetery managers, monument makers, and funeral florists—was vulgarity, not avarice. Their missing virtues were refinement and sincerity. In the end humor rather than indignation carries *The American Way of Death,* which eggs on its readers not so much to scorn as to laugh at the ghoulish artificiality of the ill-bred funeral director and his ill-appointed chapels.[30]

Mitford was lionized, in short, because the cultural tide was turning. Less than a year after Pope Paul VI lifted the ban on cremation and only months after the publication of *The American Way of Death,* President Kennedy was killed on November 22, 1963, in Dallas, Texas. Looking back at that moment through the prism of the Vietnam conflict and the flurry of succeeding assassinations—of Malcolm X, the Reverend Martin Luther King, Jr., and Robert Kennedy—the sixties seem to have begun not on the first day of 1960 but on November 22, 1963. On that day America began to turn from optimism toward cynicism, from conformity to nonconformity, from excess toward simplicity. The new cultural mood reached into all areas of American life, including the funeral industry, which after 1963 witnessed what even the NFDA recognized as a "shift toward simpler... and less expensive funerals." That shift, however, was gradual.[31]

In 1963 cremating a fallen president, especially a Catholic one, was still unthinkable. Kennedy's obsequies were dignified, but by no measure simple. A caisson pulled by six gray horses transported the body of the martyred president in a mahogany coffin from the White House up Pennsylvania Avenue to the Capitol. Enlisted men carried the coffin up thirty-six marble steps, placing the president's body in the center of the rotunda on the same catafalque that had supported Abraham Lincoln's corpse nearly a century earlier. After a series of eulogies, over 100,000 mourners filed past the coffin, which in a nod to the emerging funerary style was closed. Hundreds of millions worldwide then watched on television as the president's body was carried in a state procession to Arlington National Cemetery and buried with full military honors. Fifty jets, one for each state, roared over the grave site. Military men performed a twenty-one-gun salute. An Army bugler played taps. Then Mrs. Kennedy, Senator Edward Kennedy, and Robert Kennedy lit the eternal flame at the head of the President's grave, and Cardinal Cushing sprinkled holy water on the coffin, which was promptly lowered into the ground and covered with earth.[32]

The obsequies that followed President Dwight D. Eisenhower's death in 1969 were, by contrast, a model of the emerging austerity. While Kennedy's funeral, by fixing the minds of Americans on death and con- spiracies, helped to create a vast audience for Mitford's fulminations, Eisenhower's funeral demonstrated that the Mitfordian style was as- cending. Like Kennedy, Eisenhower lay in state in the Capitol. Mourn- ers celebrated his life at a funeral service at Washington's National Ca- thedral. But Eisenhower's body was not interred in Arlington National Cemetery. Instead, Eisenhower chose to be buried alongside his boy- hood friends at the modest Chapel of Meditation in his hometown of Abilene, Kansas. This time the coffin was simple: an $80 G.I.-style cas- ket. The service, held on the library steps, was brief. And the family requested that charitable donations be sent in lieu of flowers.[33]

Both Mitford's reputation and the cremation alternative benefited from, even as they contributed to, this new mood. When *The American Way of Death* appeared, Mitford was like a VW Bug in a Cadillac cul- ture. But by the time her book was being read widely, Cadillacs were going out of style, and Bugs, propelled by a timely advertising campaign that urged Americans to "Think Small," were selling fast. Thanks to Mitford, the memorial societies, and the FTC, burial and the "tradi- tional American funeral" were losing the aesthetic high ground to cre- mation and the memorial service. After 1963 many self-respecting Americans wouldn't be caught dead in an "Eterna-Crib." Excess had lost its dignity, and the funeral directors were the high priests of excess. The high priests of simplicity were, by contrast, Thomas Weber and Charles Denning, nonconforming direct cremation providers who came to prominence as minimalism overtook the American art scene, the counterculture hit the cover of *Time,* and "small is beautiful" became a countrywide cliche.

During their three-front battle with Mitford, the memorial societies, and the FTC, some funeral directors took Mitford to task not for her communism but for her ethnocentrism. One told the *New York Times* she was pushing "a white, Anglo-Saxon Protestant view of funeral rit- ual with no regard for ethnic, racial, or religious considerations." In the 1990s, the *Funeral Monitor* called her a closet aristocrat. "The common folk invariably came off in her writings as a good-natured subspecies in clear need of a firm hand from those like herself who were more in- formed and knowledgeable," it wrote. "It is hardly the democratic ideal."[34]

There is some truth in both charges. Mitford claimed to be pro-choice in death rites, but it is impossible to read her writing without seeing that she regarded embalming as fake and the funeral as vulgar. Mitford was no genteel reformer, but like the cremationists of the Gilded Age, she was a refiner of American deathways who was convinced she knew what was best for poorly educated and working-class corpses. Though branded a communist, she was really a Puritan, a reincarnation not of Karl Marx but of Cotton Mather, who like other Puritan divines believed in postmortem simplicity and social purity. Like the Puritan preacher (and the nineteenth-century cremationist), Mitford was no denier of death, no friend of the postmortem euphemism. She too was wary of priestcraft and ritual. The priests she opposed, however, were the funeral directors, and the rites she condemned were the sham ceremonies of the American way of death.

In a study of U.S. immigration, historian John Higham has argued that Americans have wrestled for centuries with a fundamental contradiction between purity and practicality. Both values are deeply ingrained in American life, Higham says. The desire for purity goes back to the Puritans, who sought to purify both church (by admitting only the "elect") and community (by building a "Biblical Commonwealth"). And that desire surfaced, Higham notes, in sanitary reform. The desire for practicality can be traced to the frontier, the rise of industrial capitalism, and the thought of Enlightenment icons like Benjamin Franklin. According to Higham, Victorian Americans tried to resolve this fundamental contradiction by relegating purity concerns to the private sphere of the home (ruled—and cleaned—by godly wives and mothers) and practicality to the rough-and-tumble public sphere of work (overseen by pragmatic men). But that effort collapsed when the Progressives insisted on purifying American economic and political life—on busting trusts, passing food and drug legislation, and cleaning up corrupt elections. In the 1920s, the "passionate desire" of the Progressives "to recreate a homogeneous society" receded and practicality again gained the upper hand.[35]

Higham's analysis does an excellent job of contextualizing both the desire for purity of the Gilded Age cremationists and the pragmatic bent of the cremating businessmen of the bricks and mortar period. It also sheds light, however, on Mitford and the cremation boom. After explaining how the liberal side of Progressivism eventually triumphed over its less tolerant and less cosmopolitan purity strain, Higham notes that the desire for purity lives on in a new American tradition, namely, muckraking. Born of the double standards of the Gilded Age compromise, muckraking goes back to Progressive Era journalists like Upton Sinclair, whose *The Jungle* (1906) exposed the hypocrisy in the meat packing industry, and Samuel Hopkins Adams, whose *Collier's* articles on "The Great American Fraud" (1905–12) skewered patent medicines. But it extends forward to Mitford's unmasking of the inner workings of the casket sale and the embalming table. Her work too was, to borrow from Higham, "in revolt against equivocation and complexity." She too "concentrated fiercely on exposing sham and pretence."[36]

If cremation in the 1870s was a modern revival of a Hindu and Greco-Roman practice, cremation in the 1960s and beyond was a modern revival of Puritanism and Progressive Era moralism. As the baby boomers born after World War II entered young adulthood, they cultivated a disdain for their parents' accommodationism (which was in their view "the great American fraud"). This rebellion produced a new "culture of cool," which championed the simple and the real over the extravagant and the fake. The cremation boom owed much to this new revolt. In that sense, it had its roots in both Puritan simplicity and Progressive Era exposés.[37]

Countercultural Cremation

Mitford and her allies did not convert the country. Most of America's dead continued to be embalmed and buried through the end of the twentieth century. But a truly viable counterpoint to the American way of embalming and burying did emerge after 1963. Thumbing its nose at the establishment, this countercultural way incorporated cremation rather than burial, the memorial service rather than the funeral. And participants expected these death rites would express the unique personality of the deceased. In an age that celebrated the living body, this alternative insisted on memorializing not the corpse but the living spirit of the person. Rather than gazing with their eyes on an embalmed corpse, nonconforming mourners were urged to recall with their hearts and minds the deceased's eternal spirit. "We honor the memory of the dead person," Thomas Weber said, "not the cadaver."[38]

This new American way of cremation shared much with the old cremation way crafted by genteel reformers in the Gilded Age. Cremationists still thought of their postmortem practice largely as an alternative to burial, and they continued to associate cremation with warmth and light, and burial with cold and darkness. But the new cremationists were far less likely to describe cremation as modern, cosmopolitan, and progressive. And they spoke little of purity and cleanliness, and not at all of germ theory or sanitary science. Now when advocates said cremation was purer than burial (and they did not say that often), they meant that it did not pollute the environment. Cremation continued to be seen as an alternative to the vulgarities of burial, but supporters no longer sought to educate partisans of burial to refinement, to uplift the masses to a higher level of culture and civilization.

Like the world according to the genteel cremationists (see table 1 in chapter 3), the world of these countercultural cremationists can be expressed in a series of hierarchically ordered binary oppositions (see table 2). Here again the key contrast was between burial, which was evaluated negatively (−), and cremation, which was evaluated positively (+). But now the second most important dyad was extravagance/simplicity rather than pollution/purity:

Burial (−)   Cremation (+)
Extravagance (−)   Simplicity (+)

In short, cremation had become matter of style. Cremationists associated the embalming and burial regime with the fake and the artificial, and aligned cremation with authenticity and naturalness.

While the nineteenth-century cremationist worldview was designed by and for genteel elites, this new conception of cremation was made by and for the counterculture. During the 1870s cremation had been a project of middle-class reformers eager to distinguish themselves from the "unwashed" masses. A century later cremationists were decidedly antibourgeois. Rather than cultivating middle-class values, they rebelled against them. While their predecessors defined themselves over against the burying masses, this new generation of cremationists defined themselves over against the organizational man in the gray flannel suit. He conformed; they were nonconformists. He valued tradition, repetition, and formalism; they were innovative, spontaneous, and informal. He was a poser, blindly followed the dictates of "organized religion"; they were true to themselves, seekers after "personal spirituality." In short, he was square while they were hip. For this new generation of cremationists, a vote for cremation was no longer a vote against African Americans, immigrants, women, or the poor. Neither was it an effort to create a more homogeneous America. It was, instead, a vote against the

TABLE 2

The World According to
Countercultural Cremationists

Burial	Cremation
extravagance	simplicity
"bigger is better"	"small is beautiful"
artificial	natural
fake	authentic
hypocrisy	reality
conformity	individuality
formal	informal
tradition	innovation
ugly	beautiful
impersonal	customized
establishment	counterculture
square	hip
conspicuous consumption	economical spending
slow	fast
cold	warm
darkness	light
earth	sun
polluting	eco-friendly
West	Asia
organized religion	personal spirituality
body	soul
materialistic	spiritual
funeral (with body)	memorial service (without body)
director-run funeral	family-directed funeral
passive audience	congregational participation
self is body and soul	self is soul only
resurrection of the body	immortality of the soul

"establishment"—an effort to make a more pluralistic America in which each individual was free to be true to himself or herself, not just in life but also in death.

John Lennon's White Balloons

The world the countercultural cremationists made was on display in the cremation of Beatles superstar John Lennon, who in the evening of December 8, 1980, was shot four times outside his New York City home by a deranged fan. Lennon was rushed from the Dakota Apartments at 72d Street and Central Park West, where he had lived, to nearby Roosevelt Hospital (where Baron De Palm had died a century earlier). Lennon's shocking murder, which for many recalled the assassination of President Kennedy, instantly transformed him from a member of the British rock group the Beatles into an American icon—a symbol of the violent death of 1960s optimism.[39]

Lennon's wife, singer Yoko Ono, had been influenced not only by consumer critiques of burial but also by the countercultural commitments of Mitford and the memorial societies. In lieu of flowers, she asked for donations to the Spirit Foundation, the charitable arm of the multimillion dollar Lennon/Ono empire. And she wanted no public funeral. Lennon's fans, however, would have none of that. The Beatles star had not yet been pronounced dead when admirers began to gather in an impromptu vigil outside the hospital. When they finally got word of their hero's death, they memorialized Lennon in prayers and song. Radio stations played Lennon's music without profane commercial interruptions. Outside Lennon's apartment building mourners placed flowers, evergreens, poems, photographs, and paintings in a wrought-iron gate. Some wore black arm bands. One student, recalling Lennon's interest in Transcendental Meditation and the Hare Krishnas, meditated at the base of the newly sacred gate.

After witnessing this outpouring of grief and affection, Ono announced a memorial service slated for Sunday, December 14. No site was announced for the ceremony, which was to take place everywhere and anywhere. "Pray for his soul from wherever you are," Ono said. Convinced that family, friends, and fans alike should concentrate on Lennon's spiritual rather than his material remains, Ono saw to it that her husband's body was not part of the rite. Placed in a body bag and driven from the office of the Manhattan Medical Examiner to the Frank E. Campbell Funeral Home, it was put into a white casket before being driven randomly around in a hearse (an effort to shake the paparazzi) and finally delivered to the Ferncliff Crematory in Hartsdale, New York.

On Sunday, December 14, millions gathered to commemorate Lennon's spirit, each in his or her own way. The biggest U.S. gathering occurred in Manhattan's Central Park, where roughly 100,000 congregated around a bandstand decorated with evergreens. In keeping with the cremationists' bias for spirituality over materiality, the only tangible witness to the dead singer on display was a poster-size image of Lennon in his trademark glasses. Once again, Beatles melodies consoled the crowd. Then everyone fell as silent as Quakers for ten minutes of prayer and meditation. CBS cut into its National Football League game to carry the rite, radio stations across the country broadcasted ten minutes of silence, and in cities and towns throughout the world fans of all races and creeds gathered in living testimony to Lennon's belief in the universal brotherhood and sisterhood of humanity. Back in Central Park, in the midst of the silence, a bouquet of white balloons ascended skyward in testimony to the purity of Lennon's departing spirit. Ono later reported that looking up, she "saw John smiling in the sky."

Lennon's cremation seems to have taken place on the afternoon of December 10, 1980, but newspaper reports do not describe it in any detail. Unlike the De Palm cremation, this was not a public event. In fact, it wasn't even a private event. In keeping with the custom of the time, there were no prayers, no eulogies, no music at the crematory. Back in 1876 Olcott had announced that the first modern cremation in America was to be a purely technological and secular exercise. His actions had belied that pronouncement. But with the Lennon cremation, this vision was complete. What had been a religious rite had become a secular technology. Lennon's arm may well have risen up, and his fingers might have pointed heavenward, but there was no one there to see it or to debate the significance of those movements. There were no religious services at the crematory. The body was not lowered ceremoniously from a first-floor chapel to the basement retort after the manner of a committal service at a grave. We do not know whether the body entered the retort head- or feet-first.

Lennon's cremation would seem to symbolize the secularization of cremation. But does it? His cremation was, admittedly, an irreligious affair. And his memorial service was clearly idiosyncratic, orchestrated by neither a funeral director nor a priest. But what did Ono's "no public funeral" pronouncement do? And how did cremation function in the worldwide process of memorializing the passing star? Both served to divert attention from Lennon's bullet-ridden body to his spirit. A body must be somewhere, but a spirit can be everywhere. By banishing the body from the memorial service, Ono demonstrated her conviction that the self is both spiritual and immanent. And by relying on fire and heat to free his spirit to fly to what she awkwardly termed "the big upstairs," she demonstrated her belief in the immortality of the soul. John Lennon, she was saying, lives.

Lennon's cremation does highlight an important turn in American religion and culture, but that turn is not secularization. It is instead the ongoing pluralization of U.S. religion and ritualization. In the same period when Americans were following Lennon into religious alternatives such as Transcendental Meditation, they were crafting ritual alternatives to the old American way of death and theological alternatives to the Judeo-Christian tradition. Like Lennon's memorial, those death rites were less formal and more personal than the rites denounced by Mitford. They promoted values, such as simplicity and naturalness, cherished by the counterculture. And they helped to make plausible alternative theological universes. As the public power of the Judeo-Christian tradition faded and the belief in hell virtually disappeared, belief in the traditional Jewish and Christian conception of the self receded too. Many, perhaps most, Americans continued to view themselves as psychosomatic unities—intriguing mixtures of body and soul—but an alternative self-conception was edging its way from the margins into the mainstream of American culture. Like Lennon and Ono, many Americans, including many liberal Protestants, Catholics, and Jews, were embracing an alternative view of the self as essentially spiritual. "I have a body, but I am a soul," they were saying. And they wanted their exits from the world of bodies to reflect their alternative spiritualities. At least for them, white balloons resonated as metaphors, and cremation was the perfect rite.

7

Contemporary Ways of Cremation

ON APRIL 21, 1997, CREMATION BOLDLY went where no man had gone before. Early that morning Houston-based Celestis, Inc., rocketed into low-earth orbit portions of the cremated remains of LSD guru Timothy Leary and Star Trek creator Gene Roddenberry. As the millennium approached, Leary, Roddenberry, and twenty-two other clients of the Celestis Earthview Commemorative Spaceflight Service were safely in orbit in individual lipstick-sized aluminum capsules, passing overhead roughly once every ninety minutes. Eventually their miniaturized mausoleum will tilt back to earth and burn out in a quick flash of light. "I'll be a space pioneer," Leary boasted shortly before his death, "I will be the light."[1]

At America's latest fin de siècle, cremation continued to be associated with offbeat religions and countercultural personalities: with Jerry Garcia, the lead guitarist for the Grateful Dead, whose ashes made their way to the Ganges River; with Beat poet Allen Ginsberg, whose corpse was chanted over by Tibetan Buddhist monks and then incinerated privately in a New York crematory; and with the Reverend Howard Finster, America's most prolific outsider artist, who made plain his preference for cremation in this broadside (creative spelling and punctuation in original):

> Do you understand about creamenation.... God would not let Jesus see coruption God would not let Jesus rot in his grave and 'stink' as carion God raised him from the Grave and like Jesus didnt see any coruption I wanto be

like Jesus free from coruption. Take my body when i die. Creamanate it into clean ashes....[2]

By the 1990s cremation had not yet shaken its long-standing associations with the odd and the offbeat, but like the counterculture of the 1970s it was nonetheless going mainstream. In papers across the country Ann Landers dispensed cremation etiquette; and on the Internet evangelist Billy Graham concluded that cremation posed "no hindrance to the resurrection." The dilemma of what to do with cremated remains helped churn plots in soap operas and feature films. (On the television cartoon "The Simpsons," Joe's crematorium attracted customers with the slogan, "You kill 'em, we grill 'em.") Half the new arrivals at Arlington National Cemetery were cremated remains, and Boston's historic Old North Church was housing ashes alongside memories of the Revolutionary War. After decades of resisting cremation, casket manufacturers like the Batesville Casket Company were merchandising both urns and "cremation containers." And vault manufacturers like the Doric Vault Company were selling "urn vaults." Each of the "big three" funeral service multinationals—Service Corporation International, the Loewen Group, and Stewart Enterprises—offered cremation services. Neptune Society stock was publicly traded.[3]

The ratio of cremations to deaths reached 25 percent nationwide in 1999, when 1,366 crematories incinerated well over half a million bodies in the United States. In Hawaii, Nevada, Washington, Alaska, Oregon, Montana, and Arizona cremation was more common than burial. Cremation was especially popular among the wealthy and well-educated, and among Christian Scientists, Unitarians, Episcopalians, Buddhists, and Hindus. It was also widespread among AIDS patients (and the preferred postmortem practice in novels on AIDS). Thanks to the lifting of the Catholic cremation ban in 1963, Catholic lay people were selecting cremation about as frequently as the overall U.S. population. And women, who had held fast to burial in the Gilded Age, were now just as likely as men to choose cremation.[4]

Although the overall U.S. cremation rate throughout the 1990s trailed figures in countries such as Japan (98%), Great Britain (70%), Scandinavia (over 65%), and Australia (over 50%), where local, state, and national governments actively promoted cremation, it easily outpaced ratios in predominantly Catholic countries such as Spain and Italy, where percentages had stalled in the low single digits. There were indications, moreover, that U.S. numbers might climb. In a telephone survey in 1995, 43 percent of respondents said they were "likely to choose cremation" for themselves. Some predicted that those preferences, accompanied by ongoing immigration from pro-cremation nations in Asia, would translate into a 40 percent cremation rate in the early twenty-first century. Richard Grayson of *Mortuary Law & Business Quarterly* was even more optimistic. He foresaw a rate of nearly 80 percent by the year 2015. "The future," said Jack Springer, CANA's executive director, "is in cremation."[5]

By the late 1990s, however, that future had not quite arrived. After climbing sharply in the seventies and eighties, the cremation rate flattened out in the ensuing decade. One growth inhibitor was scandal. During the eighties and nineties, some crematory operators were accused of cremating bodies en masse and commingling the ashes of survivors. Others were charged with harvesting gold from the teeth of crematory corpses. In 1997 police found thousands of boxes of cremated remains at a San Francisco Bay area storage facility. Those remains were supposed to have been scattered from the air, but the pilot contracted to do the work did not even have a pilot's license. Shortly after the story broke, the contractor killed himself. In lawsuits emanating from scandals of this sort juries have awarded bereaved plaintiffs multimillion-dollar awards.[6]

Cremation itself remained a scandal among conservative Christians and most Muslims in America through the end of the millennium. Both groups held fast to the ancient Hebraic conception of the self as an amalgamation of body and soul, and rejected cremation as an assault on that belief. In a homily delivered at the Russian Orthodox Cathedral of St. John the Baptist in Washington, D.C., Archpriest Victor Potapov rejected cremation as an anti-Christian denial of "the truth of the psychophysical union of body and soul." In 1994 *Pentecostal Evangel* argued against cremation on the grounds that the body "is not garbage" but "a gift from God." Mormons denounced the practice for violating their distinctive theology that the body was "an essential part of the soul." Cremation was almost as unpopular among Jews, for whom it served as a grim reminder of Nazi death camps. Conservative and Orthodox Jews continued to forbid it, but the practice did make some inroads into Reform Jewish congregations on the West Coast. In the Bible Belt, where for many there was, in the words of one traditionalist, "no salvation after cremation," burial also predominated. The cremation rate stood at only 5 percent in Alabama, Mississippi, and West Virginia in 1998.[7]

Cremation was unpopular too among African Americans and Hispanics. Both groups tended to cleave to old-time religion (the Baptist

and Methodist traditions for Blacks and Roman Catholicism for Hispanics), including the traditional Christian view of the self as an amalgamation of body and spirit, and the traditional Christian belief in the
resurrection of the body. African Americans held the casketed funeral
especially dear. Lawrence Jones, past president of the National Funeral
Directors and Morticians Association, a predominantly African-
American association based in Kansas City, reported in 1997 that cremation was still "frowned upon" among his customers. But the racial
divide over the cremation question seemed to be narrowing. While a
study conducted in 1970 found that Blacks were nearly five times less
likely than whites to choose cremation, a 1990s survey found Blacks
were only about two times less likely.[8]

The Catholic Church too accommodated itself to the practice. After
1963, U.S. Catholics began to ask their priests to conduct funeral
masses over cremated remains. Those requests were initially denied. In
1989, however, the National Conference of Catholic Bishops began to
study the question. In 1996, U.S. Catholic bishops requested from the
Vatican a special dispensation called an indult giving bishops the dis-
cretion to permit cremated remains to be present at funeral masses in
their dioceses. That indult was granted on March 21, 1997. A few
months later a new *Order of Christian Funerals* with special instruc-
tions on cremation in the United States appeared. Although that text
made considerable allowances for cremation, it stated once again the
church's preference for burial and recommended that funeral masses
take place, whenever possible, before rather than after cremations (to
allow the whole body to be present). The church insisted, moreover, on
placing cremated remains in "a worthy vessel" in a grave, mausoleum,
or columbarium. "The practice of scattering cremains on the sea, from
the air, or on the ground, or keeping cremated remains in the home of a
relative or friend of the deceased," the order read, "are not the reverent
disposition that the Church requires." Like the 1886 ban on cremation,
that anti-scattering policy was ignored by many American Catholics. In
1999, following the most high-profile cremation by any American
Catholic ever, the cremated remains of John F. Kennedy, Jr., the son of
President John F. Kennedy, were scattered at sea.[9]

Ostriches and Big-Foots

In the sixties and early seventies, funeral directors had largely ignored
cremation. They had Mitford and the FTC to fight and memorial

societies to worry about. At least when it came to cremation, they were deniers: "ostriches," according to one cremation-friendly funeral director. An occasional article in *Mortuary Management* or *American Funeral Director* in the 1970s pointed to the successes of direct cremation providers like Neptune and Telophase and warned funeral directors to "read the writing on the wall." But few heeded that warning. Those who did usually associated cremation with memorial societies and direct disposal. Cremation was "burn and scatter" on the cheap, and they would have nothing to do with it. When customers came to funeral homes insisting on cremation, they were often politely turned away. Not all funeral directors, however, were so gracious. Some pulled out pictures of cremations in progress. "Are you sure you want to burn your mother?" they would ask. "If you love her, you wouldn't dare." Throughout the seventies and into the eighties, funeral directors tried to put direct cremation providers out of business. They lobbied for restrictive regulations and took direct cremation outfits to court. The tactic was to stomp out the problem—"Ostrich" had given way to "Big-Foot."[10]

In 1981 *Mortuary Management* was still reporting that "most funeral directors become choleric when [cremation] is even mentioned." But that same year the National Funeral Directors Association finally weighed in against denial and resistance. In a report entitled "Tradition in Transition," the NFDA wrote, "Many funeral directors have developed a psyche that cremation is synonymous with memorial (bodiless) services and direct disposition, when the consumer may mean it only as an alternative to earth burial or entombment of the body." The report concluded with this advice: "Funeral service in the 1980s and 1990s must *not be against* cremation as a procedure or process in final disposition. Rather, those in funeral service should be *for* post-death rites and ceremonies which have meaning and value to the survivors, no matter what the form of final disposition is."[11]

In the late 1980s the strategies of denial and resistance began to give way to a more accommodative approach. The cremation rate was moving up rapidly, and the incinerations of American icons such as Woody Guthrie, Walt Disney, Janis Joplin, Steve McQueen, Joan Crawford, Groucho Marx, and John Lennon further legitimized the practice. Attitudes of funeral directors changed fastest where cremation was gaining the most ground. In California, where the cremation rate topped 36 percent in 1985, funeral directors were the first to take notice. As CANA data on regional and national cremation rates circulated in the late

1980s, death care providers from burial strongholds began to take heed too. While many still refused to dirty their hands, others began competing with low-cost cremation providers with inexpensive packages of their own. In the eighties, the most common site for crematory installations shifted from the cemetery to the funeral home. More than half a century after cemetery superintendents had made peace with cremation, funeral directors finally joined the competition for the cremation dollar.

At the turn of the millennium many funeral directors continued to insist on the value of the "traditional American funeral" and the embalm-and-bury regime. Some saw cremation as a passing fad. Others, convinced the practice was an anomaly that would never invade their hometowns, remained oblivious to its nationwide advance. "There are many funeral directors who today have two or three dusty urns in a cabinet," Ron Hast, publisher of *Mortuary Management* and the *Funeral Monitor*, said in 1997, "because they see [cremation] as a cheap alternative to what they want to sell," namely, embalming and a casket. Even the NFDA, according to Hast, was "consistently five or more years behind the times." But gradually American funeral directors began to heed the advice of Hast's *Funeral Monitor*, which argued in 1996 that "it is going to be—or already is—a matter of adapting to cremation or finding a new line of work." The "if you can't beat 'em, join 'em" philosophy was catching on.[12]

The New Cremation Marketing

Back in 1874 writers at the *New York Daily Graphic* had predicted American businessmen would find a way to profit from cremation:

> The undertakers to a man
> Should favor the cremation plan,
> Because the more they have to burn,
> 'Tis evident, the more they'll urn [13]

For modern cremation's first U.S. century, however, few funeral directors took that advice. From the Gilded Age to the Progressive Era, funeral directors had alternately ignored and resisted cremation. In the late twenties and early thirties, a few tried to sell it. But not until the nineties did funeral directors truly embrace cremation marketing. In the 1990s ads in the *Director* blared, "Make money the modern way. Urn it!"

The biggest booster of this new approach was Michael Kubasak, the owner of the Valley Funeral Home in trend-setting Burbank, California,

and later a vice president at Service Corporation International (SCI).
The author of *Cremation and the Funeral Director* (1990), the best-
selling funeral service book of the 1990s and the Bible of the new cremation marketing, Kubasak was the Norman Vincent Peale of the death
care industry. "Cremation is not the problem," he wrote. "The problem
is attitude." The "Ostrich" and "Big-Foot" types were Kubasak's brainchild, and he used them to make this point: Instead of trying to hide
from or stomp out cremation, funeral directors should "elevate" it and
profit. "To insure your role as a funeral director in the year two thousand," Kubasak wrote, "you must open your mind to [the cremation]
opportunity." Funeral directors needed to stop thinking of themselves
as casket salesmen and start self-identifying as funeral service providers.
When you hear someone wants cremation, Kubasak said, do not as-
sume they mean "no ceremony, no embalming, no viewing, no casket."
Cremation was "no more than one method of preparing the body for its
ultimate disposition." There was no reason it should be any less
profitable than burial.[14]

Kubasak, who once praised Telophase and Neptune as "great niche
marketers," was very successful himself in "elevating" cremation. His
Valley Funeral Home, which catered to a Catholic clientele, did 101 cremations between 1981 and 1983. Seventy-eight of those (78%) were direct cremations. Of the direct cremations, only 12 percent bought a casket or container, and only 22 percent had a funeral-home-directed
ceremony. Between 1987 and 1989, however, Kubasak did 203 cremations, roughly twice as many as in the earlier period. Only 41 percent of
those were direct. And of the direct cremation customers, 71 percent
bought a casket or container and 69 percent had a ceremony.[15]

Tom Snyder of Joseph Gawler's Sons in Washington, D.C., also
cashed in on cremation. Like others in this new breed of cremation-
friendly funeral directors, Snyder required families to identify deceased
relatives in their chosen cremation casket prior to the cremation. Although this policy began as a way to ward off lawsuits alleging the cremation of mismarked remains, it paid off handsomely in casket sales. In
the late 1980s, before Snyder began working at Gawler's, 95 percent of
the cremations handled there were done in cheap cardboard boxes. But
after children were persuaded to see Mom or Dad in a casket, families
began trading up from undignified cardboard to dignified hardwood.
Gawler's brought in an average of $3,970 per cremation in 1995, up
from only $1,332 in 1990. Over the same period, the ratio of direct cre-
mations to overall cremations shrank from 77 percent to 12 percent.[16]

Out in front of this new cremation-friendly trend were Service Corporation International, the Loewen Group, and Stewart Enterprises, which during the 1990s rapidly consolidated the industry. SCI operated 198 crematories, including Joseph Gawler's Sons, in 1999. It also ran Bleitz Funeral Home, which performed approximately 2,000 cremations a year for the Seattle-based People's Memorial Association, still the nation's largest memorial society.

If articles and ads in trade journals are any indication, the new cremation marketing of Kubasak, Snyder, and the multinationals was becoming the new orthodoxy in the 1990s even among the independent funeral homes unaffiliated with the multinationals. As the *Funeral Monitor* reported in 1992, "some still do resist providing anything but traditional services" and even in California a few Tories continued to deny that the revolution had come. But the holdouts were fast becoming oddballs. In the 1990s the NFDA promoted both Kubasak's book and a video by Snyder called "Marketing for Cremation." *Funeral Service Insider* regularly carried articles with titles like "5 Tips to Creatively Boost Cremation Merchandise $$$," "4 Ways to Make Your Cremation Service Sizzle," "3 Tips to Rev Up Your Cremation Calls (and Stay Profitable)," and "One Quick Tip to Get Your Families beyond a Direct Cremation."[17]
The tips?

Watch business boom after you rent a booth at a county fair.

Make your low-end containers look inexpensive.

Contrast your 20-gauge metal sealer rental casket with your wooden cremation caskets to prevent rental casket sales from cutting into cremation casket sales.

Keep a decorative urn in your arrangement office.... When families say that they don't want an urn, they really mean they don't want something that looks like an urn.

Sell one [urn] around $2,000 so families think your mid-range prices look reasonable.

Don't list cremation products on your general price list from the most expensive to the least expensive, as you might with burial products. This turns off cremation families, who aren't easily "merchandised." Instead, list them from least expensive to most expensive.[18]

What is interesting about these hints is how precisely they matched the sales tactics of funeral directors satirized by Mitford in 1963. "Cre-

mation families" might not be easily merchandised, but it was not for
lack of trying. Like the casket pushers lampooned in *The American Way
of Death,* the cremation-savvy funeral directors, crematory operators,
and cemetery managers of the 1990s worked hard to sell their products
and services. They even constructed their own "cremationese." At least
in the presence of the "cremation family," they spoke of "preparation"
instead of "embalming," "cremation containers" instead of "caskets,"
and "ceremonial caskets" not rentals. "Ashes," an inoffensive term in
Great Britain, was *verboten* in the United States. ("I find the word
'ashes' reprehensible," Tom Snyder said.) The word "funeral" was
taboo too, since marketing surveys indicated the "cremation family"
found funerals odious. ("Memorial ceremony" was the refined alternative.) In addition to emphasizing customer-friendly terms, cremation
marketeers coined new ones, including "cremains." One term bidding
for the imprimatur of U.S. lexicographers at the end of the millennium
("cremains" was already in most American dictionaries) was "cremo-
rial," which Matthews International Corporation liked so much it
trademarked it.[19]

Options

Underlying these neologisms were two clear pitches. The first was a revival of a theme that had been circulating among cremationists since the
popularization of the "memorial idea" in the twenties: "cremation as a
preparation for memorialization." All the major death care providers
preached what SCI's Gary O'Sullivan called "the power of memorialization." "Cremation with memorialization" was also a frequent refrain
at the Cremation Association of North America, where "Cremation Is
Not the End...It Is Preparation for Memorialization" was one of the
top-selling pamphlets.[20]

The second, more contemporary pitch can be summed up in one
word: options. In an attempt to cater to the desire of baby boomers for
personalized alternatives, the death care industry emphasized choice. A
popular CANA pamphlet in the nineties was called "Choices" and
another, "Cremation Memorial Options." A new business in Ponte
Vedra Beach, Florida, called itself the Alternative Choice Cremation
Society, Inc. In 1993 the Batesville Casket Company inaugurated a
popular cremation campaign called Options® by Batesville. Advertisements for another company's line of cremation caskets and urns read,
"Cremation. It's all a matter of preference."

In the 1960s there had been roughly a dozen urns on the market—a few each in bronze, wood, and marble. All were roughly in the shape of a cube. Most were sold by crematories and cemeteries because many funeral directors refused to handle them. In the 1990s, however, urns literally came out of the closet. "Everybody and their brother's selling urns," said Pat Jones of Jones Funeral Home in Dixon, Illinois, about the exhibit halls at a 1990s NFDA convention. "It's a sign of the times." Virtually every funeral home had an urn catalog on hand, and many proudly displayed their inventory in well-lit cremation cabinets. Some forward-thinking funeral directors opened "cremation selection rooms" devoted exclusively to cremation merchandising. A few turned over entire buildings—"cremation centers"—to serving cremation customers.[21]

The array of urns was as dizzying as the army of caskets Mitford confronted in the early sixties, and those urns were as oddly named and as crassly marketed. The cube was still standard, but thanks to the new "mass customization" trend you could have that cube personalized with an emblem of, say, the Rotary Club and engraved with your loved one's name and favorite quote. Not all urns came in cubes, however. Hepburn Industries of Orange, California, offered models shaped like Japanese pagodas, Egyptian temples, closed books, and open books. Doric's Presidential Cremation Urn Series had Truman, Adams, and Washington urns in wood; Wilson, Johnson, Cleveland, and Hayes urns in bronze; and Tyler, Harrison, and Jackson urns in cultured marble. (For some reason, Chester Arthur, one of the nation's least distinguished chief executives, merited commemoration in both wood and bronze.) Kelco Supply Company, the industry's biggest direct mail supplier, offered a walnut urn shaped like a golf bag. (Advertised as termite-proof, it was guaranteed to remain "intact for many generations.") There were 300-cubic-inch urns for large people and 200-cubic-inch urns for standard-sized people. There were biodegradable urns for environmentally correct people, urns for children (among them, the "Huggable Memories" teddy bear urn), urns for members of the Army, Navy, Air Force, Marine Corps, and Coast Guard, and a "Lambda Triangle" urn for gays and lesbians. One of the most popular models on the market was also one of the most expensive: a bronze leaping dolphin urn by Batesville Casket Company marketed to the environmentally aware. Retail price? Around $2000.

For those who were willing to divide their ashes, the options multiplied. Small keepsake urns allowed families to split up ashes or to retain a portion after scattering. Matthews International Corporation offered models shaped like ocean waves, lighthouses, and pine trees—all designed, like Batesville's dolphin, to appeal to the eco-friendly. Companion Star of Hinsdale, Illinois, could embed up to one-third of your ashes into a one-of-a-kind piece of blown glass art. Madelyn Company made twenty-four-karat heart-shaped keepsake pendants. This was big business (Madelyn's pendants retailed for $950), but not everyone treated it seriously. "Have you heard about this cremation jewelry?" *Tonight* show host Jay Leno joked. "What do you do, wake up in the morning and ask, 'Who should I wear today—Aunt Grace or Uncle Joe?'"[22]

In addition to this menu of urns, there were cremation containers and urn vaults to consider. There were also competing columbaria. The Gibraltar Mausoleum Construction Company had a model "built to last an afterlifetime," and Oregon Brassworks marketed an "Eco-Niche." At Robert Schuller's Crystal Cathedral in Garden Grove, California, you could have your ashes placed in an outdoor mosaic or a stained glass window for $2,400 to $5,000. Warrensburg Memorial Gardens in Warrensburg, Missouri, had a bronze columbarium that doubled as a sundial—"light, like the sun."

Scattering cremains was also big business, and here too options were the order of the day. Despite intense opposition from "memorial idea" cremationists since at least the twenties, scattering seems to have been practiced in a little over half of cremation cases in the nineties. A survey published in *Cremationist* in 1996, for example, found that over 50 percent of cremation customers preferred scattering. Increasingly over the course of the 1990s cremated remains were scattered not only on private estates but also in public venues such as race tracks and national parks. In fact, wildcat scattering was so popular that Disney World and Wrigley Field (the home of the Chicago Cubs baseball team) found it necessary to ban it. In 1996 an AIDS activist from the group ACT UP tossed an urn containing ashes over the wrought-iron fence at the White House to protest President Clinton's AIDS policies. But unlike their predecessors earlier in the century, crematory operators and suppliers did not try to browbeat customers out of scattering. Instead they offered "scattering urns." ("Regardless of where they choose to scatter," read an ad from Wilbert, Inc., "offer them a place to hold the memories.") And scattering services. Afterlife Adventures, Inc., of Austin, Texas, for example, scattered ashes "by hot air balloon, plane, boat, or by hand" at sites as far-flung as Key West ($395), Niagara Falls ($475), the Grand Canyon ($475), and Kauai, Hawaii ($650). For a modest fee,

Jay Knudsen of Canuck's Sportsman's Memorials, Inc., in Des Moines, Iowa, would load your ashes into a shotgun shell, then pick off a duck or a deer. He also stuffed cremated remains into fishing lures, duck decoys, and golf clubs. "We can't get you to heaven," he said. "But we promise to land you in the happy hunting ground." Even Boston's august Mt. Auburn Cemetery got into the scattering business, opening a woodland garden for scattering cremated remains in the 1990s.[23]

Then there was the memorial (or "cremorial®") to consider. While many cremation consumers continued to buck the new cremation marketing by insisting on remembering their loved ones only in their hearts (or, increasingly, on the Internet), death care merchandisers sold memorial benches, bronze plaques, and even tree memorials. Batesville planted a tree for free for every urn it sold through funeral directors in its Options® by Batesville program. In 1990 a Texas entrepreneur got a patent for a "tree forest cemetery" consisting of rows of pines planted over urn vaults.[24]

From the time of Baron De Palm through the Great Depression cremationists had promoted their practice as an inexpensive alternative to burial. They gave up that refrain for a time, only to see it resurrected, thanks to Mitford and the consumer movement, in the 1960s. But according to CANA's Jack Springer, cremation in the 1990s had "nothing to do with what you spend." After all, in Japan, where cremation was nearly universal, the average funeral bill was over $10,000. The difference between the 1950s and the 1990s, said Springer, was that in the 1990s "the money [was] being spent post- rather than pre-." While the extended wake and the lavish pre-burial funeral were going the way of the black crape, post-cremation spending on memorial ceremonies, urns, columbarium niches, and scattering was brisk. The typical cremation customer was affluent, not poor, and more than willing to spend money to see loved ones go out in style.[25]

Personalization and the Fun Funeral

The target market for all these cremation options was, of course, the baby boom generation, which by the end of the millennium had elevated to the status of scripture the mantra of keeping your options open. Americans born during the postwar baby boom of 1946 to 1964 were, as a rule, well-educated, individualistic, wary of authority, and worried about the environment. Together they ushered in a new era in American ritual life, an era in which the ritual norms of the Gilded Age were soundly defeated. While Catholics, inspired by the liturgical "up-dating" of Vatican II, were strumming acoustic guitars in folk masses across the United States, baby boomers of all faiths were embracing a new style of ritual, characterized by simplicity, spontaneity, informality, flexibility, improvisation, participation, and (above all) personalization. In the process, they devised new birth rites, new wedding rites, new divorce rites, and new death rites. In all those new rituals, lay people seized authority from medical, funerary, and religious experts.

In the fifties the bereaved had typically deferred to the authority of funeral directors. The result was a "one size fits all" funeral. Beginning in the sixties Americans began to question that authority. Many families began to act as their own funeral directors. The result was a radical democratization and diversification in American ways of death. Father Henry Wasielewski, a Catholic priest and one of the nineties' most outspoken critics of the funeral industry, was such an advocate of family-run rites that he refused to refer to funeral directors as "funeral directors." ("Body deliverymen," he called them.) The family, he said, was the funeral director. This do-it-yourself trend reached its apogee in *Caring for the Dead: Your Final Act of Love* (1998) by Lisa Carlson, executive director of Funeral and Memorial Societies of America (FAMSA). Part consumer manifesto, part do-it-yourself manual, *Caring for the Dead* cast the funeral directors and death care conglomerates as the bad guys and hoped for a world in which family members would feel free to direct their own postmortem ceremonies. Frustrating that hope, however, was the unwillingness of funeral industry representatives to play the supporting roles Carlson and Wasielewski assigned to them.[26]

Funeral directors once saw it as their sacred duty to steer customers to what they condescendingly knew was best. By the time the century was drawing to a close, however, such paternalism had gone the way of the arranged marriage. Forward-thinking funeral directors now worked willingly with bereaved families to orchestrate rites that spoke not to the generic fact of death but to the idiosyncratic personality of the individual deceased. As a result, cookie-cutter funerals gave way to customized memorial services and the "fun funeral." These new services diverged widely from both standard funeral home practice and from the time-honored liturgies of Christian and Jewish clerics. Often they took place not in churches or funeral homes but at a favorite windsurfing spot or along a well-worn hiking trail. Mourners, rather than sitting passively by, were encouraged to participate actively by playing a favorite pop song or reading an original poem. And no one got too dressed up, not even the corpse. While the traditional funeral aimed to patch up a community torn asunder by death, the goal of these alternative rites was to celebrate an individual life. For themselves and their parents, baby boomers demanded rites that were cheerful rather than gloomy, plain rather than gaudy, private rather than public, informal rather than formal, personal rather than impersonal, improvised rather than traditional. And by the 1990s funeral directors were increasingly trying to accommodate those demands.

Book publishers, too, got in on this customization trend, rushing into print handbooks such as *Rituals for Living and Dying* (1990), *Final Celebrations* (1992), *Creating Meaningful Funeral Ceremonies* (1994), *The Parting: Celebrate a Life by Planning a Meaningful, Creative Funeral* (1996), *In Memoriam: A Practical Guide to Planning a Memorial Service* (1997), and *To Comfort and to Honor: A Guide to Personalized Rituals for the Passing of a Loved One* (1998)—all filled with suggestions for do-it-yourself funerals. Also popular were anthologies of prayers and eulogies for customized death rites and denominational guidebooks for planning funerals, among them *Planning a Funeral Service: A Guide to Planning a Funeral in the Episcopal Church* (1998) and *The Pagan Book of Living and Dying: Practical Rituals, Prayers, Blessings, and Meditations on Crossing Over* (1997). In *Dealing Creatively with Death* (1994), a book which had gone through thirteen editions by the end of the millennium, memorial society advocate Ernest Morgan included a variety of sample death ceremonies. He suggested readings by Kahlil Gibran and Rabindranath Tagore and wrote approvingly of a memorial walk through a golf course held to celebrate the life of an avid golfer.[27]

Monument makers, too, catered to baby boomers' needs to be remembered as unique. Where once tombstone makers engraved, by the gross, generic epitaphs like "Sweet rest in heaven" or "Not dead, but sleeping," in the 1990s these craftsmen were carving, one at a time, personalized expressions like "World's greatest truck driver," "High jumping in heaven," or (for a diamond cutter's wife) "She was a gem." There was a brisk trade too in odd-shaped tombstones. One headstone maker carved a beer mug and another a Harley-Davidson.[28]

While the desire for personalization was strong with burials, it was dominant in the cremation marketplace. When Ernest Malcolm Frimbo, "the world's greatest railroad buff," died in 1981, he had reportedly traveled nearly three million miles by rail. So his ashes were scattered over the tracks at Cumbres Pass, Colorado, the highest spot in the United States traversed by Frimbo's beloved narrow-gauge passenger trains. Baseball fans had their ashes scattered at the hallowed shrines of Yankee Stadium and Fenway Park. After a Grateful Dead fan died in a car crash, his family distributed sixty individually made Companion Star memorial stones to his closest friends. One year later, those friends gathered at a rock concert, relics in hand, to remember their lost friend in dance and song.

Some ritual innovations tested the bounds of good taste and ritual propriety. In Orlando, Florida, the ashes of a fireworks expert were blasted along with roman candles into the night sky. The cremated remains of a Marvel Comics editor were mixed with ink and made into a comic book, Villa Delirium Delftworks made cremains into commemorative plates, and another firm (Eternal Reefs, Inc.) offered to turn ashes into "ecologically sound" coral reefs. In 1993 someone took out a patent for a "Personalized Face Cremation Urn." Five years later, a minor controversy erupted when NASA sent a portion of the ashes of a deceased space scientist to the moon in a lunar probe. (Navajo Indians objected, arguing that human remains should not be deposited on the sacred soil of the moon.) Observers differed on whether these innovations were in good taste, but there was little doubt that the American way of cremation crafted in the bricks and mortar period had now fragmented into multiple ways of cremation.[29]

Re-Ritualization

Funeral directors cited stories like these as proof of their view that cremation was unceremonious and irreligious, and at least a few scholars were convinced. But in the late twentieth century, U.S. cremation provided little evidence for secularization or de-ritualization. In fact, ceremony seemed to be the rule, not the exception, in cremation cases. Admittedly, many cremation rites were informal and nontraditional and proceeded with little or no professional assistance, but the vast majority included more than a nod to spiritual matters.[30]

A 1990 Notre Dame study found that people who chose cremation were less likely than people choosing burial to have a service in a funeral home or a church. But they were almost twice as likely to have a service in a private home, and roughly three times as likely to hold a memorial service. A 1995 national telephone survey of American attitudes toward ritualization and memorialization found that 83 percent of the survey sample that preferred cremation wanted some kind of end-of-life ceremony. Thirty-three percent said they wanted a traditional public funeral service, while 23 percent said they wanted a private service and 23 percent, a memorial service. Yet another study found five types of American cremation ritualization. The most common was cremation followed by a traditional ceremony (defined as public and formal), urn burial, and the placing of some sort of memorial marker. A second pattern, nearly as popular, also included a traditional ceremony and a marker, but ended with scattering. The most secular of the five types—cremation with scattering but no traditional ceremony and no marker—was also the least common. And even in those uncommon cases some sort of informal ceremony may well have been the rule.[31]

Both formal and informal ritualizing can take place at the scattering site, at the urn burial site, at the site of the memorial marker, and at the site where the inurned ashes are placed in a columbarium, home mantel, or safe deposit box. The Reverend Mary Faith Nesmith, a Lutheran minister in Norcross, Georgia, has prayed with a parishioner while placing a spouse's ashes inside a safe-deposit box. Members of the Wampanoag Nation on Cape Cod, Massachusetts, have prayerfully floated the sacred ashes of tribe members into the Atlantic Ocean in clay urns shaped like conches. And a pilot with an air scattering service in California has reported that family members often ride up with him to say a last goodbye to their loved ones. Frequently he is asked to offer a prayer before he jettisons his cargo. "The most popular," he says, "is the Lord's Prayer or Psalm 23."[32]

Further evidence for the persistence of cremation ritualization was the increasing popularity of ceremonies at crematoria. During the nineteenth century, crematory rites were the rule rather than the exception, but over the course of the twentieth century the crematory (or at least the furnace room) was gradually secularized. Peepholes were covered up; families were ushered, first, to balconies overlooking the retorts and later, to crematory chapels out of view of the furnaces. Eventually families were encouraged to forego the crematory entirely—to celebrate their loved ones' lives instead at the funeral home or along the seashore. In this way, the crematory became, for the most part, a secular site with a technological purpose: transforming corpses into bone fragments. In the eighties and nineties, however, the crematory was progressively re-ritualized. Despite the fact that it remained illegal in at least six states for funeral homes to own and operate crematories, approximately 70 percent of the new crematories installed at the end of the century were placed in funeral homes. Increasingly, the crematory was moving, as

CANA's Jack Springer noted, "out of the back lot and the garage into the funeral home itself." In the process, crematory rituals were becoming more practical and more common. Many of the crematories built in the 1990s allowed both for pre-cremation ceremonies on site and for witnessing the cremation itself.

Although witnessing was not yet the nationwide rule, it was standard practice for many Asian Americans, who often conducted rituals at the crematory. Immigration from Asia was severely limited by the Chinese Exclusion Act of 1882 and by the Asian Exclusion Act of 1924, but it was reopened after the passage of new immigration legislation in 1965. Many of these post-1965 immigrants came from cremation-friendly countries in South, Southeast, and East Asia. Together they boosted U.S. cremation rates. They also boosted crematory ritualization. Immigrants from India, for example, adapted to American circumstances the ancient tradition in which a son lights the funeral pyre by assigning that son the task of pressing the start button on the crematory retort. And the insistence of Vietnamese Americans on viewing cremations prompted at least a few crematories to construct viewing rooms adjacent to their retorts. "Witnessing," said Springer, "is a coming trend."[33]

Michael Kubasak likes to tell the story of the Swiss watch industry as a cautionary tale. In 1968, according to Kubasak, the Swiss commanded 70 percent of the world's watch market sales and 90 percent of its profits, but by 1980 the Swiss market share had crashed to under 10 percent of sales and less than 20 percent of profits. What intervened was Japan and the electronic watch. When the watch industry underwent its revolution, the Swiss were left behind. Their big mistake was not listening to their customers. "People weren't saying they didn't want watches," Kubasak says, "they were saying they wanted the new kind of watch." His point is that the death care industry is undergoing a similar revolution—from burial to cremation—and that funeral directors would be smart to imitate the Japanese rather than the Swiss. But the story can be interpreted differently. In the nineties, many funeral directors and cemeterians looked at cremation customers, especially baby boomers, and assumed they were uninterested in religion. What they did not understand was that these customers were not saying they did not want religion; they were saying they wanted religion of a different sort.[34]

Consider the status of religion in the United States, which at the turn of the millennium was undergoing a subtle shift of its own. In the eighties and nineties Americans, and especially baby boomers, increasingly saw "organized religion" as something to avoid. But they were not becoming more secular. "I'm not religious, I'm spiritual" was an oft-heard refrain, and what it meant was that many Americans preferred to get their religion (or, as they called it, their spirituality) outside the confines of the mainline Protestant churches and Jewish synagogues—in yoga and meditation classes, on walks in the mountains, and in a host of groups frequently filed under the heading of "New Age." Sociologist Robert Wuthnow has described this trend as a shift from the "dwelling-oriented spirituality" of the communitarian fifties to the "seeker spirituality" of the individualistic sixties and beyond. And sociologists of all sorts are increasingly coming to see this development as evidence not for secularization but for religious transformation.[35]

These changes in American religion were not unrelated to changes in American ways of death. All across the United States citizens were seizing authority from previously revered experts. In churches, synagogues, and temples the laity were following less and leading more. Death rites too were democratized and personalized, diverging not only from the "traditional American funeral" but also from the earlier American way of cremation in directions that a generation earlier would have been unimaginable. But death was not becoming more secular in the process. In fact, the shift from the undertaker- or priest-directed funeral to the family-directed rite might be seen as an effort to infuse rites that according to many had gone stale through repetition and formalism with new spiritual significance. In the 1830s and 1840s Transcendentalists such as Ralph Waldo Emerson had left the Unitarian churches because they found ministers and services there "corpse-cold." But they did not leave religion behind. They simply sought it out in new places—in the poetic longings of their own hearts and the transient beauties of nature. And in the process, they created new, creole beliefs and practices.

In late-twentieth-century America there were cremations where the family called a funeral director and told him to pick up the body, cremate it, get rid of the ashes, and send them the bill. But that sort of cremation—one cemetery manager has called it "helter-skelter scattering"—was rare in the seventies, and rarer still in the nineties. Late-twentieth-century cremationists were not saying they did not want death rites. And they were not saying they did not want religion either. What these customers wanted were new death rites—rites that were informal, flexible, simple, improvised, participatory, family-directed, and personalized. But funeral directors, rather than offering them the funerary equivalent of the lay-led, post–Vatican II folk mass, offered instead something akin to the priest-led Latin mass with all the bells and smells. No wonder families were striking out on their own.[36]

Freed from the outdated traditions of the funeral home and from the conventions of the American way of cremation crafted during the bricks and mortar period, cremation families developed their own idiosyncratic rites—chanting Buddhism's Lotus Sutra as they cast the ashes of a loved one along with lotus leaves into Boston's Charles River, or constructing walking memorial pilgrimages that began with a poem at a dead woman's birth home and ended when her ashes were deposited in the rose garden outside the vacation cabin where she died. Some of these ceremonies employed religious or funerary professionals. Many did not. Unlike traditional burials, cremation ceremonies were often family-run. Occasionally they took place outside the confines of a church or synagogue. But like the De Palm cremation of 1876, these ceremonies were infused with spiritual purpose and ritualization. In lieu of a reading from the Bible, they might include the wisdom of Walt Whitman or Gautama Buddha. In lieu of a sermon, family members might say something about the deceased and something to comfort the bereaved. Instead of lowering a casket into a grave, family members might strew the ashes down the side of a mountain, or even run them around a racetrack. Without a doubt, many of these ceremonies diverged significantly from both standard funeral home practice and from the time-honored liturgical formulations of Christianity and Judaism, but they were, by most accounts, meaningful spiritual experiences for those who created and attended them.

As cremationists crafted these new rites, they also drew on alternative philosophies and theologies of death and the afterlife, body and self. Like the Spiritualists and Theosophists of the nineteenth century, many Americans in the 1990s saw cremation as a way to purify the spirit and release it from the worn-out body—as "a spiritually clean way of releasing the spirit from a lifeless shell." Others—Asian immigrants and Buddhist and Hindu converts alike—rooted their understandings of cremation in the teachings of Tibetan Buddhism or Hinduism's Upanishads. Phyllis Janik, the CEO of designer urn company Companion Star and for twenty-five years a practitioner of Hindu-style meditation, saw the cremation option as a way to articulate religious and scientific truths: that matter becomes energy and then matter again, and that life and death move in cycles. Literary critic Harold Bloom may or may not have been right when he claimed that American religion had become a democratized gnosticism, affirming the Greek view

of the self as soul and the body as disposable husk or prison. But cremationists seemed to be making this point: I am not my body; I am
spirit, soul.[37]

Small Is Beautiful

There are a number of reasons for cremation's popularity in late-
twentieth-century America. In *Western Attitudes toward Death* (1974),
historian Philippe Ariès wrote that cremation's popularity in the West
was part of a "brutal revolution" in deathways. Following the English
sociologist Geoffrey Gorer, who in an influential article in 1955 argued
that death had replaced sex as the great taboo, Ariès contended that
death had become forbidden in the modern West. "Denial of death"
was the rule, and cremation was the "most radical" means of accom-
plishing it. Ariès was right to view the rise of cremation in light of shifting attitudes. But he was wrong to link cremation so closely with death
denial. Admittedly, cremation (especially direct cremation) was for
some Americans a way to avoid confronting the reality of death. But on
the whole, cremation was unfriendly to denial. In the American way of
burial and embalming, the dead could still be said to be sleeping. Moreover, because the body remained intact, at least for a time, so could the
illusion of life. Cremation, by contrast, was more stoic, more insistent
on the real. In cremation the body was quickly reduced to ashes, and the
delivery of cremated remains into the hands of family members made
denial close to impossible. Cremation took off in America, in fact, as
the historical period Ariès identifies as "forbidden death" was waning.
In the United States at the start of the twenty-first century, death had become, at best, a poorly kept secret. Far from taboo, it was ubiquitous—
lurking on local news shows, the Internet, television miniseries, and
Hollywood movies. Cremation's American success can probably be attributed more to the eclipse of "forbidden death" in the 1960s than to
lingering effects of the denial of death.[38]

If we cannot attribute cremation's rise to the denial of death, what
might be the causes? In 1998 the Cremation Association of North
America identified "eight key trends affecting cremation":

People are dying older.

Migration to retirement locations is increasing.

Cremation is becoming more acceptable as a normal form of disposition.

Environmental considerations are becoming more important.

Level of education is rising.

Ties to tradition are becoming weaker.

Regional differences are diminishing.

Origin of immigrants is changing.

Tellingly, CANA did not include economic considerations in this list. Despite Jessica Mitford's emphasis on consumer calculations, the cremation decision was, at least in the period after 1963, strangely unaffected by financial factors. Like Mitford herself, cremation customers tended to be affluent. Many could easily afford a steel casket and a traditional funeral. They simply did not want to see their loved ones buried.[39]

Undoubtedly, many of the demographic factors highlighted by CANA contributed to cremation's growth. People were dying older, and older people are far more likely to be cremated, in part because they are, in anthropological parlance, socially dead long before their hearts stop beating. Cremation was popular in retirement areas because it allows for easy shipment of remains for burial in a hometown cemetery. Immigration, especially from Asian countries where cremation is the rule, also boosted the cremation rate.

Environmental concerns also played a role. In 1888, at a dedication ceremony for a Cincinnati crematory, Samuel Bernstein had argued that enough land had been given over to cemeteries. "The land reformer's cry of 'no more land to railroad syndicates, no more land to speculators, no more land to aliens,'" he wrote (echoing the populists and nativists of his time), "should for all time be supplemented by the still louder cry throughout this fair land, of 'no more land to the dead.'" Little did Bernstein know that he was sounding a chord—"Save the Land for the Living"—that would become a tag line for cremation in the twentieth century. The aesthetic turn in American cremation in the bricks and mortar period positioned cremation as ecologically friendly. That connection became more salient in the 1970s, when the U.S. Congress passed a series of environmental laws, including the Clean Air Act. So it should not be entirely surprising that in a 1990 telephone study an oft-cited reason for cremation was the fact that it "saves land." Nevertheless, environmental concerns were not the key driver of cremation rates in the period after 1963. Neither were economic considerations or demographic or immigration shifts.[40]

In the last third of the twentieth century the decision to cremate was
largely driven by style. Since the time of the Puritans, when death was
seen as both reward and punishment, Americans have been ambivalent
about death rites. In death, as in life, they have not wanted to make too
much of a fuss over themselves. At the same time, they have wanted to
be remembered, ideally in perpetuity. If not for themselves, then at least
for their mothers and fathers they have wanted a fine funeral. And so
American ways of death have swung back and forth between austerity
and ostentation, the plain and the gaudy.

Among the earliest colonists simplicity reigned. In keeping with the
hostility of the Protestant Reformers to Catholic "superstition," the Puritans were determined to root out ritual. And in their theological uni-
verse—where an absolutely sovereign God predestined totally depraved
humans to heaven or hell according to His own caprice—death rites
served no spiritual purpose. At least at the grave, the first generation of
New England Puritans read no scripture, listened to no sermons. Funerals were secular occasions where clergy played no official part;
graveyards were town, not church, property; and the dead seem to have
been buried without coffins, directly into the ground. Later generations
of Puritans rebelled against this austerity, however. As the Puritan pioneers—America's first heroes –died off, the coffin was introduced, as
were mourning ribbons, horse-drawn hearses, funeral sermons, and
grave markers. According to historian David Stannard, "it was not uncommon for funeral expenses to consume 20 percent of the deceased's
estate," much of it spent on hard alcohol. This new opulence, in turn,
produced its own reaction. In the early eighteenth century New En-
glanders passed a number of bills aimed at reducing funeral expenses,
and Puritan divines spoke out against postmortem drunkenness. By
1785, when Samuel Mather of the influential Massachusetts Mather
clan died, simplicity once again triumphed. Mather asked for "no funeral Encomiums" and was buried in a simple coffin.[41]

The pendulum swung back toward ostentation in the nineteenth century as America embraced Romanticism and then Victorian culture. In
this period, which spanned an era historian Gary Laderman has named
"simplicity lost," mourning was taken to sometimes hysterical extremes.
Yet as the hard Calvinism of the Puritans yielded to the softer evangeli-
calism of the revivalists, both religion and death were sentimentalized. In
the new rural cemeteries, which epitomized the new ostentation (most
notably in garish statuary), death was celebrated as beautiful, lingered
over as sublime. New embalming techniques, perfected after the Civil

War, extended the period of mourning, and new metal coffins upped the ante for dying. In the last quarter of the nineteenth century cremationists and other funeral reformers (Mark Twain among them) mocked both the Victorian funeral and its new purveyors, the undertakers. They converted few Americans to their style of simplicity, however. Throughout the Gilded Age and the Progressive Era excess still ruled.[42]

World War I and World War II extended this era of ostentation. In the post-Depression period of rapid economic expansion, coffins—like cars—became bigger, sleeker, and more expensive. The task of lampooning this latest revival of the gaudy fell now not on Twain but on Mitford, who was a far more successful missionary for simplicity than her Gilded Age forebears. In the 1990s Americans still seemed to be living in an age of Mitford. *The American Way of Death Revisited* came out in 1998, and in that same year a new generation of American consumers embraced a redesigned VW Bug.

Cremation benefited tremendously from this aesthetic turn. The secret of cremation's end-of-the-century success was not that it was cheap but that it was not tawdry. Its growth was fueled both by migration of the counterculture into the mainstream and by the migration of foreign cultures (especially Asian ones) into the United States. But high culture was as much a factor in cremation's success as foreign culture or the counterculture—the Episcopalians and the Unitarians as much as the Buddhists and Timothy Leary. By the end of the century cremation had come into its own. Cremation was stylish, in short, because simplicity was once again fashionable, preached now not by the Mathers or by Twain but by Martha Stewart, who in an eponymous magazine and television show preached a revival of the Puritan (and Mitfordian) values of prudence, self-reliance, authenticity, and simplicity. But as the history of American death rites demonstrates, simplicity will have its ups and down. Martha Stewart, once revered (at least among the high-culture set) as a saint, received her comeuppance in an unauthorized biography called *Just Desserts* (1998). Some day, the style of simplicity will once again get its comeuppance too.

By the end of the century there were already some signs that such a new era had arrived. The eighties, like the fifties, were years of consumer-driven excess—in author Tom Wolfe's phrase a "bonfire of the vanities." So also, the late nineties seemed to give birth to a new cultural preoccupation with bigness. As if to say that size really did matter, at least at the end of the millennium, Americans drove sport utility vehicles, patronized superstores, and super-sized their fries. There were some signs, too, that Americans were growing weary of ritual informality. A generation of Catholics, reared on groovy priests and Bob Dylan-inspired folk masses, began to demand a more traditional liturgy (and a more hierarchical relationship with their clerics). Some self-styled ritual experts began to question whether personalized wedding vows and customized cremation ceremonies were veering dangerously close to kitsch. Yes, the cremation rate rose throughout the eighties and nineties, but its rate of growth slowed considerably. And the memorial society movement, which seems to have peaked around the time the FTC began enforcing its new funeral rule in 1984, by the end of the 1990s was nothing like the force it once had been.[43]

Ironically, the age of Mitford may have come to an end with the death of Mitford herself. After she died of cancer at the age of seventy-eight on July 23, 1996, at her Oakland home, Mitford's friends became her funeral directors. They conducted her last rites with a combination of sardonic wit and consumer savvy that would have made Mitford proud. Pacific Interment Service, Inc., performed a "simple, no-embalming, no frills" cremation in a $15.45 cremation container. But in a wry wink at the suits at the NFDA, Mitford's memorial service employed an antique hearse pulled by six black horses to convey her remains through the eminently public space of San Francisco's Embarcadero district, all to the festive strains of a twelve-piece brass band.[44]

Still, cremation seemed poised to endure. Throughout its hundred-year American history, the practice had proven extremely resilient. It endured scorn in the Gilded Age and neglect in the early twentieth century, and despite age-old associations with unconventional religions and offbeat personalities, it gradually earned a place as a legitimate alternative to burial. Promoted at its birth by genteel reformers and during its bricks and mortar period by practical crematory businessmen, it boomed after 1963, thanks to support among baby boomers and Asian Americans, and to the entrepreneurial smarts of direct cremation providers like the Neptune and Telophase societies. In the process, it mutated from a public health necessity into a personal choice—from an urgent sanitary reform into a consumer option. Cremationists' own perceptions of their favored death rite shifted too. The genteel cremationists of the nineteenth century saw cremation as a pure alternative to the pollution of burial, and for them cremation was pure in both the sanitary and the spiritual sense. But as the hygienic arguments against burial were proven to be unfounded and gentility came to be associated with conventionality and hypocrisy, cremationists reconceived their reform. Now the problem with burial was pomp and circumstance, and cremation's key benefits were its naturalness and simplicity. Cremation, supporters said, avoided the extravagance of burial and the sham of embalming. Moreover, when combined with the broader cultural shift toward do-it-yourself rites, it also allowed for greater personalization. Cremation, in short, allowed baby boomers to do death in their own way.

Unless cremation's American future diverges radically from its American past, new critics will no doubt arise, denouncing the beliefs and practices of contemporary cremationists as irreligious and unceremonious. One such critic, in a book called *The Last Passage: Recovering a Death of Our Own* (1999), has already blasted the cremation rites of U.S. memorial societies—"bodiless rituals" he calls them—as unduly fixated on price and insufficiently attentive to ritual process. If the past is in any sense prologue, however, America's new ways of cremation will be rich in spiritual significance and ritual action. In the future, as in the past, cremation will probably continue to be buffeted about by business concerns, but it is almost certain to continue to be a religious demonstration. As such, it will contribute not only to the history of American ritual life but also to American religious diversity.

Timeline

1874   Sir Henry Thompson's "The Treatment of the Body after Death" appears in *Contemporary Review* (in London and New York).

The New York Cremation Society is formed.

Free religionist O. B. Frothingham delivers the first pro-cremation sermon in the United States in Lyric Hall in New York City.

Frank Leslie's Illustrated Weekly puts a cremation story on its front page.

Cremation hoaxes are reported in Philadelphia and Atlanta.

A minstrel show called *Cremation: An Ethiopian Sketch* opens on Broadway.

Monseigneur Gaume's *The Christian Cemetery in the Nineteenth Century: or, The Last War Cry of the Communists*, an anti-cremation tract originally produced in France, is translated into English and published in New York.

Boston Public Library publishes a cremation bibliography.

1876   In the first "modern and scientific" cremation in North America, Baron De Palm is incinerated at a private crematory on the estate of Dr. Francis Julius LeMoyne in Washington, Pennsylvania.

The undertakers' journal, *The Casket* (later *Casket and Sunnyside*), begins publication.

1877   Dr. Charles F. Winslow is cremated in Salt Lake City, Utah.

1878   Mrs. Ben Pitman becomes the first woman to be cremated in the United States.

1879   Dr. LeMoyne is cremated at his facility in Washington, Pennsylvania.

    The Western Undertaker (later *The American Funeral Director*) begins publication.

1881   The New York Cremation Society is reconstituted and the United States Cremation Company is organized.

1882   The Funeral Directors' National Association of the United States (later the National Funeral Directors Association) is established.

    Dr. Robert Koch's experiments with the tubercle bacillus prove the applicability of germ theory to disease.

1884   Lancaster Cremation and Funeral Reform Society is founded in a merger of the concerns of funeral reform and cremation.

    The first U.S. crematory for public use is dedicated in Lancaster, Pennsylvania.

    Dr. Samuel D. Gross, one of the country's most noted surgeons, is cremated.

1886   Pope Leo XIII forbids Catholics from joining cremation societies or cremating their corpses.

    American Medical Association passes but later tables a resolution recommending cremation as "a sanitary necessity in all populous cities."

    Modern Cremation, the country's first pro-cremation journal, begins publication.

1887   The "flower funeral" of the Reverend Henry Ward Beecher demonstrates a shift in American death rites away from doom and gloom and toward sweetness and light.

    The Association of the American Cemetery Superintendents (AACS) is founded.

1889   A new facility at Swinburne Island outside New York City becomes the first state-run crematory in the United States. It is designed to cremate recent immigrants who died in quarantine of infectious diseases.

1892   The Central Conference of American Rabbis, a Reform Jewish organization, passes a resolution stating that cremation is not anti-Jewish and permitting its rabbis to officiate at cremations.

1895	The International Order of the Odd Fellows opens a San Francisco crematory. This facility's columbarium will later become one of the most frequently visited sites in the city and its crematory the busiest in the country.
1896	*The Columbarium* ceases publication, signaling the end of the Gilded Age cremation debate.
1900	Mount Auburn Cemetery, the country's most famous rural cemetery, opens a crematory.
1913	The Cremation Association of America (later the Cremation Association of North America) is founded.
1914–18	World War I claims the lives of over 100,000 Americans and refocuses Americans' attention on death and mourning.
1917	Forest Lawn, the country's leading example of the memorial park style, opens in Glendale, California.
1920s	The U.S. cremation rate (ratio of cremations to deaths) reaches 1 percent for the first time.
1928	Metropolitan Life Insurance Company publishes a nationwide survey of funeral costs.
1931	The Bohemian National Cemetery in Chicago opens an elaborate columbarium.
1934	Mount Auburn Cemetery signals the migration of the columbarium out of dark basements when it retrofits the first floor of its crematory chapel for niches. It will add niches on the second floor two years later.
1937	The Reverend Fred Shorter and his nondenominational Congregational Church of the People in Seattle, Washington, establish the People's Memorial Association, the first memorial society in the United States.
1941–45	Nazis use crematories to kill Jews and others in World War II concentration camps. The war claims the lives of over 400,000 Americans.
1955	Albert Einstein is cremated.
1962	Continental Association of Funeral and Memorial Societies (later Funeral and Memorial Societies of America) is established.
1963	Pope Paul VI approves an instruction liberalizing cremation in some circumstances, effectively lifting the Roman Catholic ban on cremation instituted in 1886.
	Jessica Mitford's exposé, *The American Way of Death*, prompts a nationwide discussion of funeral costs and a Federal Trade Commission investigation into the funeral industry.

President John F. Kennedy is assassinated.

1964–72   The conflict in Vietnam claims the lives of over 50,000 Americans. Television coverage brings casualties and deaths into American homes.

1965   Federal legislation opens up immigration from cremation-friendly nations in Asia.

          National Cremation Magazine (later *The Cremationist of North America*) begins publication.

1969   Elisabeth Kübler-Ross's *On Death and Dying* prompts a nationwide conversation about "the good death" and stimulates university courses on thanatology.

          President Dwight D. Eisenhower's plain funeral illustrates a shift in U.S. death rites away from extravagance and toward simplicity.

1970   The first Earth Day symbolizes the arrival of the environmental movement.

1971   The San Diego-based Telophase Society becomes the first company to provide inexpensive "direct cremation" service.

1974   The National Funeral Directors Association issues "Considerations concerning Cremation," its first pamphlet on the subject.

1977   The Neptune Society enters the direct cremation business.

1978   The Federal Trade Commission issues a 526-page report accusing the funeral industry of a series of abuses and proposing new federal regulations.

1980   Beatles star John Lennon is cremated. In lieu of a traditional funeral, mourners gather for a ten-minute "silent vigil" in New York City's Central Park and other locations around the globe.

1981   The U.S. cremation rate tops 10 percent for the first time.

1984   The Federal Trade Commission's new funeral industry rule goes into effect.

1985   The AIDS epidemic comes into public consciousness.

1987   Lisa Carlson's *Caring for Your Own Dead* contributes to a trend toward family-directed death rites. This book was revised and republished in 1998.

1990   Michael Kubasak's *Cremation and the Funeral Director* urges funeral directors to profit from cremation rather than oppose it.

1993   Batesville Casket Company inaugurates a cremation campaign called Options® by Batesville.

1995	Cremation goes on-line with a World Wide Web page maintained by Elder Davis, Inc., a leading manufacturer of cremation caskets.
1996	Jessica Mitford is cremated.
1997	U.S. Catholic bishops receive from the Vatican a special dispensation that allows them the discretion to permit cremated remains to be present at funeral masses in their dioceses.
	Houston-based Celestis, Inc., rockets the cremated remains of counterculture hero Timothy Leary into low-earth orbit.
1998	Jessica Mitford's *The American Way of Death Revisited* is published posthumously.
1999	The Neptune Society begins trading as a public company.
	Following a fatal plane crash, John F. Kennedy, Jr., becomes the most famous American Catholic to be cremated. His ashes are scattered at sea.
	The U.S. cremation rate stands at 25 percent.

Abbreviations

AACS Proceedings	Proceedings of the Association of American Cemetery Superintendents
ACQR	American Catholic Quarterly Review
AFD	The American Funeral Director
CAA Proceedings	Report of the Proceedings of the Annual Convention of the Cremation Association of America
Cremationist	The Cremationist of North America (previously National Cremation Magazine)
Daily Graphic	New York Daily Graphic
ES	Hugo Erichsen Scrapbooks, John Crerar Library, University of Chicago
FM	Funeral Monitor
FSI	Funeral Service Insider
Herald	New York Herald
Inquirer	Philadelphia Inquirer
JAMA	Journal of the American Medical Association
JCL Pamphlets	Pamphlets on Cremation, John Crerar Library, University of Chicago
Leslie's	Frank Leslie's Illustrated Newspaper

MA Scrapbook	Mount Auburn Cemetery Cremation Scrapbook
M&SR	*Medical and Surgical Reporter*
MC	*Modern Crematist*
MM	*Mortuary Management*
P&C	*Park and Cemetery* (also known as *Park and Cemetery and Landscape Gardening*)
Times	*New York Times*
Tribune	*New York Tribune*
Urn	*The Urn*
World	*New York World*

Notes

Introduction

1. Louis-Vincent Thomas, "Funeral Rites," in *Death, Afterlife, and the Soul,* ed. Lawrence E. Sullivan (New York: Macmillan, 1989) 39.

2. In Genesis 38:24 and Leviticus 21:9 death by burning is recommended for a harlot. In Leviticus 20:14 a similar punishment is suggested for the crime of incest. Two important diversions from this interpretive tradition are the cremations of Saul and Asa, both kings of Israel, described in 1 Samuel 31:11–13 and 2 Chronicles 16:14. Each of these passages, of course, invites divergent readings.

3. Aquinas is quoted in Caroline Walker Bynum, "Bodily Miracles and the Resurrection of the Body in the High Middle Ages," in *Belief in History: Innovative Approaches to European and American Religion,* ed. Thomas Kselman (South Bend, Ind.: University of Notre Dame Press, 1991) 73. There are, admittedly, many Christian views of the body, self, and resurrection. The view I am focusing on here begins with Aquinas and triumphs in the Middle Ages. See Caroline Walker Bynum, "Material Continuity, Personal Survival and the Resurrection of the Body: A Scholastic Discussion in its Medieval and Modern Contexts," in her *Fragmentation and Redemption: Essays on Gender and the Human Body in Medieval Religion* (New York: Zone Books, 1992) 239–97; and Caroline Walker Bynum, *The Resurrection of the Body in Western Christianity, 200–1336* (New York: Columbia University Press, 1995). See also Paula Fredriksen, "Vile Bodies: Paul and Augustine on the Resurrection of the Flesh," in *Biblical Hermeneutics in Historical Perspective,* ed. Mark S. Burrows and Paul Rorem (Grand Rapids, Mich.: Eerdmans, 1991) 75–87; and Kallistos Ware, "'My Helper and My Enemy': The Body in Greek Christianity," in *Religion and*

the Body, ed. Sarah Coakley (New York: Cambridge University Press, 1997) 90–110.

4. Here again I am relying on Caroline Walker Bynum, *The Resurrection of the Body in Western Christianity*.

5. Quoted in Augustus G. Cobb, *Earth-Burial and Cremation* (New York: G. P. Putnam's Sons, 1892) 126.

6. On Native American death rites, see H. C. Yarrow, *Introduction to the Study of Mortuary Customs Among the North American Indians* (Washington, D.C.: Government Printing Office, 1880). On the cremation of Laurens, see Hugo Erichsen, *The Cremation of the Dead Considered from an Aesthetic, Sanitary, Religious, Historical, Medico-Legal, and Economical Standpoint* (Detroit: D. O. Haynes, 1887) 38.

7. "Cremation as a Mode of Interment, and Related Subjects," *Boston Public Library Bulletins* 2.30 (July 1874) 268.

8. Particularly influential are two books by Philippe Ariès: *Western Attitudes toward Death: From the Middle Ages to the Present*, trans. Patricia M. Ranum (Baltimore: Johns Hopkins University Press, 1974), and *The Hour of Our Death*, trans. Helen Weaver (New York: Knopf, 1981).

9. There are some useful studies of death in America, including David E. Stannard, *The Puritan Way of Death: A Study in Religion, Culture, and Social Change* (New York: Oxford University Press, 1977); and James Farrell, *Inventing the American Way of Death, 1830–1920* (Philadelphia: Temple University Press, 1980). *Death in America* (Philadelphia: University of Pennsylvania Press, 1974), a volume edited by Stannard that originally appeared in *American Quarterly*, contains important essays. Two recent studies make good use of the European historiography: David Charles Sloane, *The Last Great Necessity: Cemeteries in American History* (Baltimore: Johns Hopkins University Press, 1991); and Gary Laderman, *The Sacred Remains: American Attitudes toward Death, 1799–1883* (New Haven: Yale University Press, 1996). The only sustained scholarly study of U.S. cremation is Robert W. Habenstein's "A Sociological Study of the Cremation Movement in the United States" (M.A. thesis, University of Chicago, 1949).

10. Cremation Association of North America, "1999 Data and Projections to the Year 2010" (Cremation Association of North America, 2000, photocopy). The cremation rate exceeded 50% in 1999 in Hawaii, Washington, Nevada, Oregon, Montana, Arizona, Alaska, and New Hampshire.

11. Stuart Hall, "Cultural Studies: Two Paradigms," in *The Body: Social Process and Cultural Theory*, ed. Mike Featherstone, Mike Hepworth, and Bryan S. Turner (London: Sage, 1991) 520.

12. The writing on secularization is vast, both in the historical and the sociological literatures, and I will not reprise it here, except to note that the term is as polysemous as it is controversial, referring in one textual incarnation to rationalization and in others to differentiation, laicization, privatization, or disenchantment. For a careful review of some recent literature, see David Martin, "Sociology, Religion and Secularization: An Orientation," *Religion* 25.4 (October 1995) 295–303.

1. The Cremation of Baron De Palm

1. Sir Henry Thompson, "Cremation: Treatment of the Body after Death," *Contemporary Review* 23.2 (January 1874) 319–28. See also P. H. Holland's critical response, "Burial or Cremation?" *Contemporary Review* 23.3 (February 1874) 477–84; and Thompson's rejoinder, "Cremation: A Reply to Critics and an Exposition of the Process," *Contemporary Review* 23.4 (March 1874) 553–71.

2. *New York World*, quoted in "The Carpers' Club," *Daily Graphic* (May 2, 1874) 474; "Cremation: Proposed Incorporation of the New Society," *Times* (April 25, 1874) 2; "Cremation," *Philadelphia Medical Times* (April 25, 1874) 473; "Editor's Easy Chair," *Harper's New Monthly Magazine* 49.290 (July 1874) 283; Jacob Wyce Horher, "Cremation," (M.D. thesis, University of Pennsylvania, 1875) 18, 21. The patent is number 7,599 (July 28, 1874). The *World* spoke kindly of cremation in editorials on March 1, 8, 15, 22, and 29, 1874. The results of the doctors' poll appear in J. F. A. Adams, *Cremation and Burial: An Examination of their Relative Advantages* (Boston: Wright & Potter, 1875). The bibliography is "Cremation as a Mode of Interment, and Related Subjects," *Boston Public Library Bulletins* 2.30 (July 1874) 268. These are by no means the only texts from 1874. See, e.g., George Bayles, "Disposal of the Dead," *Sanitarian* 2.3 (June 1874) 97–105; Fannie Roper Feudge, "Burning and Burying in the East," *Lippincott's Magazine* 13.33 (May 1874) 593–603; and George Bayles, "Cremation and Its Alternatives," *Popular Science Monthly* (June 1874) 225–28.

3. Persifor Frazer, Jr., *The Merits of Cremation* (Philadelphia: n.p., 1874) 7, 8, 12. This paper was originally published in the *Penn Monthly* in June of 1874.

4. Frazer, *The Merits of Cremation*, 13. Frazier was quoting from "Opinion of an English Bishop," *Evening Bulletin* (April 13, 1874).

5. O. B. Frothingham, *The Disposal of Our Dead* (New York: D. G. Francis, 1874) 11, 13.

6. Frothingham, *The Disposal of Our Dead*, 13, 27–28, 18, 20.

7. Frothingham, *The Disposal of Our Dead*, 22–24.

8. Richard L. Bushman, *The Refinement of America: Persons, Houses, Cities* (New York: Knopf, 1992); John Tomisch, *A Genteel Endeavor: American Culture and Politics in the Gilded Age* (Stanford: Stanford University Press, 1971) 24; Frederick Law Olmstead, quoted in Bushman, *The Refinement of America*, 422. See also Stow Persons, *The Decline of American Gentility* (New York: Columbia University Press, 1973); John F. Kasson, *Rudeness and Civility: Manners in Nineteenth-Century Urban America* (New York: Hill and Wang, 1990); and Thomas Bender, *New York Intellect: A History of Intellectual Life in New York City, from 1750 to the Beginnings of Our Own Time* (New York: Knopf, 1987). The term "dangerous classes" comes from Charles Loring Brace, *The Dangerous Classes of New York and Twenty Years' Work among Them* (New York: Wynkoop & Hallenbeck, 1872).

9. "Call a Spade a Spade," *Urn* 4.3 (March 25, 1895) 2; *MC* 2.12 (December 1887) 177. Also appearing in a cremationist periodical was this Matthew Arnold

dictum, which some have cited as the definitive statement of American gentility: "Culture is to know the best that has been thought and said in the world" (*Urn* 3.12 [December 25, 1895] 11).

10. Eric Hobsbawm, "Mass-Producing Traditions: Europe, 1870–1914," in *The Invention of Tradition,* ed. Eric Hobsbawm and Terence Ranger (Cambridge: Cambridge University Press, 1983) 279.

11. "Cremation: The Ancient Grecian Method of Burning the Dead," *Leslie's* (April 25, 1874) 1, 101, 103. The *Philadelphia Sunday Press* published a dubious tale of a physician who cremated his deceased son in a furnace in the cellar of his home. Though intended for publication on April Fool's Day, it appeared later in the month. See "Cremation in Philadelphia," *Times* (April 20, 1874) 1; and "The Philadelphia Cremation Story a Hoax," *Times* (April 22, 1874) 1. The Princeton festivities are documented in an undated pamphlet, "Creative Ceremonials Conducted by the Sophomore Class of Princeton College, over the Remains of the Late Brig. Gen. Joseph Bocher." The doggerel appears in "The Carpers' Club," *Daily Graphic* (May 2, 1874) 474. A Georgia newspaper published an apocryphal account of a pro-cremation meeting in Augusta, Georgia. See "Cremation: The Stupid Philadelphia Hoax Imitated in Georgia," *Times* (April 28, 1874) 8. Another Augusta-based spoof is discussed in "The Funeral Pile," *Boston Herald* (November 28, 1876) 4; and "A Distinguished Cremationist," *Atlanta Daily Constitution* (December 8, 1876) 4. Both articles refer to an open-air pyre cremation, supposedly conducted by either "The Oriental Order of Humanity" or "The Oriental Order of Humilitate."

12. *Cremation: An Ethiopian Sketch* (New York: Robert M. De Witt, 1875).

13. "De Palm's Incineration," *Times* (December 7, 1876) 6. Other newspaper sources include but are in no way exhausted by: "A Fool Cremated," *Atlanta Daily Constitution* (December 6, 1876) 4; "Ashes to Ashes," *Boston Daily Advertiser* (December 9, 1876) 2; "Baron De Palm in Ashes," *Boston Daily Globe* (December 7, 1876) 8; "A Subject for Cremation," *Boston Herald* (November 27, 1876) 1; "Cremation," *Boston Herald* (December 6, 1876) 4; "Cremation," *Boston Herald* (December 7, 1876) 1; "The Cremation of Baron Palm," *Boston Medical and Surgical Journal* 95.24 (December 14, 1876) 710–712; "Cremation vs. Interment," *Boston Pilot* (December 28, 1876) 4; "The Subject for Cremation," *Boston Post* (November 30, 1876) 2; "Cremation," *Boston Post* (December 7, 1876) 2; "Cremation of the Remains of the Late Baron De Palm," *Leslie's* (December 23, 1876) 259; "Successful Cremation," *New Orleans Times Picayune* (December 7, 1876) 8; "Particulars of the De Palm Cremation," *New Orleans Times Picayune* (December 8, 1876) 8; "Baron Von Palm's Body," *Herald* (November 29, 1876) 5; "A Theosophical Roast," *Herald* (December 5, 1876) 5; "A Cremation Pilgrimage," *Herald* (December 6, 1876) 7; "The Cremation Folly," *Herald* (December 7, 1876) 6; "Baron De Palm's Cremation," *Times* (December 6, 1876) 10; untitled editorial, *Tribune* (November 20, 1876) 4; "Burning and Burial," *Tribune* (November 28, 1876) 4; "Cremation and Burial," *Tribune* (December 7, 1876) 4; "The Baron's Last Journey," *World* (December 5, 1876) 2; "Burning a Baron," *World* (December 6, 1876) 1; "Baron De Palm Cremated," *World* (December 7,

1876) 2; untitled editorial, *World* (December 7, 1876) 4; "Cremation," *Inquirer* (December 6, 1876) 8; "Some Talk on Cremation," *Inquirer* (December 6, 1876) 8; "Cremation," *Inquirer* (December 7, 1876) 1–2; "More Cremation Conversation," *Inquirer* (December 7, 1876) 2; "Cremation of Baron De Palm," *Inquirer* (December 7, 1876) 4; "De Palm's Body Reduced to Ashes," *Philadelphia Press* (December 7, 1876) 8; untitled editorial, *Philadelphia Press* (December 7, 1876) 4; "Cremation," *San Francisco Chronicle* (December 7, 1876) 1. The *Daily Graphic* also covered the event exhaustively, devoting to it a series of articles and editorials as well as a front page cartoon (November 28, December 4, 6, 7, 9, 13, and 15, 1876).

14. John Storer Cobb, *A Quartercentury of Cremation in North America* (Boston: Knight and Millet, 1901) 100; untitled editorial, *Tribune* (June 16, 1876) 4; "A Fool Cremated," *Atlanta Daily Constitution* (December 6, 1876) 4; Boyd Crumrine, *History of Washington County, Pennsylvania* (Philadelphia: L.H. Everts, 1882) 540; "Dr. LeMoyne's Furnace," *Times* (February 19, 1878) 2; "Baron De Palm Cremated," *World* (December 7, 1876) 2. For LeMoyne on cremation, see F. Julius LeMoyne, M.D., *Cremation: An Argument to Prove That Cremation Is Preferable to Inhumation of Dead Bodies* (Pittsburgh: E.W. Lightner, 1878). Additional biographical information can be found in Crumrine, *History of Washington County, Pennsylvania*, 449, 456, 540, 541, 543–48.

15. On Olcott, see Stephen Prothero, *The White Buddhist: The Asian Odyssey of Henry Steel Olcott* (Bloomington: Indiana University Press, 1996).

16. "Burning and Burial," *Tribune* (November 28, 1876) 4; "Cremation," *Boston Herald* (December 6, 1876) 4; Henry S. Olcott, *Old Diary Leaves: The History of the Theosophical Society* (Adyar, India: Theosophical Publishing House, 1974) 1:150. I discuss this funeral at some length in Prothero, *The White Buddhist*, esp. 54–57. For more contemporary accounts, see Olcott's *Old Diary Leaves*, 1:147–84; untitled editorial, *New York Independent* (June 1, 1876) 15; "A Theosophical Funeral," *Times* (May 29, 1876) 1; "A Rosicrucian in New-York," *Tribune* (May 26, 1876) 4; "'Theosophical' Obsequies," *Tribune* (May 29, 1876) 4; "Baron de Palm's Funeral," *Tribune* (May 29, 1876) 5; "A Theosophist's Obsequies," *San Francisco Chronicle* (May 29, 1876) 3; "The Theosophical Ceremonial over a Coffined Corpse," *San Francisco Chronicle* (June 6, 1876) 1. Apparently De Palm's funeral inspired imitators. See "Another Fancy Funeral," *Tribune* (March 6, 1878) 4.

17. "Burning and Burial," *Tribune* (November 28, 1876) 4; "A Theosophical Funeral," *Times* (May 29, 1876) 1.

18. "Two Lively Corpses," *Boston Herald* (December 1, 1876) 2; "A Rosicrucian in New-York," *Tribune* (May 26, 1876) 4.

19. "Dr. LeMoyne's Furnace," *Times* (February 19, 1878) 2; untitled editorial, *Tribune* (June 16, 1876) 4.

20. "Baron De Palm Cremated," *World* (December 7, 1876) 2; "A Cremation Pilgrimage," *Herald* (December 6, 1876) 7; Olcott, *Old Diary Leaves*, 1.174.

21. Olcott, *Old Diary Leaves*, 1.170.

22. "A Cremation Pilgrimage," *Herald* (December 6, 1876) 7; "Two Lively Corpses," *Boston Herald* (December 1, 1876) 2.

23. "The Subject for Cremation," *Boston Post* (November 30, 1876) 2. Robert W. Habenstein and William M. Lamers, *The History of American Funeral Directing*, 3d rev. ed., ed. Howard C. Raether (Milwaukee: National Funeral Directors Association, 1995), contains a helpful history of embalming in nineteenth-century America (197–231).

24. "The Subject for Cremation," *Boston Post* (November 30, 1876) 2; "The Baron's Last Journey," *World* (December 5, 1876) 2.

25. "A Cremation Pilgrimage," *Herald* (December 6, 1876) 7.

26. "A Cremation Pilgrimage," *Herald* (December 6, 1876) 7.

27. "A Cremation Pilgrimage," *Herald* (December 6, 1876) 7; "Burning a Baron," *World* (December 6, 1876) 1.

28. "Baron De Palm's Cremation," *Times* (December 6, 1876) 10; "Baron De Palm Cremated," *World* (December 7, 1876) 2; "A Cremation Pilgrimage," *Herald* (December 6, 1876) 7. The *Philadelphia Inquirer* writer apparently had a stronger stomach. He witnessed a corpse "in a good state of preservation" and was not horrified in the least ("Cremation," *Inquirer* [December 6, 1876] 8).

29. "Burning and Burial," *Tribune* (November 28, 1876) 4.

30. See A. Otterson, "Cremation of the Dead," in *Report of the Board of Health of the City of Brooklyn, 1875–1876* (Brooklyn: Brooklyn Board of Health, 1877) 131–32; and W. J. Asdale, J. P. McCord, and J. D. Thomas, "Cremation," *Annual Report of the Board of Health of the City of Pittsburgh for the Year 1876* (Pittsburgh: Pittsburgh Board of Health, 1877) 113–23.

31. "De Palm's Incineration," *Times* (December 7, 1876) 6; "The Baron's Cremation," *Daily Graphic* (December 6, 1876) 2; "Baron De Palm Cremated," *World* (December 7, 1876) 2.

32. "De Palm's Incineration," *Times* (December 7, 1876) 6; Olcott, *Old Diary Leaves*, 1.170.

33. Asdale, McCord, and Thomas, "Cremation," 117; "The Latest Cremation," *Inquirer* (February 15, 1878) 1.

34. "De Palm's Incineration," *Times* (December 7, 1876) 6; "Cremation of the Remains of the Late Baron De Palm," *Leslie's* (December 23, 1876) 259.

35. Olcott, *Old Diary Leaves*, 1.183. The Coney Island suggestion appears in "The End of Cremation," *Times* (October 17, 1879) 4.

36. "An Unceremonious Rite," *Times* (February 16, 1878) 5.

37. Olcott, *Old Diary Leaves*, 1.178; "Baron De Palm Cremated," *World* (December 7, 1876) 2; untitled editorial, *Daily Graphic* (December 7, 1876) 2; "The Cremation Folly," *Herald* (December 7, 1876) 6.

38. "Theosophical Obsequies," *Tribune* (May 29, 1876) 4; "The Cremation Folly," *Herald* (December 7, 1876) 6; "Baron De Palm Cremated," *World* (December 7, 1876); untitled editorial, *World* (December 7, 1876) 4; "De Palm's Incineration," *Times* (December 7, 1876) 6. Olcott would later note that the American papers, "which had made fun of the [Theosophical Society] for having too much religious ceremony at the Baron's funeral, now abused us for having none at all at his cremation" (*Old Diary Leaves*, 1.170).

39. "Baron De Palm Cremated," *World* (December 7, 1876) 2; "Burning a Baron," *World* (December 6, 1876) 1; "The Cremation Folly," *Herald* (December 7, 1876) 6.

40. Stevens and Stokley are quoted in "More Cremation Conversation," *Inquirer* (December 7, 1876) 2; Wood's remarks are from "Some Talk on Cremation," *Inquirer* (December 6, 1876) 8.

41. Untitled editorial, *Tribune* (November 20, 1876) 4.

42. "Ashes to Ashes," *Boston Daily Advertiser* (December 9, 1876) 2; untitled editorial, *World* (December 7, 1876) 4.

43. "Cremation of the Remains of the Late Baron De Palm," *Leslie's* (December 23, 1876) 268.

44. "Cremation of the Remains of the Late Baron De Palm," *Leslie's* (December 23, 1876) 268.

45. Olcott, *Old Diary Leaves,* 1.149; "A Rosicrucian in New-York," *Tribune* (May 26, 1876) 4.

46. "Baron De Palm's Remains," *Times* (December 5, 1876) 8; "Baron De Palm's Request," *Times* (December 4, 1876) 8. On cremation in Japan, see: "Walled-In Peoples," *Tribune* (August 3, 1881) 4; "Cremation in Japan," *Tribune* (May 26, 1884); "Cremation in Japan," *Popular Science Monthly* 40:48 (March 1892) 715–16; "Cremation in Japan," *MC* 1.1 (January 1886) 12. Cremation in Siam (now Thailand) was the subject of an untitled editorial in the *Tribune* on June 16, 1888 (4). Cremation in China is discussed in "Cremation," *JAMA* 2.3 (January 19, 1884) 69; and Herbert A. Giles, "A Cremation in China," *Eclectic Magazine* 29.5 (May 1879) 547–53. Hugo Erichsen's classic early treatment, *The Cremation of the Dead* (Detroit: D.O. Haynes, 1887), traces cremation back to India (7) and contains illustrations of "Cremation in Calcutta" (14) and "Cremation in Siam" (19). More on cremation in India can be found in: "Cremation in India," *MC* 1.4 (April 1886) 60–61; "Cremation in India," *MC* 2.5 (May 1887) 76–77; "Cremation in India," *Urn* (February 25, 1892) 9. See also Fannie Roper Feudge, "Burning and Burying in the East," *Lippincott's Magazine* 13.33 (May 1874) 593–603.

47. "Cremation: The Ancient Grecian Method of Burning the Dead," *Leslie's* (April 25, 1874) 1; Olcott, *Old Diary Leaves,* 1.176.

48. Olcott, *Old Diary Leaves,* 1.150.

49. On dechristianization, which I see as a more readily definable and useful construct than secularization, see Michel Vovelle, *Piété baroque et déchristianisation en Provence au XVIIIe siècle* (Paris: Plon, 1973).

50. Jonathan Z. Smith, *To Take Place: Toward Theory in Ritual* (Chicago: University of Chicago Press, 1987) 109, quoted in Catherine Bell, *Ritual Theory, Ritual Practice* (New York: Oxford University Press, 1992) 102; "De Palm's Incineration," *Times* (December 7, 1876) 6. See also Catherine Bell, *Ritual: Perspectives and Dimensions* (New York: Oxford University Press, 1997).

51. "Cremation of a Boston Physician," *Times* (July 18, 1877) 2; "The Cremation of Dr. Winslow," *Times* (August 5, 1877) 5; "The Salt Lake Cremation," *Times* (August 9, 1877) 3. See also: "Cremation," *Deseret Evening News* (August 1, 1877) 3; C. Smart, "Cremation Practically Considered," *Medical Record* 13 (February 9, 1878) 126–29; "Cremation of Dr. Charles F. Winslow," *Popular Science Monthly* (October 1877) 765–67; and a series of articles and editorials in the *Salt Lake City Daily Tribune* (July 31, August 1, August 2, 1877).

52. "Cremation of a Baby," *Times* (November 20, 1877) 8; "The Kircher Cremation Case," *Times* (November 21, 1877) 8; "No Objection to Cremating," *Times* (December 5, 1877) 8.

53. "Yesterday's Cremation," *Boston Globe* (February 16, 1878) 1; untitled editorial, *Boston Globe* (February 18, 1878) 4; untitled editorial, *Boston Post* (February 18, 1878) 1; "The Cremation Theory Again," *Chicago Tribune* (February 17, 1878) 4; "Cremation," *Tribune* (February 16, 1878) 2; "More of Cremation," *Tribune* (February 25, 1878) 4; "An Ohio Lady to Be Cremated," *Times* (February 13, 1878) 1; "The Cremation of Mrs. Pitman," *Times* (February 14, 1878) 5; "An Unceremonious Rite," *Times* (February 16, 1878) 5; "Dr. LeMoyne's Furnace," *Times* (February 19, 1878) 2; "The Latest Cremation," *Inquirer* (February 15, 1878) 1; "Mrs. Pitman Incinerated," *Inquirer* (February 16, 1878) 3; untitled editorial, *Inquirer* (February 16, 1878) 4; "Mrs. Jane Pitman's Will," *Philadelphia Press* (February 13, 1878) 1; "The State," *Philadelphia Press* (February 16, 1878) 8; untitled editorial, *Philadelphia Press* (February 16, 1878) 4.

54. "Le Moyne Cremated," *Chicago Tribune* (October 17, 1879) 1; "A Cremation at Washington, Penn.," *Tribune* (October 17, 1879) 1; "A Dead Reformer," *Tribune* (October 17, 1879) 4; "Cremation of Le Moyne," *Inquirer* (October 17, 1879) 4; untitled editorial, *Inquirer* (October 18, 1879) 4; "The Late Dr. Le Moyne's Cremation Furnace," *Philadelphia Press* (October 16, 1879) 5; "Le Moyne's Body," *Philadelphia Press* (October 17, 1879) 1; "Reduced to Ashes," *Philadelphia Record* (October 17, 1879) 1.

55. "Cremation," *Salt Lake City Daily Tribune* (August 1, 1877) 1; "The Salt Lake Cremation," *Times* (August 9, 1877) 3; "Cremation," *Salt Lake City Daily Tribune* (August 1, 1877) 2.

56. "An Ohio Lady to Be Cremated," *Times* (February 13, 1878) 1; "An Unceremonious Rite," *Times* (February 16, 1878) 5; untitled editorial, *Boston Post* (February 18, 1878) 1.

57. LeMoyne, *Cremation: An Argument,* 5, 13, 18; Hugo Erichsen, *Roses and Ashes and Other Writings* (Detroit: American Printing Company, 1917) 5; "A Dead Reformer," *Tribune* (October 17, 1879) 4; untitled editorial, *Inquirer* (October 18, 1879) 4. The poetic language is Erichsen's, not LeMoyne's.

58. On the history of religious pluralism in the United States, see Catherine L. Albanese, *America: Religions and Religion* (3d ed.; Belmont, Calif.: Wadsworth, 1999); Diana L. Eck, *On Common Ground: World Religions in America* (CD-ROM; New York: Columbia University Press, 1997); Thomas A. Tweed, *Retelling U.S. Religious History* (Berkeley: University of California Press, 1997); Thomas A. Tweed and Stephen Prothero, *Asian Religions in America: A Documentary History* (New York: Oxford University Press, 1999).

2. Sanitary Reform

1. Quoted in John Duffy, *The Sanitarians: A History of American Public Health* (Urbana: University of Illinois Press, 1990) 106; David L. Gollaher, "From Ritual to Science: The Medical Transformation of Circumcision in America," *Journal of Social History* 28.1 (Fall 1994) 23. Other useful treat-

ments of the sanitary movement include: Phyllis Palmer, *Domesticity and Dirt* (Philadelphia: Temple University Press, 1989); Nancy Tomes, *The Gospel of Germs: Men, Women, and the Microbe in American Life* (Cambridge: Harvard University Press, 1998); and Claudia and Richard Bushman, "The Early History of Cleanliness in America," *Journal of American History* 74 (1988) 1213–38.

2. See Alan M. Kraut, *Silent Travelers: Germs, Genes, and the "Immigrant Menace"* (New York: Basic Books, 1994).

3. Quoted in Felix Pascalis, *An Exposition of the Dangers of Interment in Cities* (New York: W. B. Gilley, 1823) 147; John H. Rauch, *Intramural Interments in Populous Cities, and Their Influence upon Health and Epidemics* (Chicago: Tribune Company, 1866) 17. See also Francis D. Allen, *Documents and Facts Showing the Fatal Effects of Interments in Populous Cities* (New York: F. D. Allen, 1822); Atticus [pseud.], *Hints on the Subject of Interments within the City of Philadelphia* (Philadelphia: Brown, 1838); and a long series of articles published between 1830 and 1854 in the *Boston Medical and Surgical Journal*. These same matters were debated in England. The key source there is Edwin Chadwick, *Supplementary Report on the Results of a Special Inquiry into the Practice of Interment in Towns* (London: W. Clowes & Sons, 1843). On "body reforms," see Robert H. Abzug, *Cosmos Crumbling: American Reform and the Religious Imagination* (New York: Oxford University Press, 1994) 163–82.

4. See Blanche Linden-Ward, *Silent City on a Hill: Landscape of Memory and Boston's Mount Auburn Cemetery* (Columbus: Ohio State University Press, 1989); and David Charles Sloane, *The Last Great Necessity: Cemeteries in American History* (Baltimore: Johns Hopkins University Press, 1991) 44–95.

5. John Duffy, *A History of Public Health in New York City, 1866–1966* (New York: Russell Sage, 1974) 177.

6. *JAMA* editorial quoted in Duffy, *The Sanitarians*, 135.

7. "Poison from the Dead," *Tribune* (December 18, 1878) 4; Henry D. Fulton, "Should We Burn Our Dead?" *American Medicine* (November 2, 1901) 1.

8. Mark Twain, *Life on the Mississippi* (New York: Harper, 1950) 345.

9. Frederick Peterson, "Cremation," *Buffalo Medical and Surgical Journal* 20.9 (April 1881) 385–97.

10. J. E. Chancellor, "History, Evils and Advantages of Inhumation and Cremation," *JAMA* 5.16 (October 17, 1885) 438.

11. This tidbit is widely cited in the literature. See, e.g., Augustus G. Cobb, *Earth-Burial and Cremation* (New York: G. P. Putnam's Sons, 1892) 49.

12. "Mr. Benn Pitman's Address," *MC* 4.3 (July 1889) 1.

13. "Burial or Cremation," *M&SR* 62.13 (September 24, 1887) 424. The ten-foot requirement is attributed to Rev. Dr. B. F. DeCosta in "Earth-to-Earth Burial," *Times* (November 16, 1884) 2. In an 1892 paper, "Sanitary Methods of Burial," George H. Scott endorsed this system, though he stated a preference for "ordinary or common grave burial"—burial with no coffin whatsoever (JCL Pamphlets, 6).

14. "A Novel View of the Cremation Question," *The Medical Record* (January 18, 1879) 69–70; J. Morris, "Report on Cremation," *JAMA* 8.26 (June 25, 1887); "Quicklime Coffins," *Urn* 2.6 (July 25, 1893) 5.

15. Secure mausoleums are proposed in Rev. Charles R. Treat, "Sanitary Entombment: The Ideal Disposition of the Dead," a paper read to the American Public Health Association (October 23, 1889) and later published independently. On metal caskets, see Walter H. Link, "Incineration or Adipocere," *Times* (December 25, 1876) 3. Martin's ideas are discussed in "Disposal of the Dead," *Sanitarian* 210 (May 1887) 415. Sea burial in corrosive metal coffins is explored in "Editor's Retort," *Urn* 3.6 (June 25, 1894) 4–5. George Bayles mentions desiccation in "Disposal of the Dead," *Sanitarian* 40.3 (June 1874) 101; that alternative was later propounded in *The New Mausoleum* and endorsed by the editor of *Sanitarian*. "Electrical Cremation," a reprint of an article originally published in *Electrician,* appears in *MC* 1.10 (October 1886) 159. "Cementation" is the subject of an article in *MC* 2.3 (March 1887) 44–45. Electroplating corpses is the matter at hand in "Metallic Burial," *The Sanitary Era* 1.27 (May 1, 1887) 256; "Sanitary Burial," *The Sanitary Era* 1.17 (December 1, 1886) 131; and "The Body after Death," *Modern Cemetery* 1.5 (July 1891) 59–60.

16. George Bayles, "Disposal of the Dead," *Sanitarian* 40.3 (June 1874) 101.

17. "Disposal of the Dead," *MC* 1.1 (January 1886) 9.

18. Thompson is quoted in John D. Beugless, "Incineration," *Princeton Review* 59.2 (September 1883) 145. The rejoinder appears in Samuel Bernstein, "Cremation a Sanitary Reform," *MC* 4.2 (April 1889) 21. Publishing by sanitarians on cremation roughly tracked public concerns about cholera, the century's most-feared disease. In the mid-1870s, when the cremation movement got underway, the *Sanitarian* called cholera the nation's "all-absorbing topic" and the *New York Times* was editorializing about "Cholera Panics!" (Duffy, *A History of Public Health in New York City, 1866–1966,* 144). In the mid-1880s, when writing on cremation reached its height, cholera was again a major topic of concern. Interest in cremation did not wane until shortly after the century's last great cholera scare in 1892.

19. C. N. Peirce, *Sanitary Disposal of the Dead* ([Philadelphia]: Philadelphia Cremation Society, [1891]) 10.

20. George Bayles, "Disposal of the Dead," *Sanitarian* 2.3 (June 1874) 105; "Cremation," *Leslie's* (April 25, 1874) front page, 103.

21. Hugo Erichsen, *The Cremation of the Dead* (Detroit: D. O. Haynes, 1887) 83–85, 77; Cobb, *Earth-Burial and Cremation,* 88.

22. Peirce, *Sanitary Disposal of the Dead,* 27; Erichsen, *The Cremation of the Dead,* 77; Cobb, *Earth-Burial and Cremation,* 62; John D. Beugless, "Incineration," *Princeton Review* 59.2 (September 1883) 148; John O. Marble, *Cremation in Its Sanitary Aspects: The Torch versus the Spade* (Boston: Clapp, 1885) 7. For a far more careful treatment of this issue, see Caroline Walker Bynum's *The Resurrection of the Body in Western Christianity, 200–1336* (New York: Columbia University Press, 1995) esp. 1–17.

23. "The Cemetery Problem," *Urn* 1: 3 (April 1892) 1; Cobb, *Earth-Burial and Cremation,* 44; Dr. John Marble, quoted in Samuel Bernstein, "Cremation a Sanitary Reform," *MC* 4.2 (April 1889) 18; "Homeopathists Favor Cremation," *Urn* (October 1892) 6; "Cremation and Sanitation," in ES, 33; Dr. Thomas Wildes, letter to the editor, in "Editor's Retort," *Urn* 3.9 (September 1894) 4.

24. F. Julius LeMoyne, *Cremation: An Argument to Prove That Cremation Is Preferable to Inhumation of Dead Bodies* (Pittsburgh: E. W. Lightner, 1878) 8, 9; W. H. Curtis, *The Disposal of the Dead* (Cambridge: Riverside Press, 1882) 11.

25. John D. Beugless, "Cremation as a Safeguard against Epidemics," *Sanitarian* 180 (November 1884) 445. Other articles framed pleas for cremation in terms of the dangers of infectious diseases. See J. Heber Smith, "The Desirability of Disposing of Infected Bodies by Cremation," paper read before the Boston Homoeopathic Medical Society (January 2, 1896), in JCL *Pamphlets*.

26. Lew Slusser, "Cremation as a Sanitary and Economic Measure," *Sanitarian* 222 (May 1888) 453; D. M. Skinner, "A Plea for Cremation," *M&SR* 61 (October 5, 1889) 369.

27. "Spring Cleaning," *Urn* 2.3 (April 25, 1893) 1–2; "Keep the Destroyer Out," *Urn* 2.3 (April 25, 1893) 5. René Girard presents a widely-discussed interpretation of the connection between religion and violence in his *Violence and the Sacred*, trans. Patrick Gregory (Baltimore: Johns Hopkins University Press, 1977).

28. John D. Beugless, "Cremation as a Safeguard Against Epidemics," *Sanitarian* 180 (November 1884) 444–46; Robert Newman, "Cremation and Its Importance in Cholera," *Sanitarian* 281 (April 1893) 291–92.

29. "The Future of Cremation," *Medical Record* 20 (January 9, 1886) 46; "A Plan to Cremate Paupers," *Tribune* (February 13, 1888) 8; "Cremation," *Tribune* (Feb 12, 1880) 4. In *Cremation and Burial: An Examination of Their Relative Advantages* (Boston: Wright & Potter, 1875) Dr. J. F. A. Adams reports that his study yielded 133 Massachusetts respondents. Among them, 36 stated that they "approve," 13 that they "approve in cities," and 11 that they "disapprove." Sixty-five expressed no opinion, and a total of 8 cast their lot with either "embalming," "chemical disintegration," or "encasing in Portland cement" (302). The other data comes from the pages of the *M&SR* (December 21, 1889 through February 15, 1890). See also the letters of March 15 and April 12, 1890. The reporters did not tabulate their results. My readings of the responses finds 97 unequivocally pro-cremation, 25 clearly anti-cremation, and 21 straddling the fence.

30. "Report on Cremation," *JAMA* 6.22 (May 29, 1886) 606–607.

31. "Cremation: A Hasty Endorsement," *JAMA* 7.4 (July 24, 1886) 98; "Domestic Correspondence," *JAMA* 6.14 (April 3, 1886) 387–88; "Cremation and Health: A Paper by Dr. Frank H. Hamilton," *Tribune* (March 12, 1886) 5. Exactly how idiosyncratic Hamilton's views were is difficult to gauge. A newspaper report indicates that the paper was "frequently applauded," and at least two listeners responded to the paper by standing up to testify against cremation.

32. "The Conservative View of Cremation," *Medical Record* (June 14, 1884) 666; Adams, *Cremation and Burial*, 310, 311; A. Otterson, "Cremation of the Dead," *Report of the Board of Health of the City of Brooklyn, 1875–1876* (Brooklyn: Brooklyn Board of Health, 1877) 131; "Cremation: What Is Thought of It by Physicians" (Fourth Series) *M&SR* 62 (January 11, 1890) 45; "Cremation: What Is Thought of It by Physicians" (Seventh Series) *M&SR* 62 (February 1, 1890) 138; "Correspondence," *M&SR* 62 (April 12,

1890) 441. These views were supported later in a carefully researched review of the relevant literature: A. K. Stone, "The Hygienic Argument for Cremation Considered from a Bacteriological Standpoint," *Boston Medical and Surgical Journal* 129.18 (November 2, 1893) 433–35; and 129.19 (November 9, 1893) 462–65. Following the De Palm cremation, Adams reiterated his views in "The Sanitary Aspect of Cremation," *Boston Medical and Surgical Journal* 95 (December 14, 1876) 715–16. He wrote: "The over-crowded, pestilential grave-yards upon which the cremationists build their sanitary argument are things of the past, and, both in this country and in Europe, the sanitary laws are sufficient to render them hereafter impossible: cremation, therefore, becomes merely a question of sentiment and convenience, especially in our own sparsely-populated country" (716). England also had its skeptics. In the 1870s, the *Lancet,* a London medical journal, repeatedly downplayed the sanitary evils of burial, arguing that the dangers to well water were minimal and could be virtually eliminated simply by digging deeper wells. Great Britain's most celebrated anti-cremationist was Mr. Philip Holland, the Medical Inspector of Burials in England and Wales, whose 1874 reply to Sir Henry Thompson's essay of the same year was received by cremationists as something akin to doubting the Word of God. Holland believed that the defects in burial practice were minimal and could be easily remedied. See P. H. Holland, "Burial or Cremation?" *Contemporary Review* 23.3 (February 1874) 477–84.

33. Mrs. P. T. Lamb, "Disapproves Cremation," *Detroit Commercial Advertiser* (n.d.) in ES; "Not a Cremationist," *Modern Cemetery* 1.12 (February 1892) 146; "Cremation: What Is Thought of It by Physicians" (Fifth Series) *M&SR* 62 (January 18, 1890) 75–76.

34. George H. Scott, "Sanitary Methods of Burial," paper read at the annual convention of the Association of American Cemetery Superintendents (September 1892) 3, in ES; W. H. Washburn, "Sanitation," *Modern Cemetery* 2.8 (October 1892) 86. Scott also disputed the claim that buried bodies were magnets for worms. He offered as evidence not only an anecdote (he had himself seen hundreds of bodies exhumed but never seen any engorged worms) but also this claim: worms prefer to inhabit topsoil and corpses are not their preferred food.

35. "Correspondence," *M&SR* 62 (March 15, 1890) 328; Chairman of the Sitting-Room, "An Opinion or Two," *Detroit Commercial Advertiser* (n.d.) in ES.

36. "Cremation: What Is Thought of It by Physicians" (Fourth Series) *M&SR* 62 (January 11, 1890) 45; "Cremation: What Is Thought of It by Physicians" (First Series) *M&SR* 61 (December 21, 1889) 695.

37. Adams, *Cremation and Burial,* 244; "Cremation Gaining," *Tribune* (January 8, 1888) 4; untitled editorial, *Tribune* (January 7, 1884) 4.

38. A. Cleveland Coxe, "Vulcan, or Mother Earth?" *Forum* 1 (March 1886) 70; George H. Scott, "Sanitary Methods of Burial," paper read at the annual convention of the Association of American Cemetery Superintendents, September 1892, in JCL *Pamphlets*; "Cremation: What Is Thought of It by Physicians" (Fourth Series) *M&SR* 62 (January 11, 1890) 45.

39. Untitled editorial, *Tribune* (March 11, 1881) 4.

40. "Fair Play for Cremation," *Tribune* (April 6, 1878) 4; "Burning and Burial," *Tribune* (November 28, 1876) 4; "Cremation," *Inquirer* (December 6, 1876) 8.

41. "The Better Way," *Columbarium* 2.8 (October 1895) 1–2; "Be Thou Clean!" *MC* 1.1 (January 1886) 1.

42. Mary B. Comyns, "A Plea for Cremation," *Urn* 1.12 (January 25, 1893) 6; Alice N. Lincoln, "On Cremation," *Urn* 3.2 (February 25, 1894) 5; Erichsen, *The Cremation of the Dead,* 177.

43. Anonymous, *Cremation: By an Eyewitness* (New York: A. S. Barnes, 1880) 12; George W. Barnes, "A Paper on Cremation," *MC* 4.2 (April 1889) 25; untitled note, *Urn* 4.3 (March 25, 1895) 4.

44. Anonymous, *Cremation: By an Eye-Witness,* 5; John D. Beugless, *Incineration* (n.p.: United States Cremation Company, 1883) 150; "Cremation: What Is Thought of It by Physicians" (Seventh Series) *M&SR* 62 (February 1, 1890) 137; Max Levy, *Why Cremation Should Replace Earth-Burial* (San Francisco: Bacon, 1885) 20.

45. R. E. Williams, *Cremation and Other Modes of Sepulture* (Philadelphia: Lippincott, 1884) 34; Levy, *Why Cremation Should Replace Earth-Burial,* 19.

46. Frederick Peterson, "Cremation," *Buffalo Medical and Surgical Reporter* 20.9 (April 1881) 397.

47. "Views on Cremation: By a Visitor to Milan," *Urn* 4.9 (September 1895) 5.

48. Mary Douglas, *Purity and Danger: An Analysis of the Concepts of Pollution and Taboo* (Boston: Ark, 1984) 29, 35.

3. Resurrection and the Resurrectionists

1. "Skulls on Fence Posts," *MC* 2.8 (August 1887) 122–23; "An Object Lesson," *Urn* 4.5 (May 1895) 10–11.

2. "Odds and Ends," *Urn* 4.8 (August 1895) 8; "Grave Robberies," *Urn* 3.12 (December 1894) 10; "Play with Human Bones," *Urn* 4.1 (January 1895) 8–9; Hugo Erichsen, "The Torch vs. the Spade," *MC* 2.9 (September 1887) 136; "Opinions on Cremation," *MC* 4.4 (October 1889) 56–57; Hugo Erichsen, *The Cremation of the Dead* (Detroit: D. O. Haynes, 1887) 214; T. G., "Cremation," *MC* 1.10 (October 1886) 159.

3. *Urn* 4.5 (May 1895) 5; R. E. Williams, *Cremation and Other Modes of Sepulture* (Philadelphia: Lippincott, 184) 36; *Urn* 4.7 (July 1895) 11.

4. "An Object Lesson," *Urn* 4.5 (May 1895) 10.

5. Max Levy, *Why Modern Cremation Should Replace Earth-Burial* (San Francisco: Bacon & Company, 1885) 18–19.

6. "Dr. Gross on Cremation," *Medical Record* 14 (December 7, 1878) 460; Hugo Erichsen, "Urn or Grave?" *MC* 1.9 (September 1886) 139.

7. C. N. Peirce, *Sanitary Disposal of the Dead* ([Philadelphia]: Philadelphia Cremation Society, [1891]) 9; Felix Adler, quoted in "The New Crematory Temple," *Times* (November 20, 1884); Samuel Bernstein, "Cremation a Sanitary Reform," *MC* 4.2 (April 1889) 20.

8. *Urn* 2.6 (July 1893); "Posthumous Revelations: From the Diary of a Corpse," *Urn* 4.6 (June 1895) 1–2. For more postmortem photographs, see *Photographic Likeness of Bodies Taken from the Cemeteries of Paris,* a brochure published around 1900 by the Odd Fellows Cemetery Association of San Francisco.

9. Carolyn Walker Bynum, "Bodily Miracles and the Resurrection of the Body in the High Middle Ages," in *Belief in History: Innovative Approaches to European and American Religion,* ed. Thomas Kselman (South Bend, Ind.: University of Notre Dame Press, 1991) 77.

10. *Ziemssen's Cyclopoedia of the Practice of Medicine,* cited in Augustus G. Cobb, *Earth-Burial and Cremation* (New York: G. P. Putnam's Sons, 1892) 93; A. W., "To Prevent Premature Burial," *Tribune* (January 11, 1880) 5; New York Cremation Society, *Urn Burial* (New York: New York Cremation Society, 1882) 10. On grave signals, see Robert W. Habenstein and William M. Lamers, *The History of American Funeral Directing,* 3d rev. ed., ed. Howard C. Raether (Milwaukee: National Funeral Directors Association, 1962) 180–88; and "Grave Signal," *Urn* 3.2 (November 1894) 4. The voluminous literature on premature burial has yet to be mined by historians of American religion. An interesting exchange appears in G. Eric Mackay, "Premature Burials," *Popular Science Monthly* 10 (January 1880) 389–97; and Dr. William See, "The Extreme Rarity of Premature Burials," *Popular Science Monthly* 17 (August 1880) 526–30.

11. Hartmann quoted in "Apparent Death and Cremation," *Urn* 4.11 (November 25, 1895) 2. A gruesome premature burial tale appears in Jacob Wyce Horher, "Cremation" (M.D. thesis, University of Pennsylvania, 1875): "It is stated that about two years ago a young mother, shortly after the birth of her child, was one evening seized with a fainting-fit, so severe as to be mistaken for death even by the physician, who considering the great heat of the body prevailing at the time, advised the inhumation within six hours. This was unhappily carried out, but its frightful results only came to light the other day when, the young widower having expressed his intention of marrying again, the mother of his dead wife claimed her daughter's body, intending to have it reinterred.... The vault was opened, and to the grief and horror of all present, the coffin was found broken open, and the corpse lying by its side with hair and garments torn, and hands bitten through" (37–38).

12. Cobb, *Earth-Burial and Cremation,* 17–18; Erichsen, *The Cremation of the Dead,* 196; "Chicago Clergymen," *Urn* 4.7 (July 25, 1895) 11.

13. Quoted in "Cremation or Earth-Burial?" *Urn* 1.6 (July 25, 1892) 7; "The Church and Cremation," *ACQR* 11 (June 1886) 361; "Paupers Must Be Buried," *Tribune* (February 18, 1888) 1; James P. Murphy, "The Cremation Movement is Anti-Catholic," *Catholic World* 73.436 (July 1901) 459; "Against Heathenism and the Devil's Furnace," *Sunnyside* (July 15, 1912) in ES.

14. "Ohio Freemasons," *Urn* 4.7 (July 25, 1895) 3; "Masonic Stage Thunder," *Urn* 4.5 (May 1895) 1; "An Infidel Cremated," *Times* (June 20, 1885) 1; "The Processes of Cremation," *MC* 1.1 (January 1886) 11; "The Death of God," *Urn* 1.12 (January 1893) 10–11. Robert Ingersoll's "Effect of the World's Fair on the Human Race" appeared in the *Urn* 1.3 (April 25, 1892)

5–6. His admonition—"It is a responsibility to think and act for yourself. Most people hate responsibility"—appeared in *Urn* 1.11 (December 25, 1892) 8.

15. "A Blow at Cremation," *Urn* 1.3 (April 25, 1892) 4; Henry M. Taber, "Conservatism as a Clog," *Urn* 3.9 (September 25, 1894) 3; Augustus G. Cobb, *Earth-Burial and Cremation*, 11. The connection between the cremation movement and freemasonry is not only admitted but celebrated in "Masonic Stage Thunder," *Urn* 4.5 (May 1895) 1–2: "Cremation has many warm friends among freemasons. They have in fact been staunch supporters of that cause from the very beginning of its modern revival" (1).

16. "Light and Shadow," *Urn* 2.4 (May 1893) 1–2.

17. The Reverend J. Hogan is quoted in *Urn* 3.8 (August 25, 1894) 2. Another critic is quoted in "Cremation," *MC* 2.11 (November 1877) 172.

18. Mrs. P. T. Lamb, "Disapproves Cremation"; "A Work of More Importance," *Detroit Commercial Advertiser;* Hugo Erichsen, "A Plea for Cremation." All these sources can be found in ES.

19. Monseigneur Gaume, *The Christian Cemetery in the Nineteenth Century; or, the Last War-Cry of the Communists* (New York: Benziger Brothers, 1874) 12, 14, 133, 134. The rabbi is quoted in Jacob Wyce Horher, "Cremation," 27.

20. M. C. Lockwood, "Relation of Cremation to Christianity," in *Addresses Incidental to the Dedication of the Crematory of Cincinnati* (Cincinnati: The Cremation Company, 1889) 5; A. Cleveland Coxe, "Vulcan, or Mother Earth?" *Forum* 1 (March 1886) 71–72.

21. Quoted in J. D. Beugless, "Mr. Beecher on Cremation" (letter to the editor), *Tribune* (July 16, 1884) 7.

22. These excerpts, which may have first appeared in the *Detroit Commercial Advertiser,* can all be found in ES.

23. Wordsworth quoted in John D. Beugless, "Incineration," *Princeton Review* 59.2 (September 1883) 155; Stevens quoted in "More Cremation Conversation," *Inquirer* (December 7, 1876) 2; "It Is Raised a Spiritual Body," *MC* 1.3 (March 1886) 38.

24. "The Church and Cremation," *ACQR* 11 (June 1886) 360, 358.

25. H. A. Brann, "Christian Burial and Cremation," *ACQR* 10 (October 1885) 678, 681, 693.

26. "The Church and Cremation," *ACQR* 11 (June 1886) 362; H. A. Brann, "Christian Burial and Cremation," *ACQR* 10 (October 1885) 682.

27. On Buddhists and cremation, see "A Theosophist Incinerated with Hindoo Rites," *Urn* 1.4 (May 25, 1892) 8. The article actually describes the "first Buddhist incineration ever performed in the United States."

28. Dr. Hugo Erichsen, "Cremation and Freemasonry," *MC* 1.11 (November 1886) 168; Lawrence quoted in "The New England Cremation Society," *Urn* 3.1 (January 25, 1894) 5; "Disposal of the Dead," *MC* 1.1 (January 1886) 8.

29. Quoted in Hugo Erichsen, *The Cremation of the Dead,* 186.

30. Henry Houston Bonnell, *Cremation: Scientifically and Religiously Considered* (Philadelphia: D. C. Chalfant, 1885) 8; Rev. Howard Henderson, *Cremation: Rational Method of Disposing of the Dead* (Cincinnati: Geo. P.

Houston, 1891) 42; Dr. W.H. Curtis, *The Disposal of the Dead* (Cambridge: Riverside Press, 1882) 18.

31. "What Shall We Do with Our Dead," *Urn* 3.5 (May 1894) 9; "Cremation as a Practical Issue," *World* (March 15, 1874) 4. Caroline Walker Bynum discusses versions of this theory throughout her *Resurrection of the Body in Western Christianity, 200–1336* (New York: Columbia University Press, 1995). She notes that "from the second to the fourteenth centuries, doctrinal pronouncements, miracle stories, and popular preaching continued to insist on the resurrection of exactly the material bits that were laid in the tomb" (10). The conviction that personal identity would be secured in the afterlife by material continuity, she continues, "showed remarkable persistence even where it seemed almost to require philosophical incoherence, theological equivocation, or aesthetic offensiveness" (11). Bynum interprets the theory of material continuity as "both a defense against and an articulation of the threat of decay" (27).

32. "Cremation Strongly Favored," *Times* (May 20, 1884) 1; *Deseret News,* quoted in Hugo Erichsen, *The Cremation of the Dead,* 194.

33. "The Resurrection of a Cremationist: Revelation XXI, 27," *Urn* 4.8 (August 1895) 1–2; Shaftesbury quoted in Williams, *Cremation and Other Modes of Sepulture,* 71.

34. William Lawrence, quoted in "The New England Cremation Society," *Urn* 3.1 (January 1894) 5.

35. J.P. M'Caskey, "'Be Thou Clean!,'" *MC* 1.1 (January 1886) 2; "Resurrection," *Urn* 1.7 (August 1892) 2; Gallia, "Cremation As It Is, Not Burial As It Was," *MC* 1.2 (February 1886) 18; *MC* 1.4 (April 1886) 55.

36. Harold Bloom, *The American Religion: The Emergence of the Post-Christian Nation* (New York: Simon & Schuster, 1992).

37. "Making Too Much of the Body," *MC* 1.2 (February 1886) 26; George Hodges, "Ashes to Ashes," address given at the annual meeting of the New England Cremation Society, January 15, 1895, 7–10.

38. Bishop of Manchester quoted in Williams, *Cremation and Other Modes of Sepulture,* 72; Adler quoted in "The Belief in Immortality," *Urn* 3.4 (April 1894) 7; Gallia, "Cremation As It Is, Not Burial As It Was," *MC* 1.2 (February 1886) 18.

39. Cobb, *Earth-Burial and Cremation,* 18; J.P. M'Caskey, "'Be Thou Clean!'" *MC* 1.1 (January 1886) 2.

40. Col. Olcott, "Cremation," *Medical Record* 16 (July 12, 1879) 48; "California Physicians," *Urn* 3.9 (September 1894) 9.

41. "Spiritualism and Cremation," *Urn* 1.7 (August 1892) 3; "Spiritualists Favor Cremation," *Urn* 1.10 (November 1892) 4; "Our Columbarium," *Urn* 1.9 (October 1892) 11.

42. "Our Columbarium," *Urn* 1.3 (April 1892) 9; "Our Friends the Theosophists," *Urn* 2.10 (November 25, 1893) 6.

43. D.M. Skinner, "A Plea for Cremation," *M&SR* (October 5, 1889) 370.

44. Ben H. Pratt, "Funeral Reform.—'Interment Private,'" *MC* 1.2 (February 1886) 21; "Cheap Dying," *Medical Record* (October 10, 1885) 408; Howard M. Holmes, "Incineration of the Dead," *MC* 2.8 (August 1887) 117.

45. Habenstein and Lamers, *The History of American Funeral Directing*, 125.

46. Ben H. Pratt, "Funeral Reform—'Interment Private,'" *MC* 1.2 (February 1886) 22–23. Historians have long observed a shift in religious practice during the nineteenth century from the public sphere of the church to the private sphere of the home. See Ann Douglas, *The Feminization of American Culture* (New York: Knopf, 1977); Colleen McDannell, *The Christian Home in Victorian America, 1840–1900* (Bloomington: Indiana University Press, 1986); and A. Gregory Schneider, *The Way of the Cross Leads Home: The Domestication of American Methodism* (Bloomington: Indiana University Press, 1993).

47. "Burial Reform," *Urn* 3.10 (October 1894) 10; "A Liberal Minister," *Urn* 4.3 (March 1895) 3.

48. "Precept and Practice," *Urn* 4.1 (January 1895) 4.

49. Rabbi Joseph Stolz, "Funeral Agenda," paper read before the Central Conference of American Rabbis at Montreal, Canada, July 9, 1897, 14, 17, 14.

50. "The Floral Element of Grief," *MC* 1.7 (July 1886) 101.

51. "Facts about Funerals: Undertakers and Their Charges," *Pilot* (December 16, 1876) 1–2; "Facts about Funerals," *Pilot* (December 16, 1876) 4.

52. Bruce Lincoln, *Discourse and the Construction of Society: Comparative Studies of Myth, Ritual, and Classification* (New York: Oxford University Press, 1989) 21. Lincoln argues that sentiments of affinity construct and maintain societies.

53. "Current Opinion," *Urn* 1.3 (April 1892) 9; Henderson, *Cremation: Rational Method of Disposing of the Dead*, 26.

54. J. P. M'Caskey, "'Be Thou Clean!'" *MC* 1.1 (January 1886) 2; J. Heber Smith, "The Desirability of Disposing of Infected Bodies by Cremation," paper read before the Boston Homoeopathic Medical Society (June 2, 1896) 3, in JCL *Pamphlets;* "Cremation," *World* (March 15, 1874) 2; *Urn* 2.1 (February 1893) 7; "A Request," *MC* 1.8 (August 1886) 113.

55. Reverend Charles Reilly, "Pagan or Christian," 10–11, in ES; H. A. Brann, "Christian Burial and Cremation," *ACQR* 10 (October 1885) 678; James P. Murphy, "The Cremation Movement is Anti-Catholic," *Catholic World* 73.436 (July 1901) 456.

56. Dr. P. F. Hyatt, "The Disposal of the Dead," *MC* 3.4 (October 1888) 54; "Of Interest to Spiritualists," *Urn* 4.8 (August 1895) 5; L. D. Z., "Passe," *MC* 2.12 (December 1887) 185; J. P. M'Caskey, "'Be Thou Clean!'" *MC* 1.1 (January 1886) 2; "What Cremation Is Not," *Columbarium* 2.5 (July 1895) 2; Williams, *Cremation and Other Modes of Sepulture,* 73. The *Lynn Press* called the corpse "so much refuse" ("Editor's Retort," *Urn* 3.5 [May 1894] 4). Cremationists did not typically go that far.

57. *MC* 2.7 (July 1887) 110.

58. "The Process Explained," *Columbarium* 2.5 (July 1895) 4; Anonymous, *Cremation, by an Eyewitness* (New York: A. S. Barnes, 1880) 9.

59. David L. Gollaher, "From Ritual to Science: The Medical Transformation of Circumcision in America," *Journal of Social History* 28.1 (Fall 1994) 12–13; H. A. Brann, "Christian Burial and Cremation," *ACQR* 10 (October 1885) 695;

"Report on Cremation," *JAMA* 6.22 (May 29, 1886) 607. This sort of division has operated in many other societies, notably in India where ritual bathing has been one of the main ways that pure, high-caste Brahmins differentiate themselves from polluted "untouchables." Like America's cremationists, those Brahmins are "pure" in both the ritual and the sanitary sense of the term. It should be noted, however, that Brahmins are forbidden from tending to cremations themselves. That work, which is considered polluting, is performed by "untouchables."

60. Catherine Bell, *Ritual Theory, Ritual Practice* (New York: Oxford University Press, 1992) 101–104. This approach has its critics. See Louis Dumont, *Essays on Individualism: Modern Ideology in Anthropological Perspective* (Chicago: University of Chicago Press, 1986) 223–33. See also Rodney Needham's rejoinder in his *Counterpoints* (Berkeley: University of California Press, 1987) 102–86.

61. Mary Douglas, *Purity and Danger: An Analysis of the Concepts of Pollution and Taboo* (Boston: Ark, 1984) 128.

62. J. Wetherbee, "Cremation in Boston" (Roxbury, 1895), handwritten manuscript in Countway Library of Medicine, Harvard University.

63. Wetherbee, "Cremation in Boston."

4. The Business of Cremation

1. "The End of Cremation," *Times* (October 17, 1879) 4; "Dr. LeMoyne's Furnace," *Times* (February 19, 1878) 2; "Cremation as a Science," *Medical Record* (December 16, 1876) 816; John Storer Cobb, "Abstract of an Address," in *Information regarding Cremation* (Boston: New England Cremation Society, 1899) 12.

2. "Professor Gross Dead," *Philadelphia Record* (May 7, 1884) 1. The *Boston Transcript* is quoted in "Cremation," *Modern Cemetery* 2.11 (January 1893) 128.

3. "Cremation," in *Chamber's Encyclopedia* (Philadelphia: Lippincott, 1897) 3:556; George Hodges, "Ashes to Ashes," *Urn* 4.2 (February 1895) 2; "Cremation Approved," *Tribune* (May 14, 1899) S5; "Cremation," *Times* (April 21, 1902) 8; "More about Incineration," in ES, 17; "The Progress of Cremation in the United States," *Urn* 1.11 (December 1892) 1; "Cremation at Detroit," *Urn* 1.10 (November 1892) 6.

4. "In Union There is Strength," *MC* 1.5 (May 1886) 65; "A National Cremation Society," *MC* 1.5 (May 1886) 72; "Propaganda," *Urn* 1.4 (May 1892) 1. The *Lancaster Examiner* is quoted in "Slow but Steady," *Urn* 2.9 (October 1893) 4.

5. There are a number of sources for nineteenth-century cremation data. I have relied on John Storer Cobb, *A Quartercentury of Cremation in North America* (Boston: Knight and Millet, 1901) 117–21. See also James R. Chadwick, *The Cremation of the Dead* (Boston: Geo. H. Ellis, 1905) 14–16; Lodovico Foresti, *Statistica delle Cremazioni Eseguite in Europa nel Secolo XIX* (Bologna: Stabilimento Giuseppe Civelli, 1901) 6–10; Sir Henry Thompson, *Modern Cremation* (London: Smith, Elder, & Co., 1901) 16, 25; "Cremation Statistics—1885–1935," *Pharos* 2.4 (July 1936) 25.

6. "Our Columbarium," *Urn* 2.3 (April 1893) 11; Louise Rockwood Wardner, "Plea for Cremation," *Modern Cemetery* 3.4 (June 1893) 42; "Dealing with the Dead," *World* (March 29, 1874) 4.

7. "Le Moyne's Body," *Philadelphia Press* (October 17, 1879) 1; "Cremating Prof. Gross," *Philadelphia Record* (May 8, 1884) 1; untitled editorial, *Times* (November 17, 1885) 4; Robert Marsena Stone, "Cremation," *JAMA* 34.8 (February 24, 1900) 473; Massachusetts Cremation Society, *Fifteenth Annual Report for the Year 1908* (Boston: Geo. H. Ellis, 1909) 5; "Cremation versus Burial," *Sunnyside* (June 15, 1916) 24.

8. Untitled editorial, *Tribune* (November 18, 1882) 4. Bierce is quoted on cremation in "Editor's Retort," *Urn* 1.7 (August 1892) 5; and "Cremation and Poverty," *Urn* 1.6 (July 1892) 2. The famous Bierce line about death and litigation appears in Lewis O. Saum, *The Popular Mood of America, 1860–1890* (Lincoln: University of Nebraska Press, 1990) 107.

9. Cobb, *A Quartercentury of Cremation in North America*, 63.

10. "Cremation and Freemasonry," *MC* (November 1886) 168. The best source of information on Erichsen's life is the biographical sketch contained in Dr. Hugo Erichsen, *Roses and Ashes and Other Writings* (Detroit: American Printing Company, 1917) 9–20.

11. "A Semi-Centennial: From *The Urn*, December 5, 1935," *Urn* 4.9 (September 1895) 1–3. All subsequent descriptions of this "model crematory" and its rites are from this source.

12. S. F. Balcom, "The Columbarium of the Future," *P&C* 24.11 (January 1915) 267–68.

13. S. F. Balcom, "The Columbarium of the Future," *P&C* 24.11 (January 1915) 267–268.

14. "Cremation and Crematories," *American Architect and Building News* 12.341 (July 8, 1882) 22.

15. "Omaha's New Model Chapel and Crematory," *P&C* 24.9 (November 1914) 293–95.

16. "Lakewood's New Chapel is a Model Building," *P&C* 21.3 (May 1911) 547.

17. Mr. Hargrave, "Crematories I Have Met," *CAA Proceedings* (1925) 32.

18. *The American Architect* 88.1557 (October 28, 1905) 143. The data come from Chadwick, *The Cremation of the Dead,* 14.

19. Robert W. Habenstein, "A Sociological Study of the Cremation Movement in the United States" (M.A. thesis, University of Chicago, 1949) 145, 154; "Statistical Report," *CAA Proceedings* (1929) 11–13; "Operating Crematories," *CAA Proceedings* (1932) 56–57.

20. For an application of this truism to American religious history, see Laurie Maffly-Kipp, *Religion and Society on the California Frontier* (New Haven: Yale University Press, 1994).

21. David Charles Sloane, *The Last Great Necessity: Cemeteries in American History* (Baltimore: Johns Hopkins University Press, 1991) 152.

22. Hugo Erichsen, "Cremation and the Undertaker," *Sunnyside* (April 15, 1912) 27.

23. "Cemetery Notes," *Modern Cemetery* 2.8 (October 1892) 94; James Currie, "The Crematory in the Modern Cemetery," *P&C* 27.8 (October 1917) 214; *The Cemetery Handbook: A Manual of Useful Information on Cemetery Development & Management* (Chicago: Allied Arts Publishing, [1921?]) 276, 275. The statistics come from William B. Currie, "Cremation as a Part of the Cemetery," *AACS Proceedings* (1939) 110.

24. J. Henderson, "Cremation and the Cemetery," *P&C* 30.8 (October 1920) 215. In 1930, Mount Auburn performed 479 cremations and 588 total interments. Of those total interments, however, 142 were interments of ashes and only 446 whole-body burials. During the 1930s, Mount Auburn recorded 5,942 cremations and 5,932 total interments (whole-body burials and burials of cremated remains included). In 1933, cremations outran burials at the other Massachusetts crematory at Forest Hills Cemetery, which conducted 652 whole-body burials and 658 cremations. See Mount Auburn Cemetery, "Standard Report" (January 12, 1998) and Forest Hills Cemetery, "Record of Burials and Cremations," 1.

25. "The Cincinnati Crematorium," *Modern Cemetery* 2.7 (September 1892) 78.

26. Frank Bates Flanner, "How to Conduct a Cremation Funeral," *Sunnyside* (September 15, 1915) 37; "Progress in Cremation," *Boston Transcript* (June 10, 1908), in MA Scrapbook, 2.26.

27. Los Angeles Crematory, "Time Changes All Things" [1920s?]; "Phrases for Use in Promoting Cremation," undated typescript in Forest Hills Archives, 6.

28. Andrew W. Blackwood, *The Funeral: A Source Book for Ministers* (Philadelphia: Westminster, 1942) 156–58.

29. "Crematories on Liners," *Times* (September 8, 1910) 1; "Urn for the Reception of the Ashes of the Dead" (Patent 232,782), *Official Gazette of the United States Patent Office* 18.13 (September 28, 1880) 727; "A Patent Urn," *Urn* 1.7 (August 25, 1892) 4.

30. Lawrence Moore, "Crematories and Cremation," *AACS Proceedings* (1929) 34.

31. Lawrence Moore, "Lift Up Their Hearts," *CAA Proceedings* (1948) 55.

32. Frank Gibson, quoted in *CAA Proceedings* (1929) 23–26.

33. Lawrence F. Moore, "Technology of Cremation," *AACS Proceedings* (1940) 68.

34. Edgar King, "History and Practice of Cremation," *P&C* 25.1 (March 1915) 15. See *The Official Gazette of the United States Patent Office* 139.13 (February 16, 1909) 579–80 (Patent 912,585); and 24.12 (September 18, 1883) 1105 (Patent 285,034). In a study on "Cremation in Chicago and the Central States" *CAA Proceedings* (1933) 32, W.B. Currie reported that "the great majority" of the crematories in the area used oil, while three used gas, one used gas and coke, and one used coke (32).

5. The Memorial Idea

1. Quincy L. Dowd, *Funeral Management and Costs: A World Survey of Burial and Cremation* (Chicago: University of Chicago Press, 1921); and edito-

rial staff of the *Cremationist*, "Cremation Figures from 1876 to Present" (1995, photocopy).

2. See Karen Isaksen Leonard, *Making Ethnic Choices: California's Punjabi Mexican Americans* (Philadelphia: Temple University Press, 1992) 7, 49, 129–30, 181–82, 201.

3. Peter Jupp, *From Dust to Ashes: The Replacement of Burial by Cremation in England, 1840–1967* (London: Congregational Memorial Hall Trust, 1990). See also Peter Jupp, "Cremation or Burial? Contemporary Choice in City and Village," in *The Sociology of Death: Theory, Culture, Practice,* ed. David Clark (Oxford: Blackwell, 1993) 169–97.

4. *Urn* 4.4 (April 1895) 5; "The Advance of Cremation," *Boston Herald* (January 30, 1896), in ES.

5. David Charles Sloane, *The Last Great Necessity: Cemeteries in American History* (Baltimore: Johns Hopkins University Press, 1991) 225; C. J. Buchanan, "Cremation and the Funeral Director," *CAA Proceedings* (1925) 12.

6. "The Progress of Cremation," *American Cemetery* (August 1935) 12.

7. Charles Lowel Cooder, "Christian Aspect of Cremation," *MC* 1.1 (January 1886) 5.

8. Sir Henry Thompson, *Cremation: The Treatment of the Body after Death* (London: Henry S. King, 1874) 10, 11, 13; "Cremation: What Is Thought of It by Physicians" (Eighth Series) *M&SR* (February 8, 1890) 170; Prof. G. Barricelli, *After the End of Life: A Positive Dissertation* (n.p., [1880?]) 4–5; "The Cremation Movement: Singular Testament Directing Its Adoption," *Tribune* (April 13, 1974) 2. Barricelli may have intended his dissertation as satire. Using corpses as kindling was put forward seriously by a Dr. Rudler of Paris. (See R. E. Williams, *Cremation and Other Modes of Sepulture* [Philadelphia: Lippincott, 1884], 68.) Some anti-cremation physicians claimed corpses were more valuable to medical students as cadavers than they were to plants as fertilizer. It should be noted that cremationists were not the century's only vulgar utilitarians. Dr. George Hay, a chemist, advocated pulverizing and drying corpses and then selling them for manure ("Disposing of Corpses," MA Scrapbook, 1.5).

9. P. H. Holland, "Burial or Cremation," *Contemporary Review* 23.3 (February 1874) 483; "The Kindling Pyre," *World* (April 5, 1874) 4. Some opposed cremation on equally crass grounds. A Dr. Fishe of Missouri claimed it would "destroy a certain amount of matter which by no means can be restored to the world, and which lessens the amount of ordinary animal or vegetable life which otherwise could be used in the service of ourselves" ("Discussion" of Dr. Robert Marsena Stone, "Cremation," *JAMA* 34.8 [February 24, 1900] 476).

10. "Cremations, 1876–1901, LeMoyne Crematory," a list compiled by Washington County Historical Society; "Table of Cremations in the United States, 1876 to 1893," *Urn* 2.11–12 (December 1893) 4; "Reduced to Ashes," *MC* 3.2 (April 1888) 25; "The Usefulness of Cremation," *M&SR* 39.14 (October 5, 1878) 300. Of the 2,713 total cremations reported in the *Urn* in December 1893, 1,746 (69%) were males and 792 (31%) females. And of the 4,152 cremations examined in C. O. Probst, "Report of the Committee on the Disposal of the Dead," *JAMA* (December 14, 1895) 1028–1034, there were 2,783 males and 1,369 females—a ratio again of roughly 2:1.

11. "A Woman on Cremation," *MC* 4.1 (January 1889) 2; "Women Favoring the Method," *MC* 4.1 (January 1889) 12; Louis Lange, *Church, Woman and Cremation* (New York: United States Cremation Company, 1903) 26–27; "The New York Cremation Society," *Urn* 4.1 (January 1895) 2; "Women Favoring the Method," *MC* 4.1 (January 1889) 13.

12. "The Dedication at Fresh Pond," *Urn* 2.6 (July 1893) 2. On developments in the American funeral industry, see Robert W. Habenstein and William M. Lamers, *The History of American Funeral Directing*, 3d rev. ed., ed. Howard C. Raether (Milwaukee: National Funeral Directors Association, 1995); and Gary Laderman's fine cultural history, *The Sacred Remains: American Attitudes toward Death, 1799–1883* (New Haven: Yale University Press, 1996) esp. 164–175.

13. These papal edicts, grounded in the perception that cremationists, especially in Italy, were fiercely anti-clerical and strongly inclined toward freemasonry, forbade Roman Catholics to join cremation societies or to request cremation. Recalcitrant Catholics were to be denied church burial.

14. Monseigneur Gaume, *The Christian Cemetery in the Nineteenth Century* (New York: Benziger Brothers, 1874) 137.

15. F. Julius LeMoyne, *Cremation: An Argument to Prove That Cremation Is Preferable to Inhumation of Dead Bodies* (Pittsburgh: E. W. Lightner, 1878) 15, 17.

16. "Opening the Crematory," *New York Sun* (December 5, 1885) 1; Hodges quoted in "Public Meeting in Boston," *Urn* 4.6 (June 25, 1895) 5.

17. See the discussion reprinted in *CAA Proceedings* (1943) 34–35. On cremation as Aryan, see Lawrence Moore, "Crematories and Cremation," *AACS Proceedings* (1929) 33.

18. "Items of Interest," *Columbarium* 2.8 (October 1895) 4; "'United We Stand,'" *Urn* 1.10 (November 1892) 1. The following occupations for individuals cremated at the Fresh Pond crematory are listed in Augustus G. Cobb, *Earth-Burial and Cremation* (New York: G. P. Putnam's Sons, 1892) 148:

34 Merchants	6 Professors
28 Physicians	6 of Dramatic Profession
17 Journalists	5 Druggists
15 Brokers	4 Scientific Engineers
12 Artists	4 Chemists
7 Teachers	2 Authors
2 Clergymen.	

19. "Religion and Cremation," in JCL *Pamphlets*, 12–13; Stevens quoted in "More Cremation Conversation," *Inquirer* (December 7, 1876) 2.

20. Rabbi Louis Wolsey, "Attitude of the Jewish People toward Cremation," *CAA Proceedings* (1940) 18–24; Abraham I. Shinedling, "Cremation," in *The Universal Jewish Encyclopedia*, ed. Isaac Landman (New York: The Universal Jewish Encyclopedia, Inc., 1941) 405. See also Walter Jacob, ed., *American Reform Responsa: Collected Responsa of the Central Conference of American Rabbis, 1889–1983* (New York: The Conference, 1983) 341–48.

21. "A Cremation Catechism," *Urn* 2.9 (October 1893) 2. This article also provides the data. West Coast statistics tell a different story. Of the first 200 cre-

mations in San Francisco, "130 were natives of America" and "46 of Germany." Still, German Americans heavily outnumbered the English-born, who accounted for only seven of the bodies (*Urn* 4.5 [May 1895], 8).

22. W. B. Currie, "Cremation in Chicago and the Central States," *CAA Proceedings* (1933) 30. See "Fire-Burial among Our Germanic Forefathers," *MC* 2.4 (April 1887) 50–55. This article is continued in 2.5 (May 1887) 65–71; and 2.6 (June 1887) 81–87.

23. George Hodges, "Ashes to Ashes," *Urn* 4.2 (February 1895) 2.

24. Emmett L. Ross, "Cremation," *MC* 1.9 (September 1886) 129; *MC* 1.1 (January 1886) 16. This battle came into public view again in San Francisco early in the middle period of cremation's American history. The catalyst was a decision by the Odd Fellows crematory to begin conducting funerals. The United Undertakers of San Francisco and Alameda Counties, intent on rebuffing this foray onto what it saw as its turf, had convinced the local Stable Keepers' Association and Hack Drivers' Union to refuse to drive for Odd Fellows' funerals unless and until the crematory manager belonged to the local funeral directors association. So the manager applied and was rebuffed. In 1902, the crematory responded with an unusual broadside addressed "to the friends of cremation and the public." While noting that cremation was not a money saver in all cases, the crematory pointed out that cremation did reduce expenses in "the preparation of bodies, THE COST OF CEMETERY LOTS, CASKETS, METALLIC, AND OTHER USELESS ORNAMENTATION" (Odd Fellows' Cemetery Association broadside, "To the Friends of Cremation and the Public," May 30, 1902). Unfortunately, I have not been able to determine how this dispute was settled.

25. "Our Friends the Undertakers," *Urn* 2.9 (October 1893) 4; "Mind Your Own Business," *Urn* 3.2 (February 1894) 1–2; untitled advertisement, *Urn* 1.3 (March 1892); *Urn* 3.7 (July 1894) 5; Hugo Erichsen, "Cremation and the Undertaker," *Sunnyside* (April 15, 1912) 27, in ES; Leslie Hoagland, "Cremation Sales," *CAA Proceedings* (1926) 32. For Erichsen's earlier views, see "The Torch versus the Space," *Detroit Commercial Advertiser* (n.d.), in ES.

26. Leslie Hoagland, "Cremation Sales," *CAA Proceedings* (1926) 36; Lawrence Moore, quoted in *CAA Proceedings* (1928) 18; Frank Bates Flanner, "How to Conduct a Cremation Funeral," *Sunnyside* (September 15, 1915) 37; and Frank B. Flanner, *Cremation and the Funeral Director* (Buffalo, N.Y.: Cremation Association of America, 1915).

27. Lawrence F. Moore, "Progress Knows No Barriers," in *Cemetery Handbook and Buyers' Guide* (American Cemetery Owners Association, 1937) 23; Henry S. Adams, "Cremation Problem in the East," *CAA Proceedings* (1935) 33; Frank Gibson, quoted in *CAA Proceedings* (1929) 25.

28. Vernon L. Thompson, "The Cremation Trend," *AACS Proceedings* (1941) 91. *Casket* and *Western Undertaker* are quoted in "Cemetery Notes," *Modern Cemetery* 2.8 (October 1892) 94. *Mortuary Management* is discussed in Robert W. Habenstein, "A Sociological Study of the Cremation Movement in the United States" (M.A. thesis, University of Chicago, 1949) 173. Results of the survey appear in "President's Report," *CAA Proceedings* (1931) 13. A later survey found that roughly one-quarter of crematory operators reported "ill-will"

from local funeral directors. See Lloyd M. Smith, "Is the Operation of a Crematory an Advantage to a Cemetery?" *CAA Proceedings* (1943) 34.

29. Franklin Edson Belden, *Temples of Peace or the Endowed Community Mausoleum* (Seattle: published by the author, 1916) 44–48. Belden described the involuntary contraction of the muscles in the arms he witnessed—a movement interpreted by witnesses to the De Palm cremation as a spiritual sign—as an act of "agonizing protest" (47).

30. R. E. Williams, *Cremation and Other Modes of Sepulture*, 68; "Cincinnati Red Pepper," *Urn* 1.8 (September 1892) 4. Harrison explains his position in his *Realities and Ideals: Social, Political, Literary and Artistic* (New York: Macmillan, 1908) 156–66.

31. "California Physicians," *Urn* 3.9 (Sept 25, 1894) 9; George Hodges, "Ashes to Ashes," *Urn* 4.2 (February 1895) 3; ES, 73; New England Cremation Society, *Information Regarding Cremation* (Boston: New England Cremation Society, 1899) 17; Erichsen quoted in "The First National Cremation Convention," *Sunnyside* (circa 1913), in JCL *Pamphlets*.

32. "Cremation at Fresh Pond," *Urn* 2.5 (June 1893) 3; "A Cremation Catechism," *Urn* 2.9 (October 1893) 2; "Our Columbarium," *Urn* 2.9 (October 1893) 10. For a similar description of the goings-on at the Philadelphia Crematorium, see "The Process Explained," *Columbarium* 2.5 (July 1895) 4.

33. Howard Henderson, *Cremation: Rational Method of Disposing of the Dead* (Cincinnati: Geo. P. Houston, 1891) 6, 18; Hodges quoted in "Public Meeting in Boston," *Urn* 4.6 (June 25, 1895) 5.

34. Charles Kerney, "'Why I Am a Crematist,'" *MC* 1.3 (March 1886) 34.

35. *Urn* 4.6 (June 1895) 8; "A Triumph of Science," *MC* 1.7 (July 1886) 99; "What the Poets Say," *World* (March 29, 1874) 2.

36. "Lotus and Jewel: Buddhism Saranam Gak Khammi," *Los Angeles Herald* (April 30, 1892) 3. See also "Buddhist Cremation in California," *Brooklyn Daily Eagle* (April 30, 1892) 6.

37. James Currie, "The Crematory as an Adjunct to the Modern Cemetery," *AACS Proceedings* (1917) 36.

38. Massachusetts Cremation Society, *Cremation: What Thoughtful People of the Day Have Said about It* (n.p., n.d.) 29–30; W. B. Currie, "Cremation in Chicago and the Central States," *CAA Proceedings* (1933) 33; "What Cremation Is Not," *Columbarium* 2.5 (July 1895) 2. Currie referred to his geographical region as "the Central States" and defined it as follows: "Western Pennsylvania on the east, Colorado on the west, Minnesota on the north, and Texas on the south" (29).

39. Leslie Hoagland, "Your Obligation as a Crematory Owner Today," in *CAA Proceedings* (1934) 25.

40. Walter B. Londelius, "Cremation and Modern Crematory Construction," *AACS Proceedings* (1928) 26–27; and Walter B. Londelius in *CAA Proceedings* (1927) 26. In *The Comemoral: The Cemetery of the Future* (Los Angeles: Interment Association of America, 1954) Hubert Eaton of Forest Lawn claimed credit for discovering the memorial idea, which by 1954 he was calling "the memorial impulse" (11).

41. Henry S. Adams, "Cremation Problem in the East," *CAA Proceedings* (1935) 33; American Cemetery Owners Association, *Cemetery Handbook* (1937) 23.

42. Hubert Eaton, "Who Wants to Be Forgotten?" in American Cemetery Owners Association, *Cemetery Handbook* (1937) 46; Roy Hatten, "Little Courtesies That Help Sales," in *CAA Proceedings* (1938) 52; Hugo Erichsen, "A Quarter of a Century of Achievement, Its Past, Present, and Future Significance," in *CAA Proceedings* (1938) 49; Harold L. Wright, "The Funeral Director Looks at Cremation," *CAA Proceedings* (1939) 19.

43. *CAA Proceedings* (1948) 53; Leslie Hoagland, "Cremation Sales," *CAA Proceedings* (1926) 37.

44. Herbert R. Hargrave, "Customs and Practices of U.S. Crematories," in *CAA Proceedings* (1940) 22–23; Cremation Association of America, *Manual of Standard Crematory-Columbarium Practices* (Cremation Association of America, 1941) 8.

45. Lawrence F. Moore, "Technology of Cremation," *AACS Proceedings* (1940) 69.

46. http://www.peoples-memorial.org/history.htm (August 16, 1999).

47. Dr. Kenneth W. Dumars, Jr., quoted in "Medical Magazine Publishers Memorial Society Propaganda," *AFD* 85.3 (March 1962) 59; Herb Klein, *Don't Waste Your Death...It Could Save a Life!* (Farmington, Mich.: ad-Creators, Inc., 1975). The slogan appears as the epigram to Klein's book.

48. C. O. Probst, "Report of the Committee of the Disposal of the Dead," *JAMA* (December 14, 1895) 1030–31; James Currie, "Crematory in the Modern Cemetery," *P&C* 27.8 (October 1917) 214; S. Adolphus Knopf, "Cremation versus Burial—A Plea for More Sanitary and More Economical Disposition of Our Dead," *American Journal of Public Health* 12.5 (May 1922) 391; Lawrence Moore, "Crematories and Cremation," *AACS Proceedings* (1929) 35.

49. Lawrence Moore, "Crematories and Cremation," *AACS Proceedings* (1929) 36.

50. Missouri Crematory Association, *Cremation a Growing Custom* (St. Louis: Missouri Crematory Association, 1916); and Kenneth Robb, "I Restore to Nature," *Reader's Digest* 64.382 (February 1954).

51. Frances Newton, *Light Like the Sun* (New York: Dodd, Mead, 1937). In the 1990s, Funeral and Memorial Societies of America was continuing to make use of this essay. See http://vbiweb.champlain.edu/famsa/light.htm (August 24, 1999).

52. "Wisdom's Weavings," *MC* 3.3 (July 1888) 46. On nature religion, see Catherine L. Albanese, *Nature Religion in America: From the Algonkian Indians to the New Age* (Chicago: University of Chicago Press, 1990).

53. William Devlin, "Cremation," in *The Catholic Encyclopedia*, ed. Charles G. Herbermann et al. (New York: Appleton, 1908) 482–83; Bertrand L. Conway, "The Ethics and History of Cremation," *Catholic World* 117.702 (September 1923) 735; "A Leading Article on Cremation of the Dead," *Catholic Medical Guardian* (July 1928), quoted in Habenstein, "A Sociological Study," 118; "The Sign-Post," *Sign* 16.11 (July 1937) 750; "The Sign-Post,"

Sign 26.5 (December 1946) 49; Most Rev. J. Duhig, D.D., "The Church and Cremation," *Catholic Mind* 39.934 (November 22, 1941) 10–11. *The Catholic Encyclopedia* of 1908 held out the possibility of future reconsideration of the matter: "It must be remembered that there is nothing directly opposed to any dogma of the Church in the practice of cremation, and that, if ever the leaders of this sinister movement so far control the governments of the world as to make this custom universal, it would not be a lapse in the faith confided to her were she obliged to conform" (William Devlin, "Cremation," in *The Catholic Encyclopedia,* ed. Charles G. Herbermann et al. [New York: Appleton, 1908], 482–83).

54. Quoted in William E. Phipps, *Cremation Concerns* (Springfield, Ill.: Thomas, 1989) 25; James P. O'Hara, "Cremation," *Catholic Digest* 4.8 (June 1940) 42–45.

55. "Cremation Forbidden by Church," *Sign* 16.11 (July 1937) 749–50; "Selling Cremation," *Catholic Digest* 1.12 (October 1937) 24–25.

6. Consumers' Last Rites

1. Paul Bryan, "The Challenge to Cremation in America," paper delivered at the Congress of the International Cremation Federation, Berlin, June 1963.

2. "Cremation and the Canon Law," *Pharos* 27.1 (February 1961) 3. For later developments, see "Cremation: Permissible," *Time* (June 12, 1964) 85; P. Herbert Jones, "The Pope Lifts the Ban," *Pharos* 30.3 (August 1964) 54–55; Paul E. Irion, *Cremation* (Philadelphia: Fortress Press, 1968) 73–84; and John F. McDonald, "A Decade of Cremation in the Roman Catholic Church," *Pharos* 42.1 (February 1976) 35–40. On the new, post-Conciliar liturgical style, the key source is Vatican Council, *Constitution on the Sacred Liturgy* (Collegeville, Minn.: Liturgical Press, 1963).

3. Jessica Mitford, *The American Way of Death* (New York: Simon & Schuster, 1963) 58. The long quotation is from Jessica Mitford, "The Funeral Salesmen," *McCall's* (November 1977) 190.

4. Jessica Mitford, "Death, Incorporated," *Vanity Fair* (March 1997) 110.

5. "Cremation: Expense of the Present Mode of Burial," *World* (March 8, 1874) 1; Mark Twain, *Life on the Mississippi* (New York: Harper & Row, 1951) 350, 353.

6. Quincy L. Dowd, *Funeral Management and Costs: A World Survey of Burial and Cremation* (Chicago: University of Chicago Press, 1921) 3–4; John C. Gebhart, *Funeral Costs* (New York: G.P. Putnam's Sons, 1928); Arnold Wilson and Hermann Levy, *Burial Reform and Funeral Costs* (New York: Oxford University Press, 1938); FCC survey quoted in "High Cost of Dying," *Newsweek* (November 20, 1944) 84.

7. Howard C. Raether includes a comprehensive list of these and similar titles in his *Funeral Service: A Historical Perspective* (Washington, D.C.: National Funeral Directors Association, 1990) 17–25.

8. Mitford, *The American Way of Death,* 231, 18–19, 60, 77–78, 236. Reviews included: Orville Prescott, "The High Cost of Dying," *Times* (August 28, 1963) 31; Francis Russell, "Merchants of Death," *National Review* 15.16 (Oc-

tober 22, 1963) 362–64; Richard Gilman, "The Loved One Is in the Slumber Room, Laid Out in Style," *New York Times Book Review* (August 25, 1963) 4, 25. See also Jessica Mitford, *The American Way of Death Revisited* (New York: Knopf, 1998).

9. http://www.peoples-memorial.org (August 16, 1999).

10. Alfred C. Longley, "Make Christian Burial Christian," *Ave Maria* 99.25 (June 20, 1964) 10; Feuerstein quoted in "Lavish Funerals Scored by Jews," *Times* (January 8, 1966) 13; Krol quoted in "Archbishop Scores Burial 'Escapism,'" *Times* (October 16, 1966) 62.

11. "Giving Undertakers Something to Cry About," *Business Week* (October 6, 1975) 93.

12. "Taking on the Undertakers," *Times* (July 2, 1978) 4.14.

13. "FTC Staff Report Echoes Earliest Charges, Demands," *AFD* 101 (July 1978) 18.

14. Mitford, *The American Way of Death*, 265; Howard C. Raether, "There Are None So Lost," *AFD* 85.11 (November 1962) 48.

15. "Two More Magazines Publish Attacks on Burial Practices," *American Cemetery* 23.8 (August 1951) 23; "Collier's Fails to Correct Untruths in Davidson Story," *American Cemetery* 23.7 (July 1951) 21; Utt quoted in "Jessica Mitford Called Pro-Red," *Times* (October 18, 1963) 63; Julius J. Nodel, *Death and Human Dignity*, pamphlet (1963) 7, 5; "British-Born Mitford Still is Raking in Those Good Yankee Dollars!" *AFD* 88.7 (July 1965) 39; "Let Us Prove That Funerals Do Not Cost Too Much," *AFD* 99.5 (May 1976) 49. Mitford and her husband had been members of the Communist Party. Both were called before the House Committee on Un-American Activities in 1952, and they resigned together from the Party in 1958.

16. Charles O. Kates, "We Are No Longer Optimistic," *AFD* 99 (June 1976) 31; Jessica Mitford, "The Funeral Salesmen," *McCall's* (November 1977) 192, 312; "Regulating Death?" *Newsweek* (July 3, 1978) 59; Paul E. Irion, *The Funeral: Vestige or Value?* (Nashville: Abingdon Press, 1966) 71; "Giving Undertakers Something to Cry About," *Business Week* (October 6, 1975) 93.

17. Irion, *The Funeral: Vestige or Value?* 7.

18. "Funeral and Memorial Societies and Memorial Services," *Director* 41.4 (April 1971) 5.

19. "General Comments," *Director* 41.4 (April 1971) 3; "Used Cars, Eyeglasses, and Coffins" *Times* (November 28, 1978) 22.

20. "NFDA Ratio Analysis Shows Minimal Price Increases," *AFD* 101.11 (November 1978) 43–44.

21. Gerald Gold, "Wide Range of Funeral Prices Found Here in Consumer Study," *Times* (April 7, 1974) 38; Richard Severo, "Disputed Practices of Undertakers Are Defended by Some in Business," *Times* (April 24, 1978) 1; The *Sun-Times* series comes in for criticism in "Once Again: Why?" *AFD* 104.8 (August 1981) 30.

22. The NFDA's cost estimate for 1999 was $5,778. See http://www.nfda.org/resources/99gpl.html (March 31, 2000).

23. Jessica Mitford, "Bake and Shake," *New York* (January 21, 1980) 50–52.

24. Consumer Reports, *Funerals: Consumers' Last Rights* (New York: W.W. Norton, 1977) 178; "A Move to Embalm 'Cremation Clubs,'" *Business Week* (September 21, 1974) 89. See also "Cheap Cremation Wins a Lease on Life," *Business Week* (August 12, 1972) 31.

25. "'Barbaric, Nightmarish,' Argues Kate Holliday," *Good Housekeeping* (February 1968) 182; "Cremated Remains Lost by Post Office," *AFD* 99 (June 1976) 16; "One Must Treat the Dead with Reverence and Respect," *AFD* 103 (January 1980) 39; James W. Fraser, *Cremation: Is It Christian?* (Neptune, N.J.: Loizeaux Brothers, 1965) 19, 11.

26. Quoted in "Funeral Customs Raising Protests," *Times* (September 3, 1963) 35.

27. Raether quoted in Steven V. Roberts, "Cremation Gaining Favor in U.S.," *Times* (December 6, 1970) 73. Public opinion was changing too. In 1971, *Psychology Today* asked over 30,000 of its readers, "If it were entirely up to you, how would you like to have your body disposed of after you have died?" Thirty-one percent said cremation. (Edwin S. Schneidman, "You and Death," *Psychology Today* 5.1 [1971] 43–45, 74–80.)

28. Amy Seidel Marks and Bobby J. Calder, *Attitudes toward Death and Funerals* (Chicago: The Center for Marketing Sciences, J.L. Kellogg Graduate School of Management, Northwestern University, 1982) 157.

29. Steven V. Roberts, "Cremation Gaining Favor in U.S.," *Times* (December 6, 1970) 73, 1.

30. Herb Klein, *Don't Waste Your Death...It Could Save a Life!* (Farmington, Mich.: ad-Creators, Inc., 1975) 7–8.

31. "A Shift in Attitude on Funerals Noted," *Times* (October 28, 1967) 25.

32. The Kennedy funeral was widely covered in the U.S. media. For an insightful interpretation, see Lawrence E. Sullivan, *Histories and Rituals: The Case of a National Rite of Mourning* (Tempe, Ariz.: Arizona State University, Department of Religious Studies, 1991).

33. "Ritual: A Changing Way of Death," *Time* (April 11, 1969) 60; "The State Funeral of Dwight D. Eisenhower," *AFD* 92.5 (May 1969) 43, 46.

34. Richard Severo, "Funeral Industry is Striving to Improve Its Image in Face of Charges of Deception and Abuses of the Public," *Times* (April 25, 1978) 20; "Famed Funeral Service Critic Jessica Mitford Dies: A Farewell To Arms," *FM* 5.30 (August 5, 1996) 3. For a rebuttal, see a letter to the editor by Mitford's long-time assistant, Karen J. Leonard: "'You Only Hurt the One You Love' Dept.: Striking Back for Jessica," *FM* (September 9, 1996) 3–4.

35. John Higham, *Send These to Me: Immigrants in Urban America* (rev. ed.; Baltimore: Johns Hopkins University Press, 1984) 194.

36. John Higham, *Send These to Me*, 196. Mitford and her pro-cremation contemporaries diverged from Puritan divines (and Gilded Age cremationists) in their tolerance of postmortem merry-making. Puritan elites wouldn't have railed so much against funeral fun if workaday colonists weren't getting a little tipsy at the funeral feast. Such revelry would have irked Cotton Mather, but Mitford wouldn't have minded it in the least.

37. On this new countercultural style, see Thomas Frank, *The Conquest of Cool: Business Culture, Counterculture, and the Rise of Hip Consumerism* (Chicago: University of Chicago Press, 1997).

38. Consumer Reports, *Funerals: Consumers' Last Rights,* 176.

39. This account is culled from these sources: Thomas E. Kelley, "Grief for John Lennon Neared Mass Hysteria," *AFD* (February 1981) 24–26, 70; "Yoko Ono Asks Mourners to Give to a Foundation Lennon Favored," *Times* (December 10, 1980) 2.7; ""Beatles' Songs Played in Memory of Lennon," *Times* (December 10, 1980) 2.7; Paul L. Montgomery, "Suspect in Lennon's Slaying Is Put under Suicide Watch," *Times* (December 11, 1980) 2.3; Clyde Haberman, "Silent Tribute to Lennon's Memory Is Observed throughout the World," *Times* (December 15, 1980) 1, 2.8; Yoko Ono Lennon, "In Gratitude," *Times* (January 18, 1981) 4.24.

7. Contemporary Ways of Cremation

1. Stephen Prothero, "Timothy Leary is Dead and Well and Blasting through Outer Space," *Salon,* April 22, 1997 (http://www.salonmagazine.com/april97/news/newsreal970422.html, August 25, 1999).

2. Untitled broadside obtained from Thomas E. Scanlin of Dahlonega, Georgia.

3. Billy Graham, "Cremation: My Answer" (http://www.capitalfuneral.com/csc/rel/index.html, May 20, 1999).

4. Cremation Association of North America, "1999 Data and Projections to the Year 2010" (CANA, 2000 photocopy). CANA's "1996/97 Cremation Container, Disposition, and Service Survey" found that 58% of the Americans cremated in 1996 were Protestant, 26% Catholic, 11% Buddhist, 3% Jewish, and 2% Hindu. A comparison of these data with U.S. demographics indicates that Catholics, Protestants, and women were being cremated at roughly the same rate as the overall U.S. population while Buddhists and Hindus were far more likely than the average American to be cremated. For a useful overview of the literature on the demography of cremation, see "Who Chooses Cremation?" (http://www.flash.net/~leimer/cremate3.html, August 18, 1999).

5. The Wirthlin Group, *1995 Study of American Attitudes toward Ritualization and Memorialization* (McLean, Va.: The Wirthlin Group, 1995) 19; Grayson predictions in "Plotting the Future in Funeral Service," *FM* 5.37 (September 23, 1996) 3; Jack Springer interview (June 1997).

6. "Human Ashes Found in Storage," *Boston Globe* (June 7, 1997) A16; "Man Tied to Remains Is Reported a Suicide," *Boston Globe* (June 26, 1997) A31; "Ashes to Ashes: Funeral Homes Face Lawsuit for Use of Bogus Scattering Service," *FM* 6.24 (June 23, 1997) 1–3.

7. Archpriest Victor Potapov, "Cremation: Earth Thou Art and unto Earth Shalt Thou Return" (http://www.stjohndc.org/homilies/homcremt.htm, August 17, 1999); Michael P. Horban, "Cremation or Burial?" *Pentecostal Evangel* (May 29, 1994) 7; Bruce L. Olsen, "Cremation," in *Encyclopedia of Mor-*

monism, ed. Daniel H. Ludlow (New York: Macmillan, 1992), quoted in www.mormons.org/daily/health/Cremation_EOM.htm (August 26, 1999); "Cremation Earns a Following," *Atlanta Journal-Constitution* (October 22, 1989) C6. The cremation rates appear in Cremation Association of North America, "1998 Data and Projections to the Year 2010" (1999). On Jewish cremation, see the web site of Temple Akiba of Culver City, California: http://www.shamash.org/reform/uahc/congs/ca/ca008/cremate.html (August 26, 1999).

8. Lawrence Jones interview (July 1997). The surveys are: Richard A. Kalish and David K. Reynolds, *Death and Ethnicity: A Psychocultural Study* (Farmingdale, N.Y.: Baywood Publishing, 1981); Wirthlin Group, *1995 Study;* CANA, "1996/97 Cremation Container, Disposition, and Service Survey" (1999). The last survey found that, of the Americans cremated in 1996, 6% were African American and 3% Hispanic. Since Blacks constituted about 12% of the U.S. population and Hispanics about 9%, those two groups were two and three times less likely, respectively, to be cremated than the average American.

9. National Conference of Catholic Bishops, *Order Of Christian Funerals,* appendix 2: *Cremation* (Totowa, N.J,: Catholic Book Publishing Co., 1997) 6.

10. Bud Noakes, "The Future of the Traditional Funeral," *MM* 64.11 (November 1977) 17.

11. Tom Fisher, "How Young People Feel about Cremation: Is American Funeral Service Ready?" *MM* 68.3 (March 1981) 24; National Funeral Directors Association, *Tradition in Transition: The Report of the Twenty-First Century Committee of the National Funeral Directors Association* (NFDA, 1981) 16.

12. "Attracting Cremation Business—and Making It More Profitable," *FM* (October 14, 1996) 5.

13. "The Carpers' Club," *Daily Graphic* (May 2, 1874) 474.

14. Michael W. Kubasak, *Cremation and the Funeral Director: Successfully Meeting the Challenge* (Malibu, Calif.: Avalon Press, 1990) 136, 5, 3, 15, 10.

15. Michael Kubasak interview (June 1997).

16. "Rocket Cremation Dollars with Independent Showroom," *FSI* 20.44 (November 20, 1995) 3–4.

17. "Jessica Mitford Again?" *FM* (December 21–28, 1992) 5; "5 Tips to Creatively Boost Cremation Merchandise $$$," *FSI* 22.6 (February 10, 1997); "4 Ways to Make Your Cremation Service Sizzle," *FSI* 22.9 (March 3, 1997) 2–3; "3 Tips to Rev Up Your Cremation Calls (and Stay Profitable)" *FSI* 22.3 (January 20, 1997) 3–4; "One Quick Tip to Get Your Families beyond a Direct Cremation," *FSI* 21.39 (October 14, 1996) 4.

18. "Skyrocket Cremation Leads with First-Rate Marketing Tips," *FSI* 22.9 (March 3, 1997) 3; "Super Scattering Options = More Cremation Services," *FSI* 22.18 (May 5, 1997) 3; "FSI's Top 8 Tips for Boosting Cremation Profits," *FSI* 20.38 (October 9, 1995) 3; "5 Tips to Creatively Boost Cremation Merchandise $$$," *FSI* 22.6 (February 10, 1997) 3; "Make Cremation Merchandise Sales Hum with These 5 Tips," *FSI* 21.20 (May 13, 1996) 3; "5 Secrets of Cremation Success," *FSI* 21.40 (October 2, 1996) 3; "4 Ways to Keep your Cremation Profitability High," *FSI* 21.44 (November 18, 1996) 4.

19. William V. Forsberg, "What Wilbert Found Out about Cremation Customers," *AFD* 118.11 (November 1995) 46.

20. Gary O'Sullivan, "Buying the Idea, and Promoting the Concepts," *Cremationist* 32.4 (1996) 9.

21. "Cremation Merchandise Dominates NFDA Exhibit Hall," *FSI* 18.41 (November 1, 1993) 3.

22. The Leno quotation appeared at http://www.cremationconsultants. com/crem8me (August 1, 1998).

23. John Greiwe, "Listening and Responding to the Cremation Consumer," *Cremationist* 32.4 (1996) 36; *AFD* (November 1996) 75; "Cremains of the Day," *Sports Illustrated* (March 28, 1994) 10.

24. Patent 4977652 (http://patent.womplex.ibm.com) (August 18, 1999).

25. Jack Springer interview (June 1997).

26. Quoted in http://www.xroads.com/~funerals (August 9, 1999). This is the web site of Father Wasielewski's Interfaith Funeral Information Committee (IFIC), an ecumenical consumer rights group. See also Lisa Carlson, *Caring for The Dead: Your Final Act of Love* (Hinesburg, Vt.: Upper Access, 1998).

27. Ernest Morgan, *Dealing Creatively with Death: A Manual of Death Education and Simple Burial* (13th revised ed; New York: Zinn Communications, 1994). See also earlier works such as Paul Irion, *A Manual and Guide for Those Who Conduct a Humanist Funeral Service* (Baltimore: Waverly Press, 1971); and Meg Bowman, *Memorial Services for Women* (San Jose: Hot Flash Press, 1986).

28. John Gary Brown, *Soul in the Stone: Cemetery Art from America's Heartland* (Lawrence: University Press of Kansas, 1994) 37.

29. "More Than We Wanted to Know Department," *New Yorker* 33.3 (November 3, 1997) 61; "Washington Whispers," *U.S. News and World Report* (September 8, 1997) 21; http://www.booksatoz.com.artatoz/krafft/funerary. htm (August 5, 1999); http://www.eternalreefs.com (August 5, 1999); Patent 5230127 (http://patent.womplex.ibm.com) (August 18, 1999); "A Lunar Probe Settles into Orbit 60 Miles above the Moon," *Boston Globe* (January 14, 1998) A13.

30. Scholarly work associating cremation with secularity includes: Robert Fulton, *Death and Identity* (New York: John Wiley & Sons, 1965); Edwin S. Schneidman, "You and Death," *Psychology Today* 5.1 (1971) 43–45, 74–80; Grace D. Dawson, John F. Santos, and David C. Burdick, "Differences in Final Arrangements between Burial and Cremation as the Method of Body Disposition," *Omega* 21.2 (1990) 129–46; Peter Jupp, "Cremation or Burial? Contemporary Choice in City and Village," in *The Sociology of Death,* ed. David Clark (Cambridge, Mass.: Blackwell, 1993) 169–97; and J. Douglas Davies, *Cremation Today and Tomorrow* (Brancote, Nottingham: Grove Books, 1990). The last two works address cremation in Great Britain, not the United States. One problem with these studies is that they rely far too heavily on traditional markers of religiosity, such as church attendance or belief in God. From this perspective, someone who meditates three times a day in the presence of a "higher power" would be considered unreligious.

31. Grace D. Dawson, John F. Santos, and David C. Burdick, "Differences in Final Arrangements between Burial and Cremation as the Method of Body Disposition," *Omega* 21.2 (1990) 136; National Research and Information Center, "Project Understanding: A National Study of Cremation," 16–17; Wirthlin Group, *1995 Study,* 21; http://www.flash.net/~leimer/cremate2.html (August 17, 1999).

32. The Reverend Mary Faith Nesmith interview (July 1996); Sean Gonsalves, "Farewell to a Friend," *Cape Cod Times* (November 2, 1997) B1–B4; "Getting Funerals off the Ground," *Times* (July 5, 1978) 4.2.

33. Jack Springer interview (June 1997). A 1999 CANA study found that Buddhists and Hindus accounted for 13% of U.S. cremations ("And Who Is Choosing Cremation?" *FM* [June 7, 1999] 6).

34. Michael Kubasak quoted in "Paradigm Shift," *AFD* 118.7 (July 1995) 26.

35. Robert Wuthnow, *After Heaven: Spirituality in America since the 1950s* (Berkeley: University of California Press, 1998). See also Wade Clark Roof, *Spiritual Marketplace: Baby Boomers and the Remaking of American Religion* (Princeton: Princeton University Press, 1999).

36. Bud Hanson interview (July 1997).

37. "Cremation and the Baby Boomer," *AFD* 118.8 (August 1995) 28.

38. Philippe Ariès, *Western Attitudes toward Death: From the Middle Ages to the Present,* trans. Patricia M. Ranum (Baltimore: Johns Hopkins University Press, 1974) 85, 91. See Geoffrey Gorer, *Death, Grief, and Mourning* (Garden City, N.J.: Doubleday, 1965).

39. Cremation Association of North America, "1998 Data and Projections to the Year 2010" (1999) 20.

40. Samuel Bernstein, "Cremation as a Sanitary Reform," *MC* 4.2 (April 1889) 20; Wirthlin Group, *American Attitudes and Values Affected by Death and Deathcare Services* (McLean, Va.: The Wirthlin Group, 1990) 25. "Concern for use of land" was an insignificant factor in the cremation decision among the 407 families surveyed in Grace D. Dawson, John F. Santos, and David C. Burdick, "Differences in Final Arrangements between Burial and Cremation as the Method of Body Disposition," *Omega* 21.2 (1990) 129–46.

41. David E. Stannard, *The Puritan Way of Death: A Study in Religion, Culture, and Social Change* (New York: Oxford University Press, 1977) 113, 161.

42. Gary Laderman, *The Sacred Remains: American Attitudes toward Death, 1799–1883* (New Haven: Yale University Press, 1996) 39–50.

43. On gigantism in American culture, see Kenneth S. Goldstein, "Notes toward a European-American Folk Aesthetic: Lessons Learned from Singers and Storytellers I Have Known," *Journal of American Folklore* 104.412 (Spring 1991) 164–78; and Richard Stengel, "Living Large," *New Yorker* (April 27/May 4, 1998) 50.

44. "Famed Funeral Service Critic Jessica Mitford Dies: A Farewell To Arms," *FM* 5.30 (August 5, 1996) 1–3.

Selected Bibliography

Primary Sources

Interviews

Margaret Adams, Service Corporation International, August 1999.

Joe Allen, J. S. Waterman & Sons, Boston, Mass., July 1997.

Lisa Carlson, Funeral and Memorial Society of America, June 1997, February 1999, August 1999.

Rabbi Earl Grollman, August 1999.

Bud Hanson, Forest Hills Cemetery, Jamaica Plain, Mass., July 1997.

Ron Hast, *Mortuary Management,* June 1997.

Phyllis Janik, Companion Star, July 1997.

Edward C. Johnson, Johnson Mortuary, Chicago, Ill., August 1997.

Lawrence Jones, National Funeral Directors and Morticians Association, July 1997.

Michael Kubasak, Service Corporation International, June 1997.

Marilyn Lux, People's Memorial Association, August 1997.

Barry Mackintosh, National Park Service, February 1999.

The Reverend Mary Faith Nesmith, St. James Lutheran Church, Norcross, Ga., July 1996.

Howard Raether, National Funeral Directors Association, June 1997.

Bob Rosenthal, Allen Ginsberg Trust, January 1998.

Jean Scribner, Cremation Association of North America, June 1997.

Jack Springer, Cremation Association of North America, June 1997, August 1999.

Books, Periodicals, and Articles

Adams, J. A. *Project Understanding: A National Study of Cremation.* Des Plaines, Ill.: National Foundation of Funeral Services, 1986.

Adams, J. F. A.. *Cremation and Burial: An Examination of Their Relative Advantages.* Boston: Wright & Potter, 1875.

Allen, Francis D. *Documents and Facts Showing the Fatal Effects of Interments in Populous Cities.* New York: F. D. Allen, 1822.

Bermingham, Edward J. *The Disposal of the Dead: A Plea for Cremation.* New York: Bermingham & Co., 1881.

Bonnell, Henry Houston. *Cremation: Scientifically and Religiously Considered.* Philadelphia: Press of D. C. Chalfant, 1885.

Browne, Sir Thomas. *Hydriotaphia, Urne-Buriall.* London: Printed for Hen. Brome, 1658.

Carlson, Lisa. *Caring for the Dead: Your Final Act of Love.* Hinesburg, Vt.: Upper Access, 1998.

Carney, Karen L. *Our Special Garden: Understanding Cremation.* Wethersfield, Conn.: n.p., 1995.

Chadwick, James R. *The Cremation of the Dead.* Boston: Geo. H. Ellis, 1905.

Cobb, Augustus G. *Earth-Burial and Cremation.* New York: G. P. Putnam's Sons, 1892.

Cobb, John Storer. *A Quartercentury of Cremation in North America.* Boston: Knight & Millet, 1901.

———. *The Torch and the Tomb.* Boston: The New England Cremation Society, 1891.

Comyns, Mary B. *A Plea for Cremation.* Boston: Ellis, 1892.

Conway, Bertrand Louis. *Ethics and History of Cremation.* New York: Paulist, 1923.

The Columbarium. Philadelphia. 1895–96.

"Cremation as a Mode of Interment, and Related Subjects." *Boston Public Library Bulletins* 2.30 (July 1874), 268.

Cremation; By an Eyewitness. New York: Barnes, 1880.

Cremation: History of the Movement in Lancaster, Pennsylvania. Lancaster, Penn.: Lancaster Cremation and Funeral Reform Society, 1884.

The Cremationist of North America (previously *National Cremation Magazine*). Incline Village, Nev. 1965–.

Erichsen, Hugo. *The Cremation of the Dead Considered from an Aesthetic, Sanitary, Religious, Historical, Medico-Legal, and Economical Standpoint.* Detroit: D. O. Haynes, 1887.

———. *Cremation versus Burial.* Louisville, Ky.: Morton, 1886.

Flanner, Frank B. *Cremation and the Funeral Director.* Buffalo, N.Y.: Cremation Association of America, 1915.

Fraser, James W. *Cremation: Is It Christian?* Neptune, N.J.: Loizeaux Brothers, 1965.

Frazer, Persifor, Jr. *The Merits of Cremation.* Philadelphia: n.p., 1874.

Freehof, Solomon B. *Reform Jewish Practice and Its Rabbinic Background.* Cincinnati: Hebrew Union College Press, 1944.

Frothingham, O. B. *The Disposal of Our Dead*. New York: D. G. Francis, 1874.

Gaume, Monseigneur. *The Christian Cemetery in the Nineteenth Century; or, the Last War-Cry of the Communists*. New York: Benziger Brothers, 1874.

Harrah, Barbara K., and David F. Harrah. *Funeral Service: A Bibliography of Literature on Its Past, Present, and Future, the Various Means of Disposition, and Memorialization*. Metuchen, N.J.: Scarecrow Press, 1976.

Henderson, Howard. *Cremation: Rational Method of Disposing of the Dead*. Cincinnati: Press of Geo. P. Houston, 1891.

Hodges, Dean George. *Ashes to Ashes*. Boston: The New England Cremation Society, 1895.

Irion, Paul E. *Cremation*. Philadelphia: Fortress Press, 1968.

Kubasak, Michael W. *Cremation and the Funeral Director: Successfully Meeting the Challenge*. Malibu, Calif.: Avalon Press, 1990.

Kübler-Ross, Elisabeth. *On Death and Dying*. New York: Macmillan, 1969.

Lange, Louis. *Church, Woman and Cremation*. New York: U.S. Cremation Company, 1903.

Lange, Martina. *A Bibliography on Cremation*. Strasbourg: Council of Europe, Parliamentary Assembly, 1987.

LeMoyne, F. Julius. *Cremation: An Argument to Prove That Cremation Is Preferable to Inhumation of Dead Bodies*. Pittsburgh: E. W. Lightner, 1878.

Marble, John O. *Cremation in Its Sanitary Aspects: The Torch versus the Spade*. Boston: Clapp, 1885.

Modern Cemetery. Chicago. 1891–95.

Modern Crematist. Lancaster, Penn. 1886–89.

Mose, H. E., ed. *A List of Books, Pamphlets, and Articles on Cremation, Including the Collection of the Cremation Association of America*. Chicago: The John Crerar Library, 1940.

National Funeral Directors Association. *Considerations concerning Cremation*. Milwaukee: National Funeral Directors Association, 1974.

Newton, Frances. *Light Like the Sun*. New York: Dodd, Mead, 1937.

Opinions on Cremation. New York: New York Cremation Society, 1889.

Park and Cemetery (later *Park and Cemetery and Landscape Gardening*). Chicago. 1895–.

Pascalis, Felix. *An Exposition of the Dangers of Interment in Cities*. New York: W. B. Gilley, 1823.

Peirce, C. N. *Sanitary Disposal of the Dead*. [Philadelphia?] Philadelphia Cremation Society, [1891].

Phipps, William E. *Cremation Concerns*. Springfield, Ill.: Thomas, 1989.

Sanitarian. New York. 1873–1904.

Smith, Donald K. *Why Not Cremation?* Philadelphia: Dorrance, 1970.

Thompson, Sir Henry. *Cremation: The Treatment of the Body after Death*. London: Henry S. King, 1874.

Townshend, John. *A Catalogue of Some Books Relating to the Disposal of the Bodies and Perpetuating the Memories of the Dead*. New York: n.p., 1887.

———. *Modern Cremation*. 4th rev. ed. London: Smith, Elder, 1901.

United States Cremation Company. *Modern Thought on Modern Cremation.*
    New York: U.S. Cremation Company, 1895.
The Urn. New York. 1892–95.
Wetherbee, J. "Cremation in Boston." Roxbury, 1895. Handwritten manu-
    script, Countway Library of Medicine, Harvard University.
Williams, R. E. *Cremation and Other Modes of Sepulture.* Philadelphia: Lippin-
    cott, 1884.

Secondary Sources

Ahlstrom, Sydney E. *A Religious History of the American People.* New Haven:
    Yale University Press, 1972.
Albanese, Catherine L. *America: Religions and Religion.* Belmont, Calif.: Wads-
    worth, 1981.
————. *Nature Religion in America: From the Algonkian Indians to the New
    Age.* Chicago: University of Chicago Press, 1990.
Ariès, Philippe. *The Hour of Our Death.* Translated by Helen Weaver. New
    York: Knopf, 1981.
————. *Western Attitudes toward Death: From the Middle Ages to the Present.*
    Translated by Patricia M. Ranum. Baltimore: Johns Hopkins University
    Press, 1974.
Baker, Francis. *The Tremulous Private Body: Essays on Subjection.* London:
    Methuen, 1984.
Bakhtin, Mikhail. *Rabelais and his World.* Translated by Hélène Iswolsky.
    Bloomington: Indiana University Press, 1984.
Barber, Paul. *Vampires, Burial, and Death: Folklore and Reality.* New Haven:
    Yale University Press, 1988.
Barrow, Logie. *Independent Spirits: Spiritualism and English Plebians,
    1850–1910.* New York: Routledge and Kegan Paul, 1986.
Becker, Carl B. *Breaking the Circle: Death and Afterlife in Buddhism.* Carbon-
    dale: University of Southern Illinois Press, 1993.
Becker, Ernest. *The Denial of Death.* New York: Free Press, 1973.
Bloom, Harold. *The American Religion: The Emergence of the Post-Christian
    Nation.* New York: Simon & Schuster, 1992.
Bourdieu, Pierre. *Outline of a Theory of Practice.* Translated by Richard Nice.
    Cambridge: Cambridge University Press, 1987.
Bowman, Leroy. *The American Funeral: A Study in Guilt, Extravagance, and
    Sublimity.* Washington, D.C.: Public Affairs Press, 1959.
Braude, Ann. *Radical Spirits: Spiritualism and Women's Rights in Nineteenth-
    Century America.* Boston: Beacon, 1989.
Brown, Peter. *The Body and Society: Men, Women, and Sexual Renunciation in
    Early Christianity.* New York: Columbia University Press, 1988.
Bynum, Caroline Walker. *Fragmentation and Redemption: Essays on Gender
    and the Human Body in Medieval Religion.* New York: Zone Books, 1992.
————. *The Resurrection of the Body in Western Christianity, 200–1336.* New
    York: Columbia University Press, 1995.

Camporesi, Piero. *The Fear of Hell: Images of Damnation and Salvation in Early Modern Europe*. Translated by Lucinda Byatt. University Park: Pennsylvania State University Press, 1991.

———. *The Incorruptible Flesh: Bodily Mutation and Mortification in Religion and Folklore*. Translated by Tania Croft-Murray and Helen Elsom. New York: Cambridge University Press, 1988.

Carnley, Peter. *The Structure of Resurrection Belief*. Oxford: Clarendon Press, 1987.

Carter, Paul. A. *The Spiritual Crisis of the Gilded Age*. De Kalb: Northern Illinois University Press, 1971.

Chidester, David. *Patterns of Transcendence: Religion, Death, and Dying*. Belmont, Calif.: Wadsworth, 1990.

Coakley, Sarah, ed. *Religion and the Body*. New York: Cambridge University Press, 1997.

Coffin, Margaret M. *Death in Early America: The History and Folklore of Customs and Superstitions of Early Medicine, Funerals, Burials, and Mourning*. Nashville: Nelson, 1976.

Collins, John J., and Michael Fishbane, eds. *Death, Ecstasy, and Other Worldly Journeys*. Albany: State University of New York Press, 1995.

Cooey, Paula M. *Religious Imagination and the Body: A Feminist Analysis*. New York: Oxford University Press, 1994.

Crissman, James K. *Death and Dying in Central Appalachia: Changing Attitudes and Practices*. Urbana: University of Illinois Press, 1994.

Cronin, Xavier A. *Grave Exodus: Tending to Our Dead in the Twenty-First Century*. New York: Barricade, 1996.

Curl, James Stevens. *A Celebration of Death: An Introduction to Some of the Buildings, Monuments, and Settings of Funerary Architecture in the Western European Tradition*. London: Constable, 1980.

Davies, John, ed. *Ritual and Remembrance: Responses to Death in Human Societies*. Sheffield: Sheffield Academic Press, 1994.

Douglas, Ann. *The Feminization of American Culture*. New York: Knopf, 1977.

Douglas, Mary. *Natural Symbols: Explorations in Cosmology*. New York: Vintage, 1973.

———. *Purity and Danger: An Analysis of Pollution and Taboo*. Boston: Ark, 1984.

Dowd, Quincy L. *Funeral Management and Costs: A World Survey of Burial and Cremation*. Chicago: University of Chicago Press, 1921.

Duffy, John. *A History of Public Health in New York City, 1625–1866*. New York: Russell Sage Foundation, 1968.

———. *A History of Public Health in New York City, 1866–1966*. New York: Russell Sage Foundation, 1974.

———. *The Sanitarians: A History of American Public Health*. Urbana: University of Illinois Press, 1990.

Elias, Norbert. *The History of Manners*. Translated by Edmund Jephcott. New York: Pantheon, 1978.

―――. *The Loneliness of the Dying.* Translated by Edmund Jephcott. New York: Basil Blackwell, 1985.

Etlin, Richard. *The Architecture of Death: The Transformation of the Cemetery in Eighteenth-Century Paris.* Cambridge: MIT Press, 1984.

Evans, Richard. *Death in Hamburg: Society and Politics in the Cholera Years, 1830–1914.* New York: Penguin, 1990.

Farrell, James J. *Inventing the American Way of Death, 1830–1920.* Philadelphia: Temple University Press, 1980.

Featherstone, Mike, Mike Hepworth, and Bryan S. Turner. *The Body: Social Process and Cultural Theory.* London: Sage, 1991.

Feher, Michel, Ramona Naddaff, and Nadia Tazi, eds. *Fragments for a History of the Human Body, Part One, Part Two, and Part Three.* New York: Urzone, 1989.

Foucault, Michel. *The History of Sexuality 1, An Introduction.* New York: Vintage, 1980.

Gallagher, Catherine, and Thomas Laquer. *The Making of the Modern Body.* Berkeley: University of California Press, 1987.

Garland, Robert. *The Greek Way of Death.* Ithaca: Cornell University Press, 1985.

Gebhart, John C. *Funeral Costs.* New York: G. P. Putnam's Sons, 1928.

Geddes, Gordon E. *Welcome Joy: Death in Puritan New England.* Ann Arbor, Mich.: UMI, 1981.

Ginzburg, Carlo. *The Cheese and the Worms: The Cosmos of a Sixteenth-Century Miller.* Baltimore: Johns Hopkins University Press, 1980.

Gittings, Clare. *Death, Burial and the Individual in Early Modern England.* London: Croom Helm, 1984.

Gorer, Geoffrey. *Death, Grief, and Mourning.* Garden City, N.J.: Doubleday, 1965.

Grimes, Ronald L. *Marrying and Burying: Rites of Passage in a Man's Life.* Boulder: Westview, 1995.

Habenstein, Robert W. "A Sociological Study of the Cremation Movement in the United States." M.A. thesis, University of Chicago, 1949.

Habenstein, Robert W., and William M. Lamers. *Funeral Customs the World Over.* Milwaukee: Bulfin, 1960.

―――. *The History of American Funeral Directing.* 3d edition. Revised and edited by Howard C. Raether. Milwaukee: National Funeral Directors Association, 1995.

Hall, David D., ed. *Lived Religion in America: Toward a History of Practice.* Princeton: Princeton University Press, 1997.

―――. *Worlds of Wonder, Days of Judgment: Popular Religious Belief in Early New England.* New York: Knopf, 1989.

Harmer, Ruth M. *The High Cost of Dying.* New York: Crowell-Collier, 1963.

Heinz, Donald. *The Last Passage: Recovering a Death of Our Own.* New York: Oxford University Press, 1999.

Hertz, Robert. *Death and the Right Hand.* Translated by Rodney and Claudia Needham. Glencoe, Ill.: Free Press, 1960.

Howarth, Glennys. *Last Rites: The Work of the Modern Funeral Director.* New York: Baywood, 1996.

Hoy, Suellen. *Chasing Dirt: The American Pursuit of Cleanliness.* New York: Oxford University Press, 1995.

Iserson, Kenneth V. *Death to Dust: What Happens to Dead Bodies.* Tucson, Ariz.: Galen Press, 1994.

Jackson, Charles O., ed. *Passing: The Vision of Death in America.* Westport, Conn.: Greenwood, 1977.

Jackson, Kenneth T., and Camilo Jose Vergara. *Silent Cities: The Evolution of the American Cemetery.* New York: Princeton Architectural Press, 1989.

Jupp, Peter. *From Dust to Ashes: The Replacement of Burial by Cremation in England, 1840–1967.* London: Congregational Memorial Hall Trust, 1990.

Kalish, Richard A., and David K. Reynolds. *Death and Ethnicity: A Psychocultural Study.* Farmingdale, N.Y.: Baywood Publishing, 1981.

Kastenbaum, Robert, and Beatrice Kastenbaum, eds. *Encyclopedia of Death.* Phoenix: Oryx, 1989.

Kselman, Thomas A. *Death and the Afterlife in Modern France.* Princeton: Princeton University Press, 1993.

Laderman, Gary. *The Sacred Remains: American Attitudes toward Death, 1799–1883.* New Haven: Yale University Press, 1996.

Laqueur, Thomas. *Making Sex: Body and Gender from the Greeks to Freud.* Cambridge: Harvard University Press, 1990.

Le Goff, Jacques. *The Birth of Purgatory.* Translated by Arthur Goldhammer. Chicago: University of Chicago Press, 1981.

Le Roy Ladurie, Emmanuel. *Love, Death, and Money in the Pays d'Oc.* New York: Penguin, 1984.

Lewis, James R. *Encyclopedia of Afterlife Beliefs and Phenomena.* Detroit: Gale Research, 1994.

Lincoln, Bruce. *Death, War, and Sacrifice: Studies in Ideology and Practice.* Chicago: University of Chicago Press, 1991.

Linden-Ward, Blanche. *Silent City on a Hill: Landscapes of Memory and Boston's Mount Auburn Cemetery.* Columbus: Ohio State University Press, 1989.

Linenthal, Edward Tabor. *Sacred Ground: Americans and Their Battlefields.* Urbana: University of Illinois Press, 1991.

Loffin, Margaret M. *Death in Early America.* Nashville: Nelson, 1976.

Lynch, Thomas. *Undertaking: Life Studies from the Dismal Trade.* New York: Penguin, 1998.

May, Melanie. *A Body Knows: A Theopoetics of Death and Resurrection.* New York: Continuum, 1995.

McDannell, Colleen, and Bernhard Lang. *Heaven: A History.* New Haven: Yale University Press, 1988.

McManners, John. *Death and the Enlightenment: Changing Attitudes to Death among Christians and Unbelievers in Eighteenth-Century France.* New York: Oxford University Press, 1981.

Metcalf, Peter, and Richard Huntington. *Celebrations of Death: The Anthropology of Mortuary Ritual.* Rev. ed. Cambridge: Cambridge University Press, 1991.

Meyer, Richard E., ed. *Ethnicity and the American Cemetery.* Bowling Green, Ohio: Bowling Green State University Popular Press, 1993.

Mitford, Jessica. *The American Way of Death*. New York: Simon and Schuster, 1963.

———. *The American Way of Death Revisited*. New York: Knopf, 1998.

Moore, R. Laurence. *In Search of White Crows: Spiritualism, Parapsychology, and American Culture*. New York: Oxford University Press, 1976.

———. *Religious Outsiders and the Making of Americans*. New York: Oxford University Press, 1986.

Morris, Ian. *Death-Ritual and Social Structure in Classical Antiquity*. New York: Cambridge University Press, 1992.

Nock, Arthur Darby. "Cremation and Burial in the Roman Empire." In *Harvard Theological Review* 25.4 (October 1932), 321–60.

Obayashi, Hiroshi, ed. *Death and Afterlife: Perspectives of World Religion*. New York: Praeger, 1991.

Oppenheim, Janet. *The Other World: Spiritualism and Psychical Research in England, 1850–1914*. New York: Cambridge University Press, 1985.

Owen, Alex. *The Darkened Room: Women, Power and Spiritualism in Late Victorian England*. London: Virago, 1989.

Pagels, Elaine. *Adam, Eve, and the Serpent*. New York: Random House, 1988.

Parry, Joan K., and Angela Shan Ryan. *A Cross-Cultural Look at Death, Dying, and Religion*. Chicago: Nelson-Hall, 1995.

Parry, Jonathan P. *Death in Banaras*. Cambridge and New York: Cambridge University Press, 1994.

Paxton, Frederick S. *Christianizing Death: The Creation of a Ritual Process in Early Medieval Europe*. Ithaca: Cornell University Press, 1990.

Pine, Vanderlyn R. *Caretaker of the Dead: The American Funeral Director*. New York: Wiley, 1975.

Power, David N., and F. Kabasele Lumbala. *The Spectre of Mass Death*. Maryknoll, N.Y.: Orbis, 1993.

Ragon, Michel. *The Space of Death: A Study of Funerary Architecture, Decoration, and Urbanism*. Translated by Alan Sheridan. Charlottesville: University Press of Virginia, 1983.

Richardson, Ruth. *Death, Dissection, and the Destitute*. New York: Penguin, 1989.

Rothman, Sheila M. *Living in the Shadow of Death: Tuberculosis and the Social Experience of Illness in America*. New York: Basic Books, 1994.

Rowell, Geoffrey. *Hell and the Victorians: A Study of the Nineteenth-Century Theological Controversies concerning Eternal Punishment and the Future Life*. Oxford: Clarendon Press, 1974.

Ruby, Jay. *Secure the Shadow: Death and Photography in America*. Cambridge: MIT Press, 1995.

Saum, Lewis O. *The Popular Mood of America, 1860–1890*. Lincoln: University of Nebraska Press, 1990.

Shively, Charley. *A History of the Conception of Death in America, 1650–1860*. New York: Garland, 1980.

Sideman, Rachel M. "Fueling the Flame: The Cremation Question in New England." M.A. thesis, Simmons College, 1997.

Sloane, David Charles. *The Last Great Necessity: Cemeteries in American History*. Baltimore: Johns Hopkins University Press, 1991.

Spencer, A. J. *Death in Ancient Egypt.* New York: Penguin, 1982.

Stannard, David. *The Puritan Way of Death: A Study in Religion, Culture, and Social Change.* New York: Oxford University Press, 1977.

———, ed. *Death in America.* Philadelphia: University of Pennsylvania Press, 1974.

Starr, Paul. *The Social Transformation of American Medicine.* New York: Basic, 1982.

Stilgoe, John R. *Common Landscape of America, 1580 to 1845.* New Haven: Yale University Press, 1982.

Strocchia, Sharon T. *Death and Ritual in Renaissance Florence.* Baltimore: Johns Hopkins University Press, 1992.

Suleiman, Susan Rubin. *The Female Body in Western Culture.* Cambridge: Harvard University Press, 1985.

Sullivan, Lawrence E., ed. *Death, Afterlife, and the Soul.* New York: Macmillan, 1989.

Synnott, Anthony. *The Body Social: Symbolism, Self, and Society.* New York: Routledge, 1993.

Tomes, Nancy. *The Gospel of Germs: Men, Women, and the Microbe in American Life.* Cambridge: Harvard University Press, 1998.

Trachtenberg, Alan. *The Incorporation of America: Culture and Society in the Gilded Age.* New York: Hill and Wang, 1982.

Turner, Bryan. *The Body and Society: Explorations in Social Theory.* 2d ed. Thousand Oaks, Calif.: Sage, 1996.

Turner, Victor. *The Ritual Process: Structure and Anti-Structure.* Ithaca: Cornell University Press, 1969.

Van Gennep, Arnold. *The Rites of Passage.* Translated by Monika Vizedom and Gabrielle Caffee. Chicago: University of Chicago Press, 1960.

Vovelle, Michel. *La Mort et l'occident de 1300 à nos jours.* Paris: Gallimard, 1983.

———. *Piété baroque et déchristianisation en Provence au XVIIIe siècle.* Paris: Plon, 1973.

Walker, D. P. *The Decline of Hell: Seventeenth-Century Discussions of Eternal Torment.* Chicago: University of Chicago Press, 1964.

Warner, W. Lloyd. *The Living and the Dead: A Study of the Symbolic Life of Americans.* New Haven: Yale University Press, 1959.

Wheeler, Michael. *Death and the Future Life in Victorian Literature and Theology.* Cambridge: Cambridge University Press, 1990.

Wiebe, Robert H. *The Search for Order, 1877–1920.* New York: Hill and Wang, 1967.

Wilson, Sir Arnold, and Hermann Levy. *Burial Reform and Funeral Costs.* New York: Oxford University Press, 1938.

The Wirthlin Group. *1995 Study of American Attitudes toward Ritualization and Memorialization.* McLean, Va.: The Wirthlin Group, 1995.

Young, Katharine. *Bodylore.* Knoxville: University of Tennessee Press, 1993.

Zaleski, Carol. *Otherworld Journeys: Accounts of Near-Death Experiences in Medieval and Modern Times.* New York: Oxford University Press, 1987.

Index

Text: 10/13 Sabon
Display: Futura
Design: Nola Burger
Composition: Impressions Book and Journal Services, Inc.
Printing and binding: Edwards Brothers